Journey Towards Home

Journey Towards Home

The Christian Life According to C. S. Lewis

S. STEVE PARK

Foreword by William Edgar

WIPF & STOCK · Eugene, Oregon

JOURNEY TOWARDS HOME
The Christian Life According to C. S. Lewis

Copyright © 2017 S. Steve Park. All rights reserved. Except for brief quotations in critical publications or reviews, no part of this book may be reproduced in any manner without prior written permission from the publisher. Write: Permissions, Wipf and Stock Publishers, 199 W. 8th Ave., Suite 3, Eugene, OR 97401.

Wipf & Stock
An Imprint of Wipf and Stock Publishers
199 W. 8th Ave., Suite 3
Eugene, OR 97401

www.wipfandstock.com

PAPERBACK ISBN: 978-1-61097-882-8
HARDCOVER ISBN: 978-1-5326-1125-4
EBOOK ISBN: 978-1-4982-8837-8

Manufactured in the U.S.A.   FEBRUARY 27, 2017

Contents

Foreword by William Edgar | *vii*
Preface | *xi*

1 Introduction: Why C. S. Lewis? | 1
    The Main Ideas
    An Overview

2 The Origin of "Mere Christianity" | 10
    The Major Influences on Lewis's "Mere Christianity"
    The Main Motives Behind "Mere Christianity"
    The Main Distinctive of "Mere Christianity"

3 Away From Home: Restlessness and Wandering as *Praeparatio Evangelica* | 48
    Signs from "the Landlord"
    The "Shepherd People" and the Pagans
    The Appearance of "the Landlord's Son"
    Conclusion

4 Homeward Turning: The Doctrine of Conversion | 84
    Repentance as "Dying to Self"
    Faith as Trust
    Active and Passive Dimensions of Conversion
    Conclusion

5 Home Away From Home: The New Life in the Fallen World | 115
    The Church
    The Guide

　　　　Prayer
　　　　The Tempters and Temptations
　　　　Conclusion

6　　The Final Home: The Consummation of the Journey | 163
　　　　Crossing the Final Brook: What Physical Death Means
　　　　Lewis on Eschatology: Real or Fictional?
　　　　The Great Divorce: Personal Eschatology
　　　　The Last Battle: Cosmic Eschatology
　　　　Conclusion

7　　"Mere Christianity": Concluding Reflections on Lewis's Theology | 193
　　　　Evaluation

Selected Bibliography | *207*

Foreword

Many Christians have had a romance with the writings of C. S. Lewis, both in his own day and ever since. And for good reason. He was, and is, a powerful voice for the Christian faith, one able to herald our religion with enviable clarity. They have also tried to package him in their own giftwrap. Evangelicals see him as an articulate, creative evangelical. Conservatives want to own him as the herald of civilization. Thomists see him as belonging to the tradition of Plato, Aristotle, and Thomas Aquinas. Even unbelievers who have discovered some of Lewis's fiction claim him as their favorite children's author or their favorite science fiction writer. There are ministers who scarcely let a Sunday sermon go by without a quote or two from C. S. Lewis. Not everyone is inclined to embrace him. Some have detected unorthodox doctrines in Lewis, such as universalism and theistic evolution. Others find him a less-than-genial literary critic. Still others fault him for his traditionalist views of women.

Who was the real C. S. Lewis? More than fifty years after his death, that issue is still being debated. We are now well-served by a number of excellent biographies and a good number of quality research tools. Walter Hooper, his personal secretary, has given us *C. S. Lewis: A Complete Guide to His Life and Works*. Several articles by Lewis's long-time friend and solicitor, Owen Barfield, have been collected by G. B. Tennyson in *Owen Barfield on C. S. Lewis*. There is even a *Cambridge Companion to C. S. Lewis*, which contains a cache of valuable articles. Though the biography by Roger Lancelyn Green and Walter Hooper (*C. S. Lewis: A Biography*) is a classic, my favorite account is by Alister McGrath, *C. S. Lewis—A Life: Eccentric Genius, Reluctant Prophet*. McGrath breaks considerable new ground, including an argument for a new date for Lewis's conversion. Besides all these there are hundreds, if not thousands of books and articles on some aspect of Lewis's work.

Still, the best way to understand him and assess his contributions, is by reading him. This should include not only the classics, such as *Mere Christianity*, *Miracles*, and *The Chronicles of Narnia*, but also the lesser-known texts, including numerous articles, his literary criticism, and of course his correspondence. There are still many riches to discover and reward the seeker. The book you hold in your hand is full of treasures, old and new.

Journey Towards Home: The Christian Life According to C. S. Lewis will plunge the reader into the depths of Lewis's world and his thought. The title is well-chosen, since Lewis himself often conceived his work and his life as a pilgrimage. Indeed, some of his best fiction is from the tradition of the quest. *The Pilgrim's Regress*, his fantasy works, and, crucially, his own account of his life, *Surprised by Joy*, which describes his quest for God as *longing*, the famous *Sehnsucht*, a journey which ends in a surprise: he did not find God; God found him. Man's search for God, he once remarked, is as absurd as the mouse's search for the cat.

Perhaps J. I. Packer summarized Lewis's contributions best, when he said (as our author notes):

> [He] was a Christian thinker and communicator without peer on three themes: the reasonableness and humanity of Christian faith; the moral demands of discipleship; and heaven as *home*, the place of all value and all contentment.

These three emphases are certainly drawn-out in the present volume. And Steve Park does so with great expertise. He also is careful to display the background for some of Lewis's work, including his favorite authors. And Park looks at related subjects: Lewis's guidance for those living in a fallen world, his free-will apologetics, and even such topics as Satan, temptation, and "practical demonology." Three of Park's most original contributions, it seems to me, are: first, the manner in which Lewis does theology, or the framework within which he does his theological thinking; second, his profound exploration of his view of the last things, or eschatology; and third, an examination of Lewis's thoughts on prayer.

As most people know, the heart of Lewis's theology was "mere Christianity," or the very basics of the Christian confession. As Lewis put it, he offers the hallway from which we may then enter a particular room with furniture and meals. Park looks carefully into the possible influence of Greek philosophy in general and Boethius in particular on Lewis's theologizing. He concludes that while these may be factors, they are not decisive. Closer to home is romantic literature. Lewis argued that Joy was a key to the meaning of life, and thus to doing theology. Park looks thoroughly at the writers who express the longing that issues in Joy, and shows their influence on Lewis. He shows the way Lewis successfully argued for the universality of the longing for the supernatural or the *numinous*. Following the enigmatic George MacDonald, Lewis celebrated the goodness of God and the dignity of the human person. Still, romanticism is not the ultimate framework for Lewis. As Park points out, the romantics too often attempted to derive their theology from nature, or naturism. Lewis does the very opposite.

Lewis's emphasis on mere Christianity bears two kinds of fruit, as Steve Park argues. The first is constructive. That is, it seeks to find the commonality between all adherents to the historic Christian position. It was, after a fashion, ecumenical, though not in the modern sense of a movement uniting different denominations. And it is evangelistic in the best sense, trying to persuade his generation of the truth and plausibility of the Christian worldview. He bases it on revelation, a special gift, first to the Hebrews and then to Christians. Some elements of it are shared with other traditions, owing to the power of their myths. (Park dismisses the canard about myth being something untrue.)

Second, Lewis meant to demolish weak or watered-down versions of the Gospel. The chief enemy of sound theology for him is moralism. To reduce Jesus to a great moral teacher is to ignore the very heart of his message, which is renovative. Lewis was a vigorous critic of modern theology, finding it lifeless and arrogant. He was also staunchly opposed to various aspects of modern education, and to modern aesthetics theory, which shy away from tried and true absolutes.

Park's second original emphasis is nestled within a larger study of the particulars of Lewis's doctrines. It is his view of "going home," or the final destination of the journey of converted people. Here we explore a range of illustrations and convictions about the end of our human pilgrimage. I do not know of any treatment of these subjects so thorough and so compelling as this one. Because he had a "sacramental" view of the universe, the reality of the final things can be experienced both now and at the very end. Lewis was not a typically Thomistic sacramentalist. His views are much less formal. But he endearingly saw heaven as a place where things are more real than their shadows on earth. The church plays a central role for Lewis. Although sharply critical of ritualism, he saw the church (at its best) as a fellowship of pilgrims, living in the light of sound teaching, provided by wise guides. This is why *The Screwtape Letters*' Wormwood is so intent on destroying the credibility and effectiveness of the church. If he could succeed, it would bar people from their awareness of the divine presence. At the highest level, the church brings people to live in Christ, to be his body.

Park helpfully draws out Lewis's views about judgment and hell. The Christian life is not one of self-improvement, but of catharsis. Why should there be a final judgment and a final destination for the unconverted? Who can forget the scene in *Voyage of the Dawn Treader*, when the stuck-up Eustace becomes a dragon, and has his scales painfully peeled off by Aslan, the Christ-figure? Without that cathartic transformation, that is, conversion, we wallow in our mediocrity when left to ourselves. Hell is when, finally, God says to the sinner, "Not my will be done, but yours." Even for believers, homecoming is not without the wrenching nature of death and grief over loss. Still, Jesus Christ tasted death for every one of us, and thus removed the power of death to keep us from the one thing that matters most, the glory of God.

One of the most refreshing sections in the book looks closely at Lewis's approach to prayer. Interestingly, and convincingly, prayer is treated along with various means of grace, such as the church, the guides we need, and Scripture. Also of interest is Park finding Lewis's theology of the Holy Spirit most thoroughly developed in his considerations on prayer. It is of interest because many commentators have found him deficient in highlighting the Third Person of the Trinity. Prayer for Lewis is not only effective, but takes the Christian up into the bosom of the Almighty. While it is right to ask, "thy will be done," that can become an easy escape in case our prayers go unanswered. Most unanswered prayers are short on faith—faith in a God able to move mountains, simply because he made the mountains. In prayer, we are most vulnerable, and yet most at home.

Steve Park does not gloss over some of the problems, even the inadequacies of Lewis's views. Evangelicals have been disappointed in his theology of the Bible, and Park shares some of their concerns. They detect a certain diffidence regarding the normative quality of the Bible. Still, Park defends Lewis's high view of biblical language, putting it in the context of his considerable knowledge of linguistics and literary criticism. His insights into reading literature are enormously helpful in avoiding the regrettable fundamentalist hermeneutic, who looks only for facts and propositions.

The book you are holding in your hands is a feast. And it winsomely accomplishes what any good study of an author should, making us want to read C. S. Lewis. As someone who has spent his life trying to commend the Christian faith, and as a huge admirer of C. S. Lewis, Steve Park's lively, in-depth study has become a great inspiration. More, it has made me want to go back over and over again to this remarkable author. Even more, it has made me want to understand Lewis's God, the Christian God, as he is in all his splendor.

William Edgar
Philadelphia
2016

Preface

C. S. Lewis came to rescue at several crucial moments in my life. It would be unnecessary to retrace them all—my stories will not come across as unique to many readers—but at least a few of these moments I feel obligated to mention at the outset of this book. The first of these was my encounter with *Mere Christianity* as a freshman in college. Unlike many who were first acquainted to Lewis through the Narnia series during their childhood years, I discovered him in my college days through his most famous apologetic piece. At the time, I was an intellectually vulnerable Christian student on a secular university campus dealing with my first crisis of faith.

Looking back, I was blessed with a devout Christian home, anchored by my mother, a woman of prayer. As a child, I would wake up to the sound of her praying by my bedside. The day would often end with an evening family devotion. Practically every day began and ended in prayers. This regular presence of Christian piety at home was the source of warmth and security in my childhood. Also, I enjoyed church life throughout my growing years. I remember a kind of conversion experience while in high school. At a Bible conference, my heart responded to a sermon on the merit of Christ's death as the atonement for my sins. I was deeply moved by the message of forgiveness and justifying grace. But for a long time, my understanding of Christian faith remained there. I was immersed in strong Christian piety but not matched by substantive theological contents. Tender at heart, yet I was not well prepared to think with a trained Christian mind.

Being at the university, I was isolated from the familiar Christian community that served as my safety net. In the lecture hall, I was exposed to a kind of humanities education that shook my religious security. Many professors were uncompromising atheists and ruthlessly attacked my softly formed religious commitment. My freshman humanities tutor, Father B., was a Roman Catholic priest, a kind man but a rigorous academician, and his brand of Christianity was very unfamiliar to me. Father B. challenged me to explain what I believe, wanting to know the Christian tradition that shaped my faith, but I could not give him a clear answer. After a few conversations, he labeled me as an "evangelical," but it wasn't until much later that I grasped what that label really meant. Father B. was extremely passionate about existentialist philosophy. With him, I read authors like James Joyce, Albert Camus, and Friedrich Nietzsche for the first time. It exposed me to a different kind of thinking that was unsettling, but after some time, I mustered up the courage to question the merit of my religious upbringing and whether I had any good reason to hold on to my simple, untested faith.

It was during that time I came across a copy of *Mere Christianity*, almost as if by accident. The book was a plain light blue covered Macmillan edition at a local bookstore. I did not know much about the author, only that he was an Oxford professor of English literature who wrote to defend Christianity. Looking back, my initial delight in the book was less about being persuaded by the logic of his arguments, and more about the relief of having someone on my side to speak up and argue on my behalf. The more I read the book, the more his words seemed to assure me that I had good, rational ground for my faith. C. S. Lewis showed me first that Christianity was intellectually defensible. This was a major turning point in my Christian formation.

More than a decade after my initial encounter with Lewis, I had another experience that would multiply exponentially my indebtedness to him. The dissertation phase of my doctoral program in theology saw more than a few frustrating changes in research direction. What began with an interest in Eucharistic controversy in nineteenth century America gave way to intrigue in religious experiences, with yet another turn to a more recent phenomenon of narrative theology. Somehow, my distracted thoughts converged on a desire to reconnect with Lewis. To my amazement, reading Lewis offered so much satisfaction on a number of issues in which I had already developed interest. To this day, I am amazed at the breadth of Lewis's writings; he addressed so many diverse issues that faced the church and Christians in his day. Lewis was indeed a substantial Christian thinker. It was only natural for me to have a desire to research his theological writings in depth for a dissertation. Encouraged by my advisors, I embarked on a journey into the Christian mind of C. S. Lewis. Rarely does anyone who survives the rigor of writing a dissertation say it was enjoyable. Rewarding, yes, but hardly joy-filled. I, on the other hand, can say in all sincerity that spending years thinking alongside Lewis was enormously entertaining and stimulating. Not only was it beneficial for my mind, but also for my heart and soul. I am deeply indebted to Lewis. At the same time, I wanted to make sure that it was an academic project for a dissertation, not a hagiographical commemoration of his life and accomplishments. I carefully endeavored to test his ideas against logical consistency and Christian orthodoxy, both of which I believe Lewis himself so desired to promote in his own ways.

This book is a result of that journey. Much of the content originates from that dissertation, but I have made several modifications to make it more suitable for a published book. Inevitably, there are vestiges of its original academic intent, and some readers in deep admiration of Lewis may find my critical comments irritating. But I left them for the sake of the integrity of this work as a whole. To all the readers, however, I offer something more than just a critical work of academic scholarship. What I tried to do in this book, to my best ability, is to exegete Lewis's theological writings and present the results in thematic organization. If you would, it is a systematic theology of C. S. Lewis. To those who find it odd that Lewis, a man of literature, would be treated systematically, I must explain that my intention is not to present him and his works themselves as a kind of systematic theology. But rather, it is similar to what systematic theologians do with Scripture. The Bible is not at all an encyclopedic book of doctrines. It is a combination of various types of literature from historical narrative to poems, practical wisdom to apocalyptic visions, and biography to personal letters. In the same way, Lewis offers literatures of various genres, from poetry to sermons, apologetic treatises to fantasy novels, and biblical reflections to imaginative letters. To understand Lewis's insights and ideas, one needs to begin with a careful exposition of his works within the context of their literary genres. It is my sincere hope that I have accomplished that with integrity.

Moreover, I have attempted to organize Lewis's theological ideas thematically to prove that his thinking was neither random nor without coherence. In doing so, readers of C. S. Lewis are aided to gain a more comprehensive view of his Christian mind. Having done this, it is my hope that I am able to do something positive in return for the debt of gratitude that I have for Lewis. But, of course, in the similar manner that a systematic theologian would never say that they have done the Bible a favor by producing a doctrinal treatise, I could never assume that I have in any way helped the cause of Lewis. His lasting legacy holds its own ground securely without any help from others, and, of course, I am the least of these.

I extend my sincere gratitude to my teachers to whom I owe everything that may be counted good in my work. All the blemishes are, on the other hand, mine and mine alone. Thank you, Dr. Sinclair Ferguson, for being an example of godly scholarship and commitment to preaching and teaching the Word. Thank you, Dr. John Frame, for showing me the truth and helping me to see it in different angles and perspectives. I have followed you from a distance like Peter (sorry for not keeping in touch), but your writings have been, over the years, my theological bread and butter. Thank you, Dr. William Edgar for your willingness to be both my teacher and colleague, always encouraging beyond measure, and never saying no to my overindulgence of your kindness.

Finally, I want to express my gratitude to my family. Mona, my loving fellow pilgrim in our journey towards home, for almost three decades, has been a constant source of friendship, healing, and inspiration. She is to me an evidence that the doctrine of sanctification is not a theological imagination but an actuality. My three boys, who are no longer boys—Justin, Austin and Chrysen—are my strength and delight; my daughter-in-law, Agnes, is the daughter I always dreamed of. My grandson, just a few months beyond his first birthday, is showing so much promise in every way. To you, Owen "SungHyun" Park, I dedicate this book.

Soli Deo Gloria!

S. Steve Park
Glenside, PA
2016

1

Introduction

Why C. S. Lewis?

On November 22, 1963, Clive Staples Lewis—an Oxford don, recognized literary critic, writer of fantasy novels, and popular Christian apologist—passed away in his Oxford home. His quiet departure was unnoticed by the world, disquieted by the news of John F. Kennedy's violent death in Dallas. Perhaps to cynics of Lewis, this coincidental masking of his death signaled what was to be the fate of Lewis's legacy. The truth is, despite his huge success as a communicator of the Christian faith, Lewis often faced severe oppositions: Alistair Cooke, for example, mocked him as a "very unremarkable minor prophet," whose memory would not last more than World War II itself.[1] A booklet, circulated in London during Lewis's active literary career, criticized his defense of Christianity as an "attempt to convince by shock tactics rather than by the use of reason,"[2] and he was not expected to have any longevity. We are told that even Lewis himself "had taken the view that his writings would fade into obscurity within five years of his death, and had no expectations of remaining a long-term presence on the literary or religious scene."[3] Then, it seemed for a time, Lewis's own self-deprecating prophecy proved to be true: McGrath observed, "Following Lewis's death, his popularity and influence declined, partly reflecting the rapid changes

---

1. McGrath, *Cloud of Witnesses*, 125.

2. Lee, *C. S. Lewis and Some Modern Theologians*, 1. Expressing contempt for Lewis, Lee contends that Lewis represents a futile reaction to the "theological revolution" that highlights the discontinuity between the old and the modern. Lewis's popularity, which he projected to be short-lived, is attributed to the war-induced anxiety that created a pervasive but temporary longing for permanence and stability.

3. McGrath, *Intellectual World of C. S. Lewis*, 1–2.

in western culture during the 1960s, which relegated many of Lewis's approaches and attitudes to the margins of culture."[4]

Then we have seen a remarkable surge of interest in Lewis and his works since the 1980s.[5] By the mid-nineties and approaching the year 1998, which marked the centenary of Lewis's birth, his books had an average reported sale of six million copies a year in the United States and Britain alone.[6] The release of a Hollywood film *Shadowlands*, which features his unusual love story with Joy Davidman, turned Lewis into a household name. His famous series of children's fantasy novels, *The Chronicles of Narnia*, began to appear as major motion pictures since 2005, along with the enormously popular *The Hobbit* and *The Lord of the Rings* series based on the fantasy literatures of his personal friend and a fellow Oxford don, J. R. R. Tolkien. His influence as a winsome and credible spokesperson for Christianity has been widening beyond the West to a world audience.[7] Lewis's popularity soared into the twenty-first century, even as many of his admirers remembered 2013 as the fiftieth year since his passing. He continues to be a mind- and culture-shaping voice in the new millennium.

The ongoing phenomenal success of Lewis as a communicator of Christianity, in terms of his popularity, size of readership, and effect, often made people ask, "Why?"[8] The right response is probably a multifaceted one, which takes into account his circumstances as well as his personal accomplishments.

Lewis's active service for the Christian cause began during World War II, when people had developed a heightened interest in seeking transcendental answers to the questions raised by their ravaged lives. In addition, as *Time* magazine noted, "Lewis is writing about religion for a generation of religion-hungry readers brought up on a diet of 'scientific' jargon and Freudian clichés."[9] During World War II, Lewis's twenty-nine radio

---

4. Ibid., 1.

5. Mary Michael reports, "By 1980, worldwide sales of his works numbered between one and two million every year." Michael, "Our Love Affair with C. S. Lewis," 34.

6. Cole, "C. S. Lewis: An Evangelical Appreciation," 102.

7. For example, I have traveled to nations in East Asia to lecture on C. S. Lewis since 2002, and I have been consistently impressed by the size of the audience and the amount of interest. In South Korea, a publisher, Hongsung Books, took upon the project of translating the most, if not the entirety, of Lewis's published works and has made significant progress to this date.

8. Graham Cole updates the figures and reports presented by Mary Michael in "Our Love Affair with C. S. Lewis," writing, "In the mid-nineties Lewis' books are selling at the rate of six million a year in the U.S.A. and Britain alone." Cole, "C. S. Lewis," 102.

9. "Don v. Devil," *Time*, 65.

broadcasts on religious subjects were heard by an average of six hundred thousand listeners.[10]

Mary Michael, on one hand, notes that Lewis's popularity in the United States has much to do with the reshaping of American evangelicalism, which "sought to distance itself from the anti-intellectual aspects of fundamentalism on the one hand and from the liberalism of the mainline denominations on the other," and that "Lewis's intellectual, articulate defenses of the Christian faith made him an ideal spokesperson."[11] These are noteworthy circumstantial explanations.

On the other hand, his success must also be attributed to what he was personally capable of accomplishing. First of all, the effectiveness of his style is frequently highlighted. *Time* noted his "talent for putting old-fashioned truths into a modern idiom."[12] John Wilson praises the fact that he was a good communicator: "He used common language," and "his arguments always appealed to commonsense."[13] J. I. Packer recalls, "As an unbeliever, I enjoyed *The Screwtape Letters* and *Mere Christianity* more for their manner than for their matter, for Lewis's writing style made him seem both a fellow schoolboy and a wise old uncle simultaneously, and that was fascinating."[14] Focusing on Lewis's apologetical value, Graham Cole notes, "Part of Lewis's genius was his ability to discern core Christian beliefs and values and then give them fresh expression."[15]

More importantly, however, Lewis's success points to the fact that he was not only an effective communicator but also a Christian thinker of substance. Doubtless, Lewis was more than a stylistic popularizer of Christianity or a craftsman of religious "propaganda," as some have accused him of.[16] As John Wilson observes, not only was he "a translator of Christian doctrines into ordinary language" and enjoyed "talking theology," but he had a theology of his own.[17] J. I. Packer also expresses his appreciation of Lewis's unique contributions to theological discourse.

---

10. Ibid.
11. Michael, "Our Love Affair With C. S. Lewis," 34.
12. "Don v. Devil," *Time*, 65.
13. Wilson, "An Appraisal of C. S. Lewis," 35.
14. Packer, "What Lewis Was and Wasn't," 11.
15. Cole, "C. S. Lewis: An Evangelical Appreciation," 106.
16. An unnamed critic said, "Lewis's Christian propaganda is cheap sophism." "Don v. Devil," *Time*, 72.
17. Wilson, "An Appraisal of C. S. Lewis," 25. Wilson briefly highlights Lewis's theology in terms of his belief "about the Scriptures, the person of Christ, salvation, and mankind's eternal destiny."

> [He] was a Christian thinker and communicator without peer on three themes: the reasonableness and humanity of Christian faith; the moral demands of discipleship; and heaven as *home*, the place of all value and all contentment.[18]

There has been a steady rise of Lewis scholarship, which has brought to light the substantive character of Lewis's thought. Especially in the field of English literature, an extensive amount of academic research has advanced in recent years. However, still many agree with a statement issued by Adam Schwartz: "Despite a steady stream of articles and monographs, satisfactory in-depth studies of Lewis's ideas remain rare, and thought as complex and rich as his demands such careful analysis."[19] In view of the fact that Lewis's main ideas were theological in nature and that he truly enjoyed theological reasoning and discussions,[20] a relatively comprehensive analysis of Lewis's theology is a great desideratum.[21] This present volume is an attempt to fill the need.

It is true that Lewis called himself "a very ordinary layman of the Church of England,"[22] and that his work was that "of a layman and an amateur" who merely attempted to restate "ancient and orthodox doctrines."[23] If so, is it really valid to deal extensively with the *theology* of C. S. Lewis? For several reasons, yes! First, Lewis was not really an amateur. He had read very

---

18. Packer, "What Lewis Was and Wasn't," 11 (emphasis his).

19. Schwartz, "Review of *Permanent Things*," 34. Angus Menuge gives support to Schwartz's observation in the introduction of Menuge, *C. S. Lewis: Lightbearer in the Shadowlands*, 13. Still, in 2010, Robert MacSwain expressed that "there has been very little sustained engagement with or critique of him in the general academy" and also in the mainstream scholarship in theology or religious studies. MacSwain and Ward, *Cambridge Companion to C. S. Lewis*, 4.

20. Lewis's meetings with the "Inklings" (see chapter 2) were often occupied by theological discussions with unusual intensity and vitality. Lewis mentioned that "the 'Inklings' . . . [meet] theoretically to talk about literature, but in fact nearly always to talk about something better. . . . Is any pleasure on earth as great as a circle of Christian friends by a good fire?" Lewis, *Letters of C. S. Lewis*, 363. Lewis also reported, "[When] Warnie, Tolkien, [Williams] and I meet for our pint in a pub in Broad Street, the fun is often so fast and furious that the company probably thinks we're talking bawdy when in fact we're v. [sic] likely talking Theology." Lewis, *They Stand Together*, 501.

21. A few notable works tried to fill this void, namely, Vaus, *Mere Theology*; reflections on Lewis as a theologian belongs to a four-volume series, Edwards, *C. S. Lewis: Life, Works and Legacy*; MacSwain and Ward, *Cambridge Companion to C. S. Lewis*. However, these works feature relatively brief articles on theological themes emerging from Lewis's work and do not measure up to being rigorous theological reflections on Lewis as a theologian.

22. Lewis, *Mere Christianity*, 6.

23. Lewis, *Problem of Pain*, 10.

widely and accumulated an amazing quantity of knowledge on theological issues. It is probably true that his self-perception as a layperson offered him a significant degree of freedom to bypass certain technical demands of theology as an academic discipline. For example, he seems less rigorous about presenting a system of theology and more concerned about offering insightful applications for specific situations, especially those of an evangelistic nature. However, in all his efforts, Lewis's system of thought shows through, in particular what this book highlights as his "mere Christianity" of supernaturalism and salvationism.

Furthermore, as a literary figure, Lewis's employment of various modes of expression created an opportunity, rather than a hindrance, to enhance his theological endeavor. He produced some noteworthy works of theology in his prose, poems, fiction, and even in his personal letter-writing. John Frame has observed that theology is not "properly something theoretical, something academic, as opposed to the practical teaching that goes on in preaching, counseling, and Christian friendship." Therefore, "It is arbitrary to insist that theology be written in a formal, academic style. Rather, theologians ought to make broad use of human language—poetry, drama, exclamation, song, parable, symbol—as Scripture itself does."[24] Lewis, in this sense, was a theologian and a very effective one.

This work is an attempt at providing a rather comprehensive look at the whole range of Lewis's theological writings, providing an analytical overview. For those who wish to get to know Lewis and his theological ideas broadly, yet substantively, I hope this volume will prove to be a helpful guide. Now let us turn to the key organizing principles in operation in this book.

THE MAIN IDEAS

In a letter written in 1939, Lewis stated, "To me the real distinction [in Christendom] is not between high and low but between religion with real supernaturalism and salvationism on one hand and all watered-down and modernist versions on the other."[25] It is evident in Lewis's theological works that this two-fold emphasis—namely that of supernaturalism and salvationism—is central to his thought. Therefore, Lewis's theology or "mere Christianity," as an abstraction or crystallization of Christian teaching, is supernaturalistic and redemptocentric in direct contrast to the naturalistic and ethicocentric (i.e., the developmental notion of improving the human

---

24. Frame, *Doctrine of the Knowledge of God*, 85.
25. Lewis, *Letters of C. S. Lewis*, 327.

condition) religion of the modern or post-Christian era. Lewis's two-fold emphasis shaped his basic Christian worldview or presupposition.

Lewis's emphasis seems to have risen from his Baxterian vision[26] for constructing a common ground for all true believers, in addition to his desire to issue a corrective challenge to the religious *Sitz im Leben*[27] of his time. In this sense, Lewis's is a contextual theology with a prophetic edge, the promoting of a transcendental worldview in the light of a decidedly immanentistic (thus, naturalistic and humanistic) religious milieu. We will see that Lewis's occasional slip into a dualistic view of reality at times unfortunately undermines his own theological vision. However, his view of Christianity consistently contradicts the tendencies of naturalism and all "non-catastrophic" developmental views of salvation.

Furthermore, Lewis's "mere Christianity" and corollary teachings seem best organized according to the paradigm of pilgrimage, because the journey motif is a dominant feature in his works in general. This motif, not surprisingly, is consistent with his two-fold emphasis on supernaturalism and salvationism. Following a presentation of his worldview, Lewis concludes, "We are strangers here. We come from somewhere else. Nature is not the only thing that exists. There is 'another world,' and that is where we come from. And that explains why we do not feel at home here."[28] Due to his supernaturalist outlook, Lewis longed for "another world," our real home, and that is none other than the very presence of God. A comment from Owen Barfield, approvingly evaluated by Lewis, accents the pilgrimage motif.

> [Barfield] thought the idea of the spiritual world as *home*—the discovery of homeliness in that wh. [sic] is otherwise so remote—the feeling that you are coming *back* tho' [sic] to a place you have never yet reached—was peculiar to the British, and thought that MacDonald, Chesterton, and I, had this more than anyone else.[29]

The idea of pilgrimage is at the heart of Lewis's thought. Taking Lewis's semi-autobiographical allegory *The Pilgrim's Regress*, the most salient

---

26. A discussion of Richard Baxter's (1615–91) contribution to Lewis's "mere Christianity" is found in chapter 3. Baxter was an English Puritan and a *reluctant* nonconformist, who stood out for his decisively ecumenical sentiment and a neonomian soteriology (emphasizing the "new law" made effective through Christ's redemption, which constitutes saving righteousness for those who obey).

27. Setting in life or context.

28. Lewis, "On Living in an Atomic Age," in *Present Concerns*, 78.

29. Lewis, *They Stand Together*, 316.

representation of this quality, this book incorporates its features as the structural resource for organizing Lewis's theology.[30]

AN OVERVIEW

This work consists of two parts: A chapter dedicated to the first part, and four chapters falling under the second part. The first part (chapter 2) focuses on the context of Lewis's theology. The chapter is titled, "The Origin of Lewis's 'Mere Christianity,'" and it identifies the major influences, both literary and contextual, on Lewis's theology. The literary influences contribute mainly to the content of his theology. The context, on the other hand, offers an impetus for the two major motives behind Lewis's "mere Christianity," namely the constructive and corrective motives.

The second part, which is the substance and the main contribution of this book, approaches Lewis's theology in terms of the paradigm of Christian pilgrimage. It contains four chapters representing various stages of the pilgrimage. Chapter 3, "Away From Home: Restlessness and Wandering as *Praeparatio Evangelica*,'" includes my discussion of Lewis's view of the human condition, both existentially and historically, prior to coming to Christ or undergoing conversion. Lewis believed that in the world and in each individual consciousness, one can discover theistic pointers (Joy, nature, Tao, the history of Israel, and the Pagan redemption myths) that serve as *praeparatio evangelica*. However, in distinction from traditional natural theology, Lewis focused on the inherent tension in the theistic pointers, which seek resolution in God. In his emphasis on a "theological psychology," Lewis offers us a significant apologetic and theological contribution.

Chapter 4, "Homeward Turning: The Doctrine of Conversion," deals with Lewis's distinctive view of repentance and faith. His notion of repentance is rooted in an in-depth view of sin and the Fall, pointing to the real and radical corruption of humanity. Although his discussion of the Fall focuses on the ontological effect brought on each individual, it begins with the ethical problem (i.e., humanity's claim to autonomy). Consequently, sin stems from an ethical corruption, not merely from human finitude. The corruption, however, accompanies an ontological disarrangement of the individual's constitutive parts, which are in themselves affected by the

---

30. It is referred to as semi-autobiographical due to Lewis's own comment in his afterword to the third edition of *The Pilgrim's Regress*. While acknowledging its autobiographical character, he urges the readers not to over-extend its implications: "[You] must not assume that everything in the book is autobiographical. I was attempting to generalise, not to tell people about my own life." Lewis, "Afterword to Third Edition," *Pilgrim's Regress*, 209.

Fall. For remedy, Lewis leans toward the substitutionary repentance view of atonement, which, although Lewis himself appears to have been oblivious to its pedigree, had been expanded earlier by John McLeod Campbell and Robert Campbell Moberly. On the other hand, Lewis views the Christian faith as more relational than notional, focusing on the quality of personal trust. In this sense, he highlights the principle of "the obstinacy of belief" in light of the critics' demand for empirical justifications of faith. Furthermore, we will briefly explore in this chapter Lewis's attempt to resolve the apparent tension between God's sovereignty and human free agency in the dynamics of salvation.

Chapter 5, "Home Away From Home: The New Life in the Fallen World," surveys the manner of Christian life lived out in a world often hostile to the newly acquired direction and purpose in life. Our discussion includes Lewis's insightful contribution to some aspects of ecclesiology, especially his concepts of Christian individuality and community, which challenge the non-Christian ideas of individualism and collectivism. An important discussion of Lewis's view of Scripture identifies his sacramental notion, which reveals the problem of radically separating the medium and the message. Also, Lewis's theology of prayer is expanded and analyzed with care, highlighting his concerns for practical spirituality. Finally, we explore the nature of the tempters and temptations with much appreciation for Lewis's practical demonology.

Chapter 6, "The Final Home: The Consummation of the Journey," represents the last and the most glorious stage of Christian pilgrimage. Due to the imaginative scope of this topic, we offer a concise yet important discussion of Lewis's view of religious and theological language. We contend that a meaningful discourse on Lewis's theology, even including some "dogmatic" assertions, is possible despite the possibility of a contrary opinion. Furthermore, as we closely examine the specifics of Lewis's eschatological vision, revealing no little irony, we find his assertions to be more biblically anchored here than elsewhere. Lewis's view of personal eschatology reveals his emphasis on the realization of the antithesis between the saved and those who refuse salvation. His vision of cosmic eschatology is both catastrophic and glorious.

In this chapter, we will advance some criticisms of the theses of two major theological works most closely associated with the current project, namely *The Image of Man in C. S. Lewis* by William Luther White and "The Evolving Eschaton in C. S. Lewis" by Clarence Francis Dye. We will see that White's work is overshadowed by an inappropriate level of emphasis on the poetic nature of religious language, guarding excessively against a literal or strictly allegorical reading (which may produce over-precise meaning) of

Lewis's "orthodox-sounding" theology. White seems to ignore the fact that Lewis clearly reserved a linguistic domain for theology and apologetics, as distinguished from common religious language. Furthermore, Lewis himself admitted that there is a real potential for abstracting a theological "moral," even from his imaginative works. Dye, on the other hand, over-spends his efforts to accent the "central importance" of the unending potential for human freedom, arguing that "the eschaton is a process of choice for each man."[31] He asserts that the power to choose is the main mechanism of the dynamic process of the "evolving eschaton," and that this is the central thesis of Lewis's theology. By contrast, we have tried to bring out the greater complexity of Lewis's thought, which embraces both the ideas of moral agency and emerging spiritual antithesis.

Chapter 7, the final chapter, titled "'Mere Christianity': Concluding Reflections on Lewis's Theology," reiterates the main thesis of this work and makes several critical observations on Lewis's theology. We find in his system a lack of transcendental normativity, mainly due to his tentative view of divine revelation. Unfortunately, this problem hinders his transcendental theological vision, inevitably resulting in an immanentistic tendency, which ironically is the very characteristic he sought to challenge in the post-Christian worldview.

Nevertheless, Lewis remains a bearer of the Christian treasure (in an earthen vessel but of an exceptional quality), which is none other than Christ himself. His eloquence and literary wit, with his densely evangelistic messages, have brought unsurpassed thrill and joy to Christian readers worldwide. His works, which he claimed targeted *tous exo* (those outside),[32] seem to be most effective in reinforcing those believers who are looking for an intellectual basis for their faith already received. He stands tall, even over thirty years after his passing, as a person who seems able to speak to skeptics with uncompromising enthusiasm when many Christians feel cornered by the powerful tides of secular humanism. He offers a model for a responsible Christian life in the modern world. It is only fitting that we carefully observe his thoughts about the meaning of Christian life as a pilgrimage, of which Lewis himself was no doubt a faithful participant.

---

31. Dye, "The Evolving Eschaton in C. S. Lewis," 263.
32. Lewis, "Rejoinder to Dr. Pittenger," in *God in the Dock*, 182.

2

The Origin of "Mere Christianity"

The objective of this chapter is to identify the origin and the context of his "mere Christianity," the key for understanding his theological "system." This is not to say that Lewis was a systematician; nevertheless, he was a cogent thinker whose theological presentations stemmed from a consistently held worldview. In that sense, Lewis's "mere Christianity" represents the crystallized theology or a distinctive worldview, which he found to be essential. It is the *kerygma*, the life-giving center of his theology.

Our major concern is to determine whether Lewis's "mere Christianity" is authentically Christian, or is a product of syncretism, a Christian labeling of non-Christian thoughts. To accomplish this, we must find out: (1) the major influences on Lewis's "mere Christianity"; (2) his main motives for identifying it; and, of course, (3) what makes it distinctive.

THE MAJOR INFLUENCES ON LEWIS'S "MERE CHRISTIANITY"

Any inquiry into these major influences should be conducted on reasonable rather than speculative grounds. A common approach is to look into Lewis's writings themselves and to speculate on their *quellenforschung*, or sources. This approach is often used with a great deal of confidence. However, Lewis himself thought it fundamentally unreliable.

> [This] sort of criticism attempts to reconstruct the genesis of the texts it studies. . . . My impression is that in the whole of my experience not one of these guesses has on any one point been right; that the method shows a record of 100 per cent failure. . . . But as I have not kept a careful record my mere impression may

be mistaken. What I think I can say with certainty is that they are usually wrong. And yet they would often sound—if you didn't know the truth—extremely convincing.[1]

A better approach would be to see if Lewis himself gave answers to the question, "What books or authors most profoundly affected your thought?" There are a few occasions on which he responded to such questions. We must look first into these.

Most Influential Authors

Lewis's essay "On the Reading of Old Books" was "originally written and published as an Introduction to St. Athanasius' *The Incarnation of the Word of God* (London, 1944)."[2] This brief article helps us to identify the classical Christian works from which Lewis derived his "mere Christianity."

In these "old books," Lewis found something of real substance, which he called "mere Christianity": "Measured against the ages, 'mere Christianity' turns out to be no insipid inter-denominational transparency, but something positive, self-consistent, and inexhaustible."[3] Reading through the old books, Lewis recognized the core substance that constituted historic Christianity, which seemed to him "like some all too familiar smell, that almost unvarying *something*."[4] What were those old books? Lewis identified the authors as Richard Hooker (an Anglican divine, author of *Of the Laws of Ecclesiastical Polity*, ca. 1554–1600), George Herbert (an English poet and divine, author of *The Temple*, 1593–1633), Thomas Traherne (an English poet and divine, author of *Centuries, Poems, and Thanksgiving*, ca. 1636–74), Jeremy Taylor (an Anglican bishop and writer, author of *The Rule and Exercise of Holy Living* and *The Rule and Exercise of Holy Dying*, 1613–67), John Bunyan (an English Puritan, author of *The Pilgrim's Progress*, 1628–88), Boethius (a Christian statesman of Rome, author of *The Consolation of Philosophy*, b. 470), St. Augustine (Bishop of Hippo, author of *Confessions* and *The City of God*, 354–430), Thomas Aquinas (a Dominican philosopher and theologian, author of *Summa Theologiae*, ca. 1225–74), Dante Alighieri (an Italian poet and philosopher, author of *Vita Nuova* and *Divina Commedia*, 1265–1321), Francois de Sales (Bishop of Geneva, a Counter-Reformation leader, author of *Introduction to the Devout Life* and *Treatise on the Love*

---

1. Lewis, "Modern Theology and Biblical Criticism," in *Christian Reflections*, 158–60.

2. Lewis, *God in the Dock*, 200n.

3. Ibid., 203.

4. Ibid.

of God, 1567–1622), Edmund Spencer (an English poet, author of *The Faerie Queene*, 1552–99), Izaak Walton (an English hagiographer, author of *Compleat Angler*, 1593–1683), Blaise Pascal (a French scientist and Christian apologist, author of *Pensées*, 1623–62), Samuel Johnson (an Anglican essayist and lexicographer, his moral essays appeared in a series under the title *Rambler*, 1709–84), Henry Vaughan (an English poet, author of *Silex Scintillans*, 1622–95), Jakob Boehme (a German Lutheran mystic, author of *Der Weg zu Christ*, 1575–1624), William Law (an English spiritual writer, author of *A Serious Call to a Devout and Holy Life*, 1686–1761), Joseph Butler (Bishop of Durham, author of *Analogy of Reason*, 1692–1752), Sir Philip Sidney (an English statesman and writer, author of *Arcadia* and *The Defense of Poesie*, 1554–86), St. Athanasius (Bishop of Alexandria, author of *De Incarnatione*, ca. 296–373), and, of course, George MacDonald (a Scottish minister, novelist, and poet, author of *Phantastes*, 1824–1905).

What Lewis found in these authors was a constant echo of what constitutes the core of Christianity. Despite their diverse expressions of faith, what Lewis called "a mixed bag, representative of many churches, climates and ages,"[5] its "sameness" was unmistakably present, "recognizable, not to be evaded, the odour which is death to us until we allow it to become life."[6]

On the Reading of New Books

A few months before his death, Lewis was interviewed by Sherwood E. Wirt of the Billy Graham Evangelistic Association. During the interview Wirt addressed the question, "What Christian writers have helped you?" To this Lewis answered, "The contemporary book that has helped me the most is Chesterton's *The Everlasting Man*. Others are Edwyn Bevan's book, *Symbolism and Belief*, and Rudolf Otto's *The Idea of the Holy*, and the plays of Dorothy Sayers."[7]

"The Christian Century" Book List

In the June 6, 1962 issue of *The Christian Century*, C. S. Lewis's book list was published. The periodical had done a survey of famous personalities who were asked, "What books did most to shape your vocational attitude and your philosophy of life?" The nature of the question was such that, if the

---

5. Ibid.
6. Ibid., 204.
7. Ibid., 260.

persons responding took it seriously, the result would reveal important facts about their intellectual heritage. Lewis answered with a list of ten books.[8]

> *Phantastes*, by George MacDonald
> *The Everlasting Man*, by G. K. Chesterton
> *The Aeneid*, by Virgil
> *The Temple*, by George Herbert
> *The Prelude*, by William Wordsworth
> *The Idea of the Holy*, by Rudolf Otto
> *The Consolation of Philosophy*, by Boethius
> *Life of Samuel Johnson*, by James Boswell
> *Descent into Hell*, by Charles Williams
> *Theism and Humanism*, by Arthur James Balfour

The list indicates the diversity of influences on Lewis. A seemingly legitimate conclusion to be drawn is that Lewis was a very eclectic thinker. However, he attempted to highlight common themes that run through these diverse thinkers. The common themes were vital to his construction of "mere Christianity."

There have been attempts to equate Lewis's Christianity with particular systems of thought, namely various forms of Hellenistic thought and Romanticism. He has been considered a syncretic thinker who placed a Christian label on either Hellenistic thought or Romanticism. These claims need to be examined. At the same time, these two intellectual traditions can serve as paradigms for evaluating the important sources of influence Lewis himself identified. It is our contention that Lewis did receive ideas from these thoughts, but only through the process of discrimination, using his consistently held presupposition of "mere Christianity" as a criterion.

Lewis and Hellenistic Thought

Lewis has been often criticized for being heavily reliant on Greek thought. We must not underestimate his interest in Hellenistic philosophy, literature, and history. From an early age, he read the Classics. Homer, as well as his Roman counterpart Virgil, shaped his early intellectual development. His initial loss of Christian faith partly stemmed from his positive reading of the Classics. Even after his conversion, Lewis continued to cherish them, believing that "Plato and Virgil and the myth-makers" really foreshadowed

---

8. Fey, *Christian Century*, 719.

the truth revealed fully in Christ.⁹ Lewis viewed Edwyn Bevan, professor of Hellenistic history and literature at Oxford, a major contemporary influence because he was deeply concerned with the relationship between Hellenistic culture and Christianity. On the other hand, we must ask whether or not Lewis was in fact dominated by Hellenistic thought.

The Greek Origin of Joy?

John Beversluis severely criticizes Lewis's "argument from desire." He asserts that the concept of Joy or humanity's longing for God arises from Greek philosophy rather than from Christianity. He interprets *Surprised by Joy* as Lewis's attempt to Hellenize the meaning of Christian conversion. He claims that he joined the movement of numerous Christian apologists who viewed Greek philosophy as a *praeparatio evangelica* and sought to interpret Christian thought in terms of Greek metaphysics. He concludes,

> If our desire for God were really as strong and systematically operative as the Platonic view suggests, we could not be as wicked as the Bible claims we are. On the other hand, if we really are that wicked, our desire for God could not be as strong as the Platonic view claims it is. To say, with Lewis, that we desire God in his attractiveness but flee from his severe side is to give birth to a philosophical hybrid, a conceptual mongrel that lacks the authentic pedigree of either parent.[10]

In the light of Lewis's radical concept of human depravity,[11] he cannot be blamed for following a strictly Platonic anthropology. First of all, Lewis held that human depravity affects an individual's whole being, requiring a supernatural redemptive operation of God to be renewed; second, he believed in a radically Christian vision of salvation, which included the bodily resurrection. Heaven must include "a bodily life," and therefore we are not looking forward to "some vague dream of Platonic paradises."[12] Our present day experience of spirit and nature quarreling within shall be corrected in the New Creation.

Beversluis's problem seems to be a simplistic anthropology. He misrepresents what he calls "the exclusivism of Pauline theology," saying that

---

9. Lewis, *Reflections on the Psalms*, 108. Lewis even said, "[We] can pray with good hope that they now know and have long since welcomed the truth; 'many shall come from the east and the west and sit down in the kingdom.'"

10. Beversluis, *C. S. Lewis and the Search for Rational Religion*, 22.

11. See the discussion on Lewis's view of sin in chapter 4.

12. Lewis, *Miracles*, 159, 161.

"[if] man is characterized by any predictable, observable, and all-consuming desire, St. Paul was convinced that it is not a desire for God but the desires of a sinful nature."[13] However, Paul's theology does not devalue what humanity is as God's chief creative accomplishment. Humanity's sinful state is highlighted by Paul in the background of the height from which humanity has collectively fallen. No sound theology should discount the fact of *sensus divinitatis* in each person, who, though fallen, still bears in a significant measure the image of God.[14]

This is not to discount the fact that there exists a severe tension. Sinful humanity distorts God's self-testimony in the Creation. Sinful humanity worships false gods by misapplying their innately operative religiosity. Lewis understood this well and, therefore, wrote of "the Fool's Way" and the "Disillusioned Way" of pursuing Joy. He evidently tried to acknowledge the devastating effects of sin. In criticizing Lewis, Beversluis attacks what he considers his religion of "self-realization". But we can hardly think this is what Lewis himself stood for. He clearly demonstrated that "self-realization" is not the way of salvation; instead, "self-surrender" in Christ is. Lewis insisted that the true personality which the Christian awaits for does not grow from his/her inner potential. He rejected the idea of salvation as a naturalistic "development from seed to flower"; "The very words *repentance, regeneration, the New Man,* suggest something very different."[15]

If we miss the paradox behind the concept of Joy (as well as other "signs from God"), we can easily misinterpret Lewis's intention, which was to highlight humanity's restlessness and wandering. Joy can be "a spilled religion,"[16] but to the fallen humanity it is an echo from a distant land. More than anything, it reminds us of our tragedy. We feel horribly empty and void, like Wordsworth the father longing for his deceased daughter in his poem "Surprised by Joy." The memory seems sweet but is, at the same time, a bitter and piercing sorrow. In the same way, we can defend Lewis's two-sided experience of awe and terror of God in the process of his conversion.

---

13. Beversluis, *C. S. Lewis and the Search for Rational Religion*, 23, 25.

14. John Calvin in *Institutes* 1:3:1 notes, "There is within the human mind, and indeed by natural instinct, an awareness of divinity (*Divinitatis sensum* [sic]). This we take to be beyond controversy. To prevent anyone from taking refuge in the pretense of ignorance, God himself has implanted in all men a certain understanding of his divine majesty. Ever renewing its memory, he repeatedly sheds fresh drops. . . . And they who in other aspects of life seem least to differ from brutes still continue to retain some seed of religion." McNeill, *Calvin: Institutes of the Christian Religion*, vol. 1, 43–44.

15. Lewis, "Membership," in *Weight of Glory*, 118.

16. Lewis, "Christianity and Culture," in *Christian Reflections*, 22.

Beversluis wrongly views this experience as a contradiction. Instead, the two-sided experience reveals the paradoxical reality of fallen humanity.

Was Lewis a Thomist?

Thomas Aquinas (1225–1274) was the most important of the medieval Christian thinkers. He attempted to address the challenge of Islamic philosophers who used the newly recovered writings of Aristotle against Christianity. In the process, Aquinas produced an impressive synthesis between Christianity and Aristotle. Because of Lewis's emphasis on the role of reason and his strong appeal for an objective view of reality and ethics, some scholars view Lewis as a Thomist. Norman Geisler, for instance, concludes from his reading of Lewis's works that he is "deeply indebted to Aquinas."[17] However, Corbin Carnell's report, based on a letter he received from Lewis in 1958, illumines the issue very clearly:

> [To] those who have read his books as modern restatements of Aquinas, Lewis says that the appearance of a strong Thomistic influence is really due to the fact that he has often (especially in ethics) followed Aristotle where Aquinas also followed Aristotle. "Aquinas," he says, "and I were, in fact, at the same school—I don't say in the same class! And I had read the *Ethics* long before I ever worked at the *Summa*."[18]

What Lewis meant by this will be explained in our later discussion of the natural moral law. Here, in brief, we may note that Lewis was deeply attracted to the Medieval discovery and implementation of Aristotelian ethics, which accepted the universal natural law as something objective and absolute, to which even magistrates must submit. On the other hand, in the light of Lewis's statement about his relation to Aquinas, we are compelled to conclude that there was no vertical influence of Thomistic thought on Lewis.

Lewis, in addition, told Carnell that he used Aquinas's *Summa Theologiae* as "a sort of dictionary of medieval belief."[19] It is not difficult to understand what Thomas Aquinas meant for Lewis. As a scholar of Medieval and Renaissance literature, he had been deeply impressed by certain characteristics of the Medieval period. Aquinas represented for him a theological

---

17. Geisler, *Thomas Aquinas: An Evangelical Appraisal*, 14n. Geisler said, "The most popular apologist of our day whose arguments are deeply indebted to Aquinas is C. S. Lewis. This is obvious in *Mere Christianity, Miracles*, and *The Problem of Pain*."

18. Carnell, *Bright Shadow of Reality*, 70–71.

19. Ibid., 70.

synthesis characteristic of the age. However, Lewis did not follow Thomistic theology as a pattern for his own theological reasoning. Aquinas remained as an important source of informative learning rather than a source of incorporative or internalized learning.

In fact, Lewis expressed a serious criticism of the Aristotelian and Thomistic view.

> Aristotle is, before all, the philosopher of divisions. His effect on his greatest disciple [Aquinas], as M. Gilson has traced it, was to dig new chasms between God and the world, between human knowledge and reality, between faith and reason. Heaven began, under this dispensation, to seem farther off. The danger of pantheism grew less: the danger of mechanical Deism came a step nearer. It is almost as if the first, faint shadow of Descartes, or even of "our present discontents" has fallen across the scene.[20]

This analysis allows us to remove a major misunderstanding in regard to Lewis's thought. He was apparently disturbed by the Thomistic tendency to dichotomize nature and grace or reason and faith. Whether or not he consistently avoided this tendency in his own thinking is a matter of dispute, as we shall see in the later chapters.

Lewis and Boethius

Of the many transmitters of Greek thought, Anicius Manlius Severinus Boethius (d. 525 or 526) is singled out by Lewis as the most important for the shaping of his mind. His references to him are numerous and deeply affectionate. As the last of the ancient Romans, Boethius sought to translate works of Aristotle and Plato into Latin. Furthermore, as a lay theologian, he produced five theological tractates, or *opuscula sacra*. But the work Lewis most often revisited was *The Consolation of Philosophy*, which he regarded as a central philosophical text of the Medieval time.

Was Boethius a Christian or a Hellenist? The same question has been asked in relation to Lewis himself. Some have concluded that the question is nullified because for Boethius Christianity and Hellenism were one and the same; some, such as Beversluis, have concluded that Lewis is likewise a "hybrid." Henry Chadwick, on the other hand, tries to demonstrate that Boethius was a deeply Christian thinker whose theology had been shaped mainly by St. Augustine. Without a doubt, Augustine himself was profoundly influenced by Hellenistic thought, especially via Plotinus's modification

---

20. Lewis, *Allegory of Love*, 88.

of it; however, Augustine was able to construct a distinctively Christian system of thought which has been regarded through the ages as a major theological foundation upon which other Christian systems are built. In general, Chadwick observes that Boethius's Christian works give much support to high Augustinianism.[21]

Lewis also defended Boethius's Christian commitment despite the methodology he used in turning to the consolation of philosophy rather than to theology or scriptural teaching to find relief from intellectual distress. First of all, Lewis did not think *The Consolation of Philosophy* represented Boethius's final words about reality in the face of imminent death; instead, he felt that there was an element of the academic in the writing of *The Consolation*. And second, as an academic exercise, Boethius simply followed the rule that he established for the work.

> If we had asked Boethius why his book contained philosophical rather than religious consolations, I do not doubt that he would have answered, "But did you not read my title? I wrote philosophically, not religiously, because I had chosen the consolations of philosophy, not those of religion, as my subject. You might as well ask why a book on arithmetic does not use geometrical methods."[22]

Lewis thought that this kind of "sticking to the method set forth" was totally consistent with the Aristotelian academics.

Apparently, there were at least three aspects of Boethius that impressed Lewis: First, the enormous influence Boethius had upon the Middle Ages deeply affected him as a scholar of the literature of that major period in history. In his celebrated lectures that became *The Discarded Image: An Introduction to Medieval and Renaissance Literature*, he presented Boethius as the greatest author of the seminal period after Plotinus.[23] Furthermore, he evaluated *The Consolation of Philosophy* as "for centuries one of the most influential books ever written in Latin."

> It was translated into Old High German, Italian, Spanish, and Greek; into French by Jean de Meung; into English by Alfred, Chaucer, Elizabeth I, and others. Until about two hundred years ago it would, I think, have been hard to find an educated man in

---

21. Chadwick, *Boethius*, 250.
22. Lewis, *Discarded Image*, 78.
23. Ibid., 75.

THE ORIGIN OF "MERE CHRISTIANITY"

any European country who did not love it. To acquire a taste for it is almost to become naturalised in the Middle Ages.[24]

Lewis appreciated the magnitude of Boethius's nourishing influence on over a thousand years of the European consciousness.

Second, the content of Boethius's *Consolation of Philosophy* shaped much of Lewis's view of time and eternity, the free will of man and the divine decree, and the problem of evil. Lewis accepted Boethius's elucidation of the Platonic concept of time and eternity as a decisive solution to the difficult theological problem of human free agency and divine providence. The issue is a recurrent one in Lewis's presentation of the Christian pilgrimage. The problem emerges particularly in the practical issue of prayer. If God coordinated all things according to his providence, how can prayer be causal?[25] Lewis thought that Boethius offered help in relation to this problem. He expressed this through the words of Screwtape:

> Why that creative act leaves room for [human] free will is the problem of problems, the secret behind the Enemy's nonsense about "Love." How it does so is no problem at all; for the Enemy does not *foresee* the humans making their free contributions in a future, but *sees* them doing so in His unbounded Now. And obviously to watch a man doing something is not to make him do it. It may be replied that some meddlesome human writers, notably Boethius, have let the secret out.[26]

Also, the chapter "Time and Beyond Time" in *Mere Christianity* largely echoes the words of Boethius. Having described the distinction between time and eternity, Lewis explains how God can give attention to millions at once and how God's knowledge of the future does not necessitate infringement upon human freedom.

Boethius asserts that God is eternal, and by understanding eternity we may perceive something about the divine nature and knowledge. "Eternity therefore is a perfect possession altogether of an endless life."[27] In eternity, past, present, and future are bound together all-at-once (*tota simul*). While man is conditioned by time, a successive motion of moments, God is free from the succession and dwells in a changeless, eternal present.

> God is everlasting and the world perpetual.... God hath always an everlasting and present state, His knowledge also surpassing

---

24. Ibid.
25. See chapter 5, where Lewis's view on prayer is discussed.
26. Lewis, *Screwtape Letters*, 127.
27. Boethius, *Theological Tractates*, 401.

all motions of time, remaineth in the simplicity of His presence, and comprehending the infinite spaces of that which is past and to come, considereth all things in His simple knowledge as though they were now in doing.... For which cause it is not called praevidence or foresight (*praevidentia*), but rather providence (*providentia*), because, placed far from inferior things, it overlooketh all things, as it were, from the highest top of things.... [The] present instant of men may well be compared to that of God in this: that as you see some things in your temporal instant, so He beholdeth all things in His eternal present.[28]

The ultimate "consolation" brought to Boethius, "a righteous sufferer of evil," is this: "There remaineth also a beholder of all things which is God, who foreseeth all things, and the eternity of His vision, which is always present, concurreth with the future quality of our actions, distributing rewards to the good and punishments to the evil."[29] Therefore, it is not in vain that a person places his hope in God and consequently prays, and it is not in futility that a person labors to do good and reject wickedness. *The Consolation of Philosophy* closes with the finale. "Wherefore fly vices, embrace virtues, possess your minds with worthy hopes, offer up humble prayers to your highest Prince. There is, if you will not dissemble, a great necessity of doing well imposed upon you, since you live in the sight of your Judge, who beholdeth all things."[30]

However, the idea of God's "eternal present" found in Boethius's *Consolation* is not without its problems. The idea of God being either "atemporal" (i.e., without any regard for time) or "supra-temporal" (i.e., totally removed and untouched by the temporal sequence) is not consistent with the biblical presentation of God working redemptively in human history. Throughout the Bible, we see God "coming down" to save his people. It is most concretely manifested in the incarnation of God in Christ. The notion of God's immanence must be accounted for in terms of our concept of Time and Eternity. It is less problematic to formulate God's relation to time as "trans-temporal," which means that he is not bound by the category of time, but he willingly engages himself in history. Time, as a category he created, is subservient to God who is the Lord over his creation. Thus, God is both transcendent and immanent in the most profound sense; to compromise either of these qualities would jeopardize the Christian concept of God and his redemptive acts. In this matter, we realize that Lewis's concept

---

28. Ibid., 405.
29. Ibid., 411.
30. Ibid.

via Boethius is more philosophical than biblical. Because Lewis's concept of God and his acts accounts for his involvement in history, the Platonic concept of time and eternity does not seem to serve his theological purpose. However, Lewis found it helpful to describe God's transcendence following the way of Boethius.

Lewis, on the other hand, did not consider the issue to be central for his "mere Christianity." His advice is, "Take it or leave it: your choice!" He said,

> This idea has helped me a good deal. If it does not help you, leave it alone. It is a "Christian idea" in the sense that great and wise Christians have held it and there is nothing in it contrary to Christianity. But it is not in the Bible or any of the creeds.[31]

We conclude that Lewis's "mere Christianity" is, therefore, not conditioned by this philosophical discourse. Rather, he introduced the discourse as "adiaphora," a nonessential, in relation to his Christian message. Something is admittedly a "Christian idea" if it is historically held by many Christians and if it does not contradict "mere Christianity." There is a major distinction between a "Christian idea" and "mere Christianity." For Lewis, the "Christian idea" can be tentative and provisionary, but "mere Christianity" is essential and true.

Finally, there are things about Boethius's own life (and death) that affected Lewis. First of all, we see a certain resemblance between Boethius, a lay philosopher-theologian, and Lewis, a lay theologian-apologist. Beside *The Consolation of Philosophy*, Boethius wrote *The Theological Tractates*, including *De Trinitate* and *De Fide Catholica*, in which he tried to explain the main articles of Christian faith as a lay person. At least in its significance and sentiment, if not in content, there is a strong tie between *De Fide Catholica* and *Mere Christianity*. Furthermore, Lewis considered the very heroic confrontation of evil and death by Boethius as a model of Good in the world. He notes, in his essay, "Evil and God,"

> Evil may seem more urgent to us. . . . But it is no more urgent for us than for the great majority of the monotheists all down the ages. The classic expositions of the doctrine that the world's miseries are compatible with its creation and guidance by a wholly good Being come from Boethius waiting in prison to be beaten to death and from St. Augustine meditating on the sack of Rome.[32]

---

31. Lewis, *Mere Christianity*, 149.
32. Lewis, "Evil and God," in *God in the Dock*, 22.

Boethius certainly is a very important figure for C. S. Lewis, and it is evident that he exerted a significant philosophical and theological influence on him. Clarence Dye points out that the influence of Platonic and Aristotelian thought in Lewis took place mainly through Boethius more than any others.[33] However, this does not mean that Lewis's theology is decisively shaped by Hellenistic thought. Through Boethius he was introduced to a synthesis of Hellenistic and Christian thought. He borrowed some concepts from Boethius to explain difficult theological problems, but his "mere Christianity" is not conditioned by them. Rather, he utilized those concepts to help explain certain corollaries of his "mere Christianity."

Lewis and Romanticism

We turn now to the second major intellectual tradition that influenced Lewis. He seems inseparable from Romanticism, even though it does not entirely explain Lewis's thought. Peter Kreeft, therefore, calls him "the romantic rationalist." Lewis struggled prior to his conversion to reconcile these two very distinctive modes of thinking. Kreeft asserts that it was Christianity which functioned as a catalyst for blending these seemingly contrasting ways.[34]

Identifying the attitude of "longing" or "nostalgia" as central to various forms of Romanticism, Corbin S. Carnell describes Lewis as an outstanding, if not the best, theorist and practitioner of the "attitude."[35] Carnell thinks that Lewis's clear definition of *Sehnsucht* exceeds, in profundity and meaning, other available Romantic theories. At the same time, as an experience, it binds together numerous Romantic writers. He states,

> Lewis's explanation of *Sehnsucht* reveals to me a basic continuity between nineteenth- and twentieth-century literature. For if we use *Sehnsucht* as a touchstone of the Romantic attitude, we discover that the various writers discussed [and] . . . share one thing in common: an interest in that dimension of experience which gives rise to nostalgia and longing, the dimension which fascinated Coleridge and Wordsworth. Where this interest is intense—as in Thomas Wolfe or Dylan Thomas—we can call

---

33. Dye, "The Evolving Eschaton in C. S. Lewis," 74.

34. Kreeft, *C. S. Lewis: A Critical Essay*, 15–16. Kreeft quotes from *Surprised by Joy* to describe Lewis's pre-conversion struggle: "[The] two hemispheres of my mind were in the sharpest contrast. On the one side a many-islanded sea of poetry and myth; on the other a glib and shallow 'rationalism.' Nearly all that I loved I believed to be imaginary; nearly all that I believed to be real I thought grim and meaningless."

35. Carnell, *Bright Shadow of Reality*, 14.

the writer Romantic without fear of contradiction. Where this interest is expressed with less intensity or is partly obscured by other emphases—as in T. S. Eliot or Virginia Woolf—we can speak of Romantic elements only with careful qualification. But the continuity remains—evidence of the basic strength of the Romantic attitude, evidence also of the amazingly similar focus taken by so much of human experience.[36]

In fact, Lewis was a romantic who struggled with the sense of displacement and alienation inherent in human experience. Lewis was a Christian romantic because he located the key to this attitude or experience in Christianity. This unquenchable longing points us to the ultimate home, the very heart of the Father, who is the origin of our beings. Lewis called Charles Williams a "romantic theologian" in the technical sense, which Williams himself invented: "A romantic theologian does not mean one who is romantic about theology but one who is theological about romance, one who considers the theological implications of those experiences which are called romantic."[37] Lewis himself was a romantic theologian who considered the theological implications (i.e., in relation to God) of *Sehnsucht*.

Carnell criticizes Lewis because he "never clearly resolves how important Joy-Longing is theologically," insisting "that longing, conscience, and myth contain divine revelation, yet they do not have the same *objective* value as the revelation in Christ."[38] I disagree with Carnell on two accounts. First, Lewis certainly thought that *Sehnsucht* is universal and has therefore an objective origin and value. The distinction is not between objective and subjective value. The real difference between Joy and Christ-manifestation is that they serve different kinds of revelatory function: Joy, as general revelation, is imbedded in the created reality (the desire to be with God), intensified by the fallen state (the sense of displacement), arousing a "hunger" or an anxiety; Christ-manifestation, on the other hand, refers to special revelation, which offers solution to the "hunger" through salvation in Christ.[39] The distinction is a major issue throughout this work.

Second, Carnell's observation that Lewis did not clearly resolve Joy's theological significance is surely erroneous. Lewis did so rather successfully. Its significance is in identifying our creaturely state as contingent beings and

36. Ibid., 158.
37. Lewis, "Preface," in *Essays Presented to Charles Williams*, vi.
38. Carnell, *Bright Shadow of Reality*, 162.
39. Lewis acknowledged the distinction between general and special revelation. For example, he said, "Theology, while saying that a special illumination has been vouchsafed to Christians and (earlier) to Jews, also says that there is some divine illumination vouchsafed to all men." Lewis, "Is Theology Poetry?," in *Weight of Glory*, 83.

in arousing in us a "pre-evangelistic" restlessness and hunger. It makes us crave for wholeness and meaning.

Furthermore, Lewis's romanticism is the very reason why his Christian theology should be arranged as a journey or a pilgrimage. This idea of the journey, found also in Lewis's favored poets (Virgil, Wordsworth, and Herbert) and his favorite Christian novelists (MacDonald, Chesterton, and Williams), offers us a paradigm of life. In this sense, the present work identifies Lewis's romantic vision. For Lewis, our quest or journey leads us to find and to experience salvation in Christ. But in the process, he highlights the paradox that it is God's quest for us that ultimately leads us to the salvific fulfillment.

Several important influences shaped Lewis's mind in regard to his romantic vision. Of those mentioned in *The Christian Century* list, William Wordsworth, Rudolf Otto, Charles Williams, G. K. Chesterton, and George MacDonald have inspired Lewis with their unique contributions to the romantic vision.

William Wordsworth (1770–1850)

Wordsworth is considered a landmark figure in English poetry. As a Romantic, he sought to bring out deep spiritual significance in ordinary persons, things, and natural events. Corbin S. Carnell points out that while some poets attempted to "make the supernatural seem real," Wordsworth's approach was "that of trying to make the real seem supernatural."[40]

The Prelude; or, Growth of a Poet's Mind: An Autobiographical Poem, published following his death in 1850, is usually considered Wordsworth's crowning achievement, "the greatest and most original long poem since Milton's *Paradise Lost*."[41] According to his letter to Arthur Greeves, Lewis first came across Wordsworth's autobiographical poem in 1919,[42] and it accompanied him throughout his life: "*The Prelude* has accompanied me through all the stages of my pilgrimage: it and the *Aeneid* . . . are the two long poems to wh. [sic] I most often return."[43]

How did Wordsworth influence Lewis? First, Lewis's idea of Joy (or *Sehnsucht*) received much shaping influence from reading Wordsworth. Of course, Lewis experienced the quality of Joy long before he met Wordsworth's poems. Nevertheless, in shaping a cogent expression of that

---

40. Carnell, *Bright Shadow of Reality*, 11.
41. Abrams et al., *Norton Anthology of English Literature*, 1448.
42. Lewis, *They Stand Together*, 261.
43. Lewis, *Letters of C. S. Lewis*, 408.

experience, Wordsworth played an important role. Lewis's autobiography, which discusses his early spiritual and intellectual journey, received its title from Wordsworth's sonnet, "Surprised by Joy—impatient as the Wind / I turned to share the transport." This sonnet, Wordsworth said, "was in fact suggested by my daughter Catherine, long after her death."[44] Catherine had died at the age of four. The poem expresses the turbulent emotion resulting from the return of her thought. "That thought's return" is described as "the worst pang that sorrow ever bore." But at the same time, memory accompanies something sweet. Joy is that bitter-sweet feeling or nostalgia which Lewis also referred to as *Sehnsucht*. James Como, in his introduction to *C. S. Lewis at the Breakfast Table*, says that the quality of Joy is what Lewis enjoyed in his reading of Wordsworth's poems:

> The experience most ubiquitous and compelling and central to Lewis's work is that which he called by the German word *Sehnsucht* and the English word *joy*: a painful longing, a nostalgia, a romantic memory of an episode or event that seemed charged by some unearthly flavor. It explains his glorious love of nature and his deep fondness for Wordsworth; it was the story of his life.[45]

Nevertheless, Lewis and Wordsworth treated this experience differently. Lewis thought that Wordsworth failed to grasp that "to desire is itself desirable" and "is the fullest possession [of Joy] we can know on earth."[46] Wordsworth had missed the point: "Wordsworth, I believe, made this mistake all his life. I am sure that all that sense of the loss of vanished vision which fills *The Prelude* was itself vision of the same kind, if only he could have believed it."[47] For Lewis, the experience of Joy itself is not the goal; its *telos* is in God, the Creator. From his own experience, Lewis warned of misusing Joy: "The dangers of romantic *Sehnsucht* are very great. Eroticism and even occultism lie in wait for it. On this subject I can only give my own experience for what it is worth."[48] But apart from the abuse of them, "the experiences themselves contained, from the very first, a wholly good element. Without them my conversion would have been more difficult."[49]

---

44. Abrams et al., *Norton Anthology of English Literature*, 1441n.

45. Como, "Introduction: Within the Realm of Plenitude," in *C. S. Lewis at the Breakfast Table*, xxvii.

46. Lewis, *Surprised by Joy*, 166.

47. Ibid., 167.

48. Lewis, "Christianity and Culture," in *Christian Reflections*, 22.

49. Ibid., 23.

Second, Wordsworth's journey motif in *The Prelude* affirmed Lewis's romantic vision of life as a pilgrimage. M. H. Abrams points out,

> As in *The Divine Comedy*, and in Augustine's *Confessions* itself, Wordsworth's recurrent metaphor is that of a journey, whose end . . . is in its beginning, and in which it turns out that the end of the journey is "to arrive where we started / And know the place for the first time." . . . Wordsworth's *Prelude* opens with a literal journey whose chosen goal is "a known Vale, whither my feet should turn" . . . In the course of the poem, however, such literal journeys become the metaphoric vehicle for an interior journey in a quest, both within the poet's memory and in his poetic enterprise itself, for his lost early self and his proper spiritual home.[50]

The resemblance of *The Prelude* with Lewis's autobiographical works, both *The Pilgrim's Regress* (in which the pilgrim's chosen goal is the unknown island) and *Surprised by Joy*, is not coincidental. The inner spiritual journey is a highlighted metaphor Lewis employed as an image of salvation, which we expand in chapters 3–6.

Rudolf Otto (1869–1937)

Otto was a German theologian whose analysis of religion appeared in *Das Heilige* (translated into English as *The Idea of the Holy*).[51] Otto's book, based on his fascination with comparative religion, was a major influence upon Lewis's thinking. It appeared in print in 1917 and was chiefly influenced by Otto's 1910–11 trip around the world, which took him to North Africa, Egypt and Palestine, India, China, Japan, and the United States.

Otto tries to identify the central theme of the many religions he encountered and thus what religious persons have in common. He extracts a "nonrational factor," which he calls the "numinous" from the Latin *numen*.[52] He argues that the idea of the holy in religion finds its ground not merely in morality but in certain inexpressible moments.

> It is true that all this moral significance is contained in the word "holy," but it includes, in addition—as even we cannot but

---

50. Abrams et al., *Norton Anthology of English Literature*, 1472.

51. The English translation by John Harvey was first published as *The Idea of the Holy: An Inquiry into the Non-Rational Factor in the Idea of the Divine and its Relation to the Rational*. London: Oxford University Press, 1923.

52. The Latin term usually means light or radiance.

feel—a clear overplus of meaning. . . . Nor is this merely a later or acquired meaning; rather, "holy," or at least the equivalent words in Latin and Greek, in Semitic and other ancient languages, denotes first and foremost only this overplus: if the ethical element was present at all, at any rate it was not original and never constituted the whole meaning of the word.[53]

When the moral and rational factors are removed from "holy," there remains "the real innermost core" without which "no religion would be worthy of the name."[54] About the numinous state of mind, Otto wrote,

> This mental state is perfectly *sui generis* and irreducible to any other; and, therefore, like every absolutely primary and elementary datum, while it admits of being discussed, it cannot be strictly defined. There is only one way to help another to an understanding of it. He must be guided and led on by consideration and discussion of the matter through the ways of his own mind, until he reach the point at which "the numinous" in him perforce begins to stir, to start into life and into consciousness.[55]

Naturally, Otto asserts that this quality cannot be taught but "can only be evoked, awakened in the mind."[56] This numinous has the dual character of *mysterium tremendum*, the sense of awe and fascination.[57]

In light of the idea of the numinous, Otto constructs the course of religious development in the world. In the first stage, most people have the religious "'predisposition,' in the sense of a receptiveness and susceptibility to religion and a capacity for freely recognizing and judging religious truth at first hand."[58] The next stage belongs to "the prophet." "The prophet corresponds in the religious sphere to the creative artist in that of art: he is the man in whom the Spirit shows itself alike as the power to hear the 'voice within' and the power of divination, and in each case appears as a creative force."[59] The stage higher still and the highest is the Christ.

> We can look, beyond the prophet, to one in whom is found the Spirit in all its plenitude, and who at the same time in His person and in His performance is become most completely the

---

53. Otto, *Idea of the Holy*, 6.
54. Ibid.
55. Ibid., 7.
56. Ibid.
57. Ibid., 41.
58. Ibid., 177.
59. Ibid., 177–78.

object of divination, in whom Holiness is recognized apparent. Such a one is more than Prophet. He is the Son.[60]

Now, we clearly see traces of Otto in Lewis. First, Lewis agreed with Otto that the experience of the numinous is a fundamental human experience. Lewis traced references to numinous awe in Romantic poets such as Wordsworth, Malory, and even Ovid and Virgil; and he concluded, "[It] seems therefore probable that numinous awe is as old as humanity itself."[61] Naturally, there is a close connection between *Sehnsucht* and the numinous. The sense of displacement is clearly present in the idea of the numinous; it evokes not only fascination but also awe, a sense of inconceivable distance.

Second, Lewis shared with Otto the view that certain stages of religious development are traceable in history culminating in the incarnation of Christ. In *The Problem of Pain*, Lewis identified these stages as follows: (1) The experience of the numinous; (2) the acknowledgment of some kind of morality; (3) "the Numinous Power of which they feel awe is made the guardian of the morality to which they feel obligation," and of those the Jews made the most decisive step of this kind; and (4) the appearance of the man "who claimed to be, or to be the son of, or to be 'one with,' the Something which is at once the awful haunter of nature and the giver of the moral law."[62] Thus, Lewis accepted the numinous—an ineffable and irreducible experience—as the basic unit of religion, which is fundamental to human consciousness.

The idea that a naked sense of divinity exists as amoral and nonrational experience and that it constitutes the basic ground of religion can hardly qualify as a Christian concept.[63] However, this is an idea Lewis borrowed from Otto and put to use in order to set forth his "mere Christianity." The language Lewis incorporated to describe "mere Christianity" seems to hint at the idea of the numinous. He called it "that almost unvarying something which met me" in various Christian authors.[64] It is hard not to notice the sense of mystery that Lewis projected.

On the other hand, Lewis's "mere Christianity," though irreducible, is not something ineffable. He tried to set forth its content in order to set it apart from that which is not Christianity. In this sense, Lewis's "mere Christianity" rises above mere Romanticism.

---

60. Ibid., 178.
61. Lewis, *Problem of Pain*, 17–19.
62. Ibid., 16–23.
63. About the sense of divinity, Rom 1:18–20 says that it serves as the basis for rendering humanity without excuse regarding their "godlessness and wickedness" and the suppression of the truth. It hardly seems to be an amoral or nonrational category.
64. Lewis, "On the Reading of Old Books," in *God in the Dock*, 203–4.

Charles Williams (1886–1945)

Williams was a fellow Inkling and a dear friend to Lewis. In the preface of *Essays Presented to Charles Williams*, Lewis described him as a "romantic theologian," saying, "The belief that the most serious and ecstatic experiences either of human love or of imaginative literature have such theological implications, and that they can be healthy and fruitful only if the implications are diligently thought out and severely lived, is the root principle of all his work."[65] As a result, Williams's novels and poems contained a "frank supernaturalism" and a shocking vitality. Williams illuminates well the ordinary world, but Lewis said that it is "only one half of a Williams story," because "[the] other half is what he tells us about a different world."[66] A strict materialist would never fathom the depth of the quality. The supernaturalistic worldview, characteristic of Williams, proves to be a central element of Lewis's "mere Christianity."

Also, Lewis learned from Williams a two-sided attitude toward life: a healthy skepticism, though often it verged on pessimism, and an intense optimism for life. It is the paradox that Lewis met earlier in William Morris's romances. About this paradoxical coexistence of pessimism and optimism, Lewis wrote,

> No full-grown mind wants optimism or pessimism—philosophies of the nursery where they are not philosophies of the clinic; but to have presented in one vision the ravishing sweetness and the heart-breaking melancholy of our experience, to have shown how the one continually passes over into the other, and to have combined all this with a stirring practical creed, this is to have presented the datum which all our adventures, worldly and otherworldly alike, must take into account.[67]

The crisscrossing of delight and longing is the central characteristic of joy, which Lewis found at the heart of Williams's attitude to life. The result was an attitude of humble delight. Of his demeanor, Lewis said, "Both in public and in private he is of nearly all the men I have met, the one whose address most overflows with love."[68] The profound effect of Williams is evident in the way Lewis described his untimely death in 1945. "No event has so corroborated my faith in the next world as Williams did simply by dying. When

---

65. Lewis, *Essays Presented to Charles Williams*, vi.
66. Lewis, "The Novels of Charles Williams," in *On Stories and Other Essays*, 25.
67. Lewis, "William Morris," in *Selected Literary Essays*, 231.
68. Lewis, *Letters of C. S. Lewis*, 363.

the idea of death and the idea of Williams thus met in my mind, it was the idea of death that was changed."[69]

A novel Lewis singled out as a major influence is *Descent into Hell*, considered one of the best Williams written. The main character, Lawrence Wentworth, undergoes a gradual damnation as he practices self-focused, self-confined sexual fantasy in his mind instead of choosing to marry the woman he adores. Several important themes emerge from the novel. The first is the idea of coming out of oneself or the imprisonment of self. The novel portrays the tragedy of falling into the abyss of self-love.[70] Williams presents the meaning of personal salvation as breaking out of oneself in order to freely love that which is outside of the self. In St. Augustine's terms, the City of Man must give away to the City of God. In the spirit of Williams, Lewis pointed out, "Hell is a state of mind . . . and every state of mind, left to itself, every shutting up of the creature within the dungeon of its own mind—is, in the end, Hell."[71] Again, "What is outside the system of self-giving is not earth, nor nature, nor 'ordinary life,' but simply and solely Hell. . . . That fierce imprisonment in the self is but the obverse of the self-giving."[72] Furthermore, he asserted, "I willingly believe that the damned are, in one sense, successful, rebels to the end; that the doors of hell are locked on the *inside*."[73]

Another important idea expressed in the novel is that of "exchange." The way of "exchange" falls within the three-fold emphasis in Williams's theology: "co-inherence, exchange, and substitution."[74] Williams emphasizes the mystical dimension of social life; our lives inevitably involve the process of living *by* and *with* each other. Christianity, according to Williams,

69. Lewis, *Essays Presented to Charles Williams*, xiv.
70. Ibid., vii-viii.
71. Lewis, *Great Divorce*, 69.
72. Lewis, *Problem of Pain*, 152.
73. Ibid., 127.
74. These ideas are explored in Hadfield, *Charles Williams: An Exploration of His Life and Work*, 32. "*Co-inherence*: Christ gave his life for us, and his risen life is in each one if we will to accept it. Simply as men and women, without being self-conscious or portentous, we can share in this life within the divine co-inherence of the Trinity, and in so doing live as members one of another. . . . *Exchange*: The whole natural and social life of the world works as a process of living by and with each other, for good or bad. We cannot be born without physical exchange, nor can we live without it. But we can each day choose or grudge it, in personal contacts, in neighborhoods, and in our society under the law. To practice this approach to co-inherence we can find strength in the risen power of Christ linking all men. *Substitution*: Another way of approach to co-inherence is by compact to bear one another's burden. One can take by love the worry of another, or hold a terror, as one member of Christ's life helping, through that life, another member in trouble."

highlights the dynamics of exchange empowered by the resurrection power of Jesus Christ, which links all people.

One of the problems we find in Williams is his mystical tendency (or, perhaps, his being overly rich with romantic imagination). This is an important concern because the idea of "death-to-self" or "self-surrender," which we find in Williams, is equally central in Lewis. It is important to ask, however, whether or not the idea is distinctively Christian or syncretistic. In the light of emerging ecumenical spirituality (via Rudolf Otto, for example) in which "Oriental" spirituality characterized by self-abandonment and the paradoxical pantheistic self-realization is introduced as compatible with the Christian notion of salvation, the danger of syncretism lingers. In fact, Lewis himself expressed his concern for Williams's enthusiasm for "gnostic theology and spirituality," which he found "obscure."[75] Furthermore, Lewis wrote of Williams, "He is largely a self-educated man, labouring under an almost oriental richness of imagination . . . which could be saved from turning silly and even vulgar in print only by a severe early discipline which he has never had."[76]

Unless Lewis's "mere Christianity" hinges on the clear notion of a Creator-creature distinction and a Christocentric view of salvation, we could suspect a mystical influence from Williams. My inquiry into the content of Lewis's theology, in chapter 4 in particular, should allow us to explore the issue further. For the moment it must suffice to notice that in Lewis's catastrophic (or eucatastrophic) notion of salvation, in contrast to various developmental notions of salvation (self-realization, self-actualization, self-improvement, mystical union with the divine, etc.), we find a distinctively evangelical, and thus Christian, view.

Gilbert Keith Chesterton (1874–1936)

Chesterton, a journalist and an essayist, an Anglican turned Roman Catholic, is generally considered, along with George MacDonald, the greatest influence on Lewis's Christian thought. Of Chesterton's impact on Lewis's time, Dorothy Sayers wrote,

> To the young people of my generation, G. K. C. was a kind of Christian liberator. Like a beneficent bomb, he blew out of the

---

75. Ford, "C. S. Lewis, Ecumenical Spiritual Director," 50. Also, in the light of Williams's membership in the Hermetic Order of the Golden Dawn, a group devoted to magic and the teaching of the Cabbala, along with Christian mystics such as Evelyn Underhill, Cavaliero concluded that Williams, at least in his younger days, had gnostic tendencies. Cavaliero, *Charles Williams: Poet of Theology*, 4–5.

76. Lewis, *Letters of C. S. Lewis*, 363.

Church a quantity of stained glass of a very poor period, and let in gusts of fresh air, in which the dead leaves of doctrine danced with all the energy and indecorum of Our Lady's Tumbler.[77]

Years before his conversion, during his military service in France, Lewis came across Chesterton's essays and he was unexpectedly moved by his words.

> I had never heard of him and had no idea of what he stood for; nor can I quite understand why he made such an immediate conquest of me. It might have been expected that my pessimism, my atheism, and my hatred of sentiment would have made him to me the least congenial of all authors. . . . I did not need to accept what Chesterton had said in order to enjoy it. His humor was of the kind which I like best . . . the humor which is not in any way separable from the argument but is rather (as Aristotle would say) the "bloom" on dialectic itself. . . . Moreover, strange as it may seem, I liked him for his goodness. . . . In reading Chesterton, as in reading MacDonald, I did not know what I was letting myself in for. A young man who wishes to remain a sound atheist cannot be too careful of his reading.[78]

Besides the fresh shock Lewis received from his first reading of Chesterton, his later reading of *The Everlasting Man* became an important incentive toward his conversion. He recalled, "Then I read Chesterton's *Everlasting Man* and for the first time saw the whole Christian outline of history set out in a form that seemed to me to make sense."[79] Chesterton came across to Lewis as the "most sensible man alive," who made Christianity sensible to the crumbling atheist on the verge of giving in. Before long, Lewis had devoured most of Chesterton's books on theological topics.[80]

The Everlasting Man has been generally considered Chesterton's most mature work, and Lewis singled it out as one of the most influential books on his view of life. Evelyn Waugh said, "In that book all [Chesterton's] random thoughts are concentrated and refined; all his aberrations made straight."[81] This insightful work is divided into two parts: The first part deals with the subject of man as a human being; the second part explores

---

77. Cited in Dale, *Outline of Sanity*, 298.
78. Lewis, *Surprised by Joy*, 190–91.
79. Ibid., 223.
80. Green and Hooper, *C. S. Lewis: A Biography*, 127. We are told that Lewis had read most of Chesterton's books on theological topics before he worked on *The Pilgrim's Regress*.
81. Cited in Ffinch, *G. K. Chesterton*, 299.

the subject of God who became a man. The parallel structure was meant not only to appeal to aesthetic senses but to communicate a pattern in human history interpreted in Christian perspective.

In the first part, Chesterton seeks to challenge the assumption of scientism and naturalism. He argues against the evolutionary view of history saying, "It is not natural to see man as a natural product."[82] Human history, on the other hand, manifests something mysterious and magnificent. Compared to other creatures, human beings act like a race of gods.

According to Chesterton, humans, in the course of their observation of the world, conceived that there was a pattern, a plan. When a seed in time turned into a tree, they perceived it as an unfolding of a plan. Also, they began to think that there was someone else in the world, though unseen. He was a stranger, a mysterious one, but a designer, even a friend, because the world seemed prepared for them by this someone. This magnificent idea was treated in two ways: one by the majority, the other by a minority. The majority turned it into a "spirit of gossip." "The world began to tell itself tales about the unknown being or his sons or servants or messengers."[83] Mythologies and poetry poured out from the gossip. It should not be forgotten, however, that "[the] gossip, like all gossip, contained a great deal of truth and falsehood."[84] On the other hand, there were those who formed a minority: sages, thinkers, and philosophers. "They were setting their minds directly to the mind that had made the mysterious world; considering what sort of a mind it might be and what its ultimate purpose might be."[85] Therefore, the ancients had handed down to us, then, two sources of information: mythologies and philosophies.

The second part deals with the coming of "the man who made the world," born in a cave in Bethlehem. That cave turned out to be the meeting point of extremes: "Omnipotence and impotence, or divinity and infancy."[86] The birthplace of the Christ-child, the very symbol of rejection and homelessness, turned out to be the very center of the universe, the real home, the heaven. The birth story is the culmination of world history. In the coming of the shepherds to their Shepherd, we see the popular traditions (or the mythologies) finding their *telos*. In the coming of the wise men of the East, we see the philosophy's search for meaning, whether in Confucius, Pythagoras,

---

82. Chesterton, *Everlasting Man*, 36.
83. Ibid., 265.
84. Ibid.
85. Ibid.
86. Ibid.

or Plato, finds its *telos*. Apparently, Lewis's idea of "Myth Became Fact" in Christ's incarnation is closely tied to Chesterton.

Chesterton, on the other hand, recognizes a strong antithesis between Christianity and other systems of thought. He finds the metaphor of "militancy" also in the birth story, in the demonic darkness of Herod's murderous soldiers. The presence of that enemy highlights Christianity's revolutionary and transformational message. Therefore, Christianity is at the same time universal and unique. No other religions or philosophies can claim the same.

> Buddhism may profess to be equally mystical; it does not even profess to be equally military. Islam may profess to be equally military; it does not even profess to be equally metaphysical and subtle. Confucianism may profess to satisfy the need of the philosophers for order and reason; it does not even profess to satisfy the need of the mystics for miracle and sacrament and the consecration of concrete things.[87]

Therefore, Chesterton says, "The Church contains what the world does not contain. . . . Nobody understands the nature of the Church, or the ringing note of the creed descending from antiquity, who does not realise that the whole world once very nearly died of broadmindedness and the brotherhood of all religions."[88]

Chesterton vehemently argues for the deity of Christ in opposition to the idea of a mere ethical Christ, which does not exist in the Gospels: "The merely human Christ is a made-up figure, a piece of artificial selection, like the merely evolutionary man."[89] His life, his deeds, his claims can be combined into only two alternatives: either he is a lunatic, "a secretive or self-centered monomaniac," or he is God.[90] The very same argument is used by Lewis in *Mere Christianity* where he pointed out that based on Jesus's claims he could be a liar, a demoniac, or God, but none other.

Chesterton also highlights the life of pilgrimage, which we find in Christ himself: Jesus's life is "a journey with a goal and an objective . . . almost in the manner of a military march; certainly in the manner of the quest of a hero moving to his achievement or his doom."[91] Christ's story as a journey naturally becomes a paradigm for interpreting the Christian life. Jesus is both the pattern and the goal of our journey. Lewis wrote,

87. Ibid., 184.
88. Ibid., 178.
89. Ibid., 196.
90. Ibid., 202–3.
91. Ibid., 207.

> [Barfield] thought the idea of the spiritual world as *home*—the discovery of homeliness in that wh. [sic] is otherwise so remote—the feeling that you are coming *back* tho' [sic] to a place you have never yet reached—was peculiar to the British, and thought that MacDonald, Chesterton, and I, had this more than anyone else.[92]

The journey image is an important literary and theological motif for Lewis. Chesterton, as well as George MacDonald, was an important influence in this regard. Green and Hooper observed that "Lewis's idea of a spiritual 'voyage' was based on an idea suggested by Chesterton in his book on *Orthodoxy*."[93]

Chesterton was an important Catholic apologist of his time who deeply influenced Lewis. It would not be an overstatement to say that Lewis's "mere Christianity" was hatched in a Chestertonian incubator; but the story would be incomplete without George MacDonald.

George MacDonald (1824–1905)

Lewis called the experience of reading MacDonald's *Phantastes* in 1916 a conversion or a baptism of his imagination.[94]

> Now *Phantastes* was romantic enough in all conscience; but there was a difference. Nothing was at that time further from my thoughts than Christianity, and I therefore had no notion what this difference really was. I was only aware that if this new world was strange, it was a dream in which one at least felt strangely vigilant; that the whole book had about it a sort of cool, morning innocence, and also, quite unmistakably, a certain quality of Death, good Death.[95]

Lewis later called that quality, which seemed to project out of the book like a "bright shadow" changing the world around it, "holiness."[96] MacDonald, through his writings, remained a life-long spiritual mentor for Lewis.

George MacDonald was a Scottish Congregational minister who turned into a literary figure. Raised in the Scottish Calvinistic tradition, MacDonald rejected certain points of Calvinism, particularly the doctrines of election, reprobation, and limited atonement; instead, he embraced

---

92. Lewis, *They Stand Together*, 316.
93. Green and Hooper, *C. S. Lewis: A Biography*, 127.
94. Lewis, "Preface," in *George MacDonald: An Anthology*, 21.
95. Ibid., 20–21.
96. Lewis, *Surprised by Joy*, 179, 181.

God's universal, impartial Fatherhood. Rolland Hein asserts that MacDonald represents "a dynamic synthesis of orthodox Calvinism and German Romanticism."[97] The result seems to be neither Calvinism nor German Romanticism. The German Romanticism's characteristic tendency "to contemplate and idealize man, his emotions, and his position in the cosmos"[98] is not necessarily that of MacDonald. With the theology of his upbringing and the outlook of life newly acquired from Germany, MacDonald reconstructed something distinctive. His theological emphases are two: First, his view of a God who is absolutely good and never severe; second, his belief in the fallenness of humanity highlighted by the symptom of self-worship.

First, MacDonald's God is always *for* his children. For him, Calvinistic theology is that which exalts God but at the expense of degrading humanity.

> They regard the Father of their spirits as their governor! They yield to the idea of . . . 'the glad Creator,' and put in its stead a miserable, puritanical, martinet of a God, caring not for righteousness but for His rights: not for the eternal purities, but the goody proprieties. The prophets of such a God take all the glow, all the hope, all the colour, all the worth, out of life on earth, and offer you instead what they call eternal bliss—a pale, tearless hell.[99]

Lewis thought that MacDonald's "history is largely a history of escape from the theology in which he had been brought up," but ironically "it is he himself, in the very midst of his intellectual revolt, who forces us . . . to see elements of real and perhaps irreplaceable worth in the thing from which he is revolting."[100] However, Lewis's latter assertion seems less evident than the former.

MacDonald apparently preached universalism believing that there is no *eternal* judgment in hell since hell has no eternal quality. Due to his absolute positive regard for humanity, God's vengeance is a means to correct and ultimately to forgive.

> Such is the mercy of God that He will hold His children in the consuming fire of His distance . . . until they drop the purse of selfishness with all the dross that is in it, and rush home to the Father and the Son and the many brethren—rush inside the centre of the life-giving fire whose outer circles burn.[101]

---

97. Hein, *Harmony Within*, 8.
98. Ibid., 7.
99. Lewis, *George MacDonald: An Anthology*, 88.
100. Lewis, "Preface," in *George MacDonald: An Anthology*, 11–12.
101. Lewis, *George MacDonald: An Anthology*, 87.

In *The Great Divorce*, Lewis's theological fantasy, George MacDonald appears as his guide in heaven. In an imaginary dialogue, Lewis asks, "In your own books, Sir . . . you were a Universalist. You talked as if all men would be saved." Lewis's MacDonald, rather than asserting his universalism, says, "Ye can know nothing of the end of all things, or nothing expressible in those terms." Lewis continued to point out in the dialogue that a high view of human freedom, which the real MacDonald consistently held, cannot be reconciled with his universalism. Either all people are saved and not free, or they are free and some are lost by their own initiative. If people are free to resist God's grace, as MacDonald says, universalism cannot be established.[102]

Lewis, on the other hand, delighted in MacDonald's attitude of joy. MacDonald's passion was to enjoy God, who is himself a joyful Creator, and to enjoy the world he has created. He said, "God is the God of the Beautiful, Religion the love of the Beautiful, and Heaven the home of the Beautiful, Nature is tenfold brighter in the sun of Righteousness, and my love of Nature is more intense since I became a Christian."[103] Such a high view of aesthetic pleasure pervades MacDonald's works. Ironically, MacDonald, in his lifetime, faced poverty, poor health, and the loss of four children through tuberculosis. Nevertheless, his entire life shows a steady trust in a personal, caring, and altogether good God. To know him is to find safety in his arms whatever the circumstances one may face. To know God is to find his presence delightful, rather than dreadful. "It is the heart that is not yet sure of its God that is afraid to laugh in His presence."[104]

Second, MacDonald highlighted humans' fallenness. Its symptom is the enjoyment of self-worship; they must, therefore, learn to follow the way of death to self in order to find salvation and life. Notice how this idea is deeply imbedded in his view of God: God who knows the best and desires to give the best to us is grieved by man's self-centeredness, which itself is hell. The death to self, which is an act of faith in God who is all good, is the only way to salvation which is to possess true life. MacDonald's view of salvation is personal, internal, experiential, even catastrophic, and, therefore, adventurous. In short, it is a personal journey from self to God.

Self-centeredness is the definition of hell. "The one principle of hell is—'I am my own!'"[105] We found the same idea pervasive in Charles Wil-

---

102. Ibid., 49. He said that God may stand at the door of one's life, but he will never "force any door to enter in. . . . The door must be opened by the willing hand, ere the foot of Love will cross the threshold."

103. Quoted in Hein, *Harmony Within*, 10.

104. Lewis, *George MacDonald: An Anthology*, 115.

105. Ibid., 85.

liams's *Descent into Hell*. Lewis's intriguing idea of hell's smallness in *The Great Divorce* is based on this principle. Why is hell so small? "For a damned soul is nearly nothing: it is shrunk, shut up in itself. Good beats upon the damned incessantly as sound waves beat on the ears of the deaf, but they cannot receive it."[106]

Therefore, MacDonald's fantasy stories are filled with the message of death, the good death. For example, in his short story, "The Golden Key," an Old Man took Mossy into a cave, to undress and to be laid in the bath (a scene very similar to what Mother Kirk does to John in Lewis's *Pilgrim's Regress*). He told Mossy, "Get up and look at yourself in the water."

> He rose and looked at himself in the water, and there was not a gray hair on his head or a wrinkle on his skin.
> "You have tasted of death now," said the Old Man. "Is it good?"
> "It is good," said Mossy. "It is better than life."
> "No," said the Old Man; "it is only more life."[107]

It is this good death Lewis found in MacDonald's *Phantastes*. The "Faerie Romance" is basically about this death and more.

In the literary work to which Lewis attributed great personal value, certain themes can be highlighted. First, *Phantastes* emphasizes the idea of the personal journey.[108] The very name of the main character, Anodos, means "one without a path."[109] A better rendering may be "a wanderer." Indeed, the story is about Anodos's "wandering" in the land of Faerie which turns into a "journey." The spiritual journey, through many hazardous moments, dictates the process of becoming a mature being. Here, MacDonald's main spiritual concern seems to be ontological in nature. His Christian hope is not a mere epistemological renewal or an ethical restoration. MacDonald's spiritual journey is to find one's true self. Ultimately, the true self is found only in the being who is the center of all beings.

Second, *Phantastes* exhorts its readers to accept the supernatural. For both MacDonald and Lewis, it is a fundamental worldview; they both vehemently rejected naturalism and materialism for these render life meaningless.

---

106. Lewis, *Great Divorce*, 123.
107. MacDonald, *Golden Key*, 31–32.
108. MacDonald, *Phantastes*. The work was first published in 1858.
109. This is not agreed beyond dispute. Hein thinks the Greek word has two meanings, "having no way" and "rising"; others have suggested, "a way back," "an upwards direction," etc. Hein, *Harmony Within*, 56, 56n.

Third, the idea of death to self is central. Self-seeking is the cause of each downfall in the story. The *telos* of the journey is the death of self that leads to freedom and unspeakable Joy. This death has a sanctifying effect. Even love, when understood correctly, must involve self-denial. Love based on desire is mere lust, a passion of the flesh.

Finally, as Lewis said, the quality of Joy or a mysterious longing pervades the story. This is what fuels and urges readers to embark on their own personal journeys to God. MacDonald points to that internal quality, a ceaseless yearning after the eternal reality that gives meaning to life. Lewis wrote of *Phantastes*, "Never had the wind of Joy blowing through any story been less separable from the story itself."[110]

All of the above ideas occupy central places in Lewis's theology as well. As Lewis himself admitted, George MacDonald was an irreplaceable influence upon him, as a major contributor to and conditioner of his "mere Christianity."

Lewis's Criticisms of Romanticism

We have surveyed and broadly evaluated romantic influences on Lewis. There are undeniable traces of them; on the other hand, he was not a mere Romantic. In his writings, he specifically rejected two tendencies central to Romanticism in general: A Romantic Primitivism and a Romantic Naturism. Regarding the first, Lewis commented,

> A Romantic Primitivism . . . prefers the merely natural to the elaborated, the un-willed to the willed. Hence a loss of the old conviction (once shared by Hindoo, Platonist, Stoic, Christian, and "humanist" alike) that simple "experience," so far from being something venerable, is in itself mere raw material, to be mastered, shaped, and worked up by the will.[111]

Lewis's comment is found in the context of his objection to Dr. I. A. Richards who rejects the tendency for "stock responses," which means "a deliberately organized attitude which is substituted for 'the direct free play of experience.'" Lewis asserted that such "deliberate organization" is "one of the first necessities of human life, and one of the main functions of art is to assist it." Lewis thought that "all solid virtue and stable pleasure" actually depended on "organizing chosen attitudes and maintaining them against

---

110. Lewis, *Surprised by Joy*, 180.
111. Lewis, *Preface to Paradise Lost*, 54.

the eternal flux (or 'direct free play') of mere immediate experience." [112] Lewis, therefore, rejected the opinion of the school of thought which maintained that the "improvement of our responses was always required in the direction of finer discrimination and greater particularity." He argued that this thought was partly due to the decay of logic (as an objective category), which gives birth to the assumption that "the particular is real and the universal is not."[113] Lewis demonstrated his deeply held conviction of the objectivity of values, which attribute proper interpretations to our experiences. According to Lewis, our simple, instinctive responses must be shaped into necessarily moral responses, properly corresponding to situations or things. Therefore, evil must be seen as evil and good as good. He realized that such an imperative does not infringe upon human freedom of expressions but rather provides the right context for the exercising of it.

Second, Lewis rejected Romantic Naturism. By Naturism we mean a tendency to nature-worship or at least a tendency to assign unwarranted functions to nature. Lewis maintained that we cannot expect to derive a sense of morality, philosophy, or theology from nature. Those who try end up projecting their own internal system of values. Nature does not provide proactive teaching of these things; instead, it provides a necessary setting (filled with corresponding images) for understanding what is taught from more appropriate sources. "Nature will not verify any theological or metaphysical proposition . . . she will help to show what it means." In order to learn propositions, "[we] must make a *detour*—leave the hills and woods and go back to our studies, to church, to our Bibles, to our knees. Otherwise the love of nature is beginning to turn into a nature religion."[114] Nature does not teach us the way of salvation. A supernatural view of the reality or "the so-called Wordsworthian concept of God-in-Nature"[115] without a recognition of the radical need for salvation, cannot be Christianity. Everything lovely, taken out of its proper context, can turn demonic; human will, depraved and fallen, can too easily spoil that which is good in itself. Romantic Naturism is a symptom of the fallen will.

Having surveyed these major sources of influence for Lewis's thought, we conclude that his theology was shaped and informed by many significant thinkers. He incorporated ideas from both philosophical (or rational) and romantic traditions. Among Christian thinkers, Boethius, Williams, Chesterton, and MacDonald were the major influences. It is equally evident that

---

112. Ibid., 53–54.
113. Ibid., 54.
114. Lewis, *Four Loves*, 37–38.
115. Carnell, *Bright Shadow of Reality*, 16.

Lewis held an essentially Christian worldview, which raised significant challenges to the ideas in conflict with it. Lewis's theology is not a compilation or redressing of a non-Christian system of thought. This is particularly evident as we identify the main motives for presenting his "mere Christianity" as a crystallization of his theology. To this we now turn.

THE MAIN MOTIVES BEHIND "MERE CHRISTIANITY"

From Lewis's writings, we can identify two distinctive motives behind Lewis's extraction of "mere Christianity": (1) Constructive, that is to build a consensus across divided denominations and Christian traditions, and (2) corrective, that is to identify the *skandalon* (or the stumbling block) which distinguishes authentically Christian thought from the "watered down version."

Constructive Motive

First, in the constructive sense, "mere Christianity" represents the "belief that has been common to nearly all Christians at all times." Lewis told readers of *Mere Christianity* that the phrase comes from Richard Baxter of the seventeenth century.[116] N. H. Keeble, comparing Lewis with Baxter, notes that both men recognized the existence of the disunity of doctrines in their respective times and sought to build bridges between them by identifying "what was common to them all." This "shared deposit of faith" alone constituted what is "essential, the mark of the true Christianity."[117] Rather than working on theological subtleties or controversial matters, these men tried to lay down a common ground among Christians, identifying the essential creeds. For Baxter, "Any man that has 'in his head, and heart, and life' the essentials contained in the Decalogue, the Creed, and the Lord's Prayer 'is certainly a member of the Catholick [sic] Church' no matter his particular doctrinal bias or liturgical practice."[118]

Lewis also attempted to establish the "positive, self-consistent, and inexhaustible" something,[119] which he found to unite all Christians at all times. In a sense, Lewis was in search of the Christian fundamentals, the absolutely essential articles of faith one must hold in order to be a Chris-

---

116. Lewis, *Mere Christianity*, 6. For a brief description of Baxter, see 5n.
117. Keeble, "C. S. Lewis, Richard Baxter, and 'Mere Christianity,'" 31.
118. Ibid.
119. Lewis, "On the Reading of Old Books," in *God in the Dock*, 203.

tian. The purpose for doing so was not to disagree with the "enterprise" of professional theologians who are able to engage in sophisticated theological reasoning. Rather, Lewis was concerned about a likely hazard of theological sophistication and diversification in his time: "One might be tempted, who read only contemporaries . . . [to think] that 'Christianity' is a word of so many meanings that it means nothing at all."[120] Lewis was confident that instead of "insipid interdenominational transparency," there is an essentially Christian (thus distinctive) message which is positive. Lewis confessed that as "a very ordinary layman of the Church of England," he held certain views he considered distinctively Anglican. He did not want to set forth his religion but "to expound 'mere' Christianity, which is what it is and was what it was long before [he] was born and whether [he] likes it or not."[121] He thought this was necessary in order to reach those outside of the Christian faith, who without it would be confused and discouraged. Therefore, in a constructive sense, Lewis's aim was both ecumenical and evangelistic.

Apparently, Lewis was assured of his accomplishment through *Mere Christianity*. "So far as I can judge from reviews and from the numerous letters written to me, the book, however faulty in other respects, did at least succeed in presenting an agreed, or common, or central, or 'mere' Christianity."[122] He illustrated the function of "mere Christianity" this way: "It is more like a hall out of which doors open into several rooms. If I can bring anyone into that hall I shall have done what I attempted. But it is in the rooms, not in the hall, that there are fires and chairs and meals."[123]

Corrective Motive

Second, in the corrective sense, "mere Christianity" is that which stands against the false representation of Christianity according to the spirit of his time. It is the *skandalon* that distinguishes Christianity from that which is not. As an extension of the "hall with many doors" illustration, Lewis reminded his readers of the importance of entering through the "true" door. He urged frankly,

> In plain language, the question should never be: "Do I like that kind of service?" but "Are these doctrines true: Is holiness here? Does my conscience move me towards this? Is my reluctance

---

120. Ibid.
121. Lewis, *Mere Christianity*, 7.
122. Ibid., 8.
123. Ibid., 12.

to knock at this door due to my pride, or my mere taste, or my personal dislike of this particular door-keeper?"[124]

Lewis clearly wanted to set something forth as true in contrast to what is false. He found his context to be in urgent need for assertions of the truth.

Keeble finds the context of Lewis and Baxter to be similar.

> In their respective ages each man was confronted by a significant break with the Christian tradition of the past and a consequent weakening of the authority and influence of the church. Baxter had to face the divisiveness and contentiousness consequent upon England's protracted and uncertain Reformation, Lewis the disillusion and apostasy which followed two world wars. They responded in an identical way.[125]

Their responses, therefore, were historically or contextually conditioned ones. Lewis was particularly critical of the spirit of his time and the version of Christianity that was in vogue among professional theologians and clergymen (what Lewis called "Christianity-and-water").

Having identified diverse carriers of "mere Christianity," expanding from the English Puritans to the German mystics, Lewis claimed that there is something concrete about it. Christianity is not something with so many meanings that it means nothing at all. Rather, he found in it "immensely formidable unity," which is seen particularly clearly from without. Lewis recalled his own atheistic days:

> In the days when I still hated Christianity, I learned to recognize, like some all too familiar smell, that almost unvarying *something* which met me, now in Puritan Bunyan, now in Anglican Hooker, now in Thomist Dante.[126]

Lewis suggested that the way to regain a proper perspective is to take our eyes off the current controversies and look behind the present time, through the books left by old and wise Christians who went before us, to get a hold of that essence. "The only safety is to have a standard of plain, central Christianity ('mere Christianity' as Baxter called it), which puts the controversies of the moment in their proper perspective."[127]

Lewis was an effective critic of modernity and modernism in theology. In his address, "*De Descriptione Temporum*," he proposed a three-fold

124. Ibid.
125. Keeble, "C. S. Lewis, Richard Baxter, and 'Mere Christianity,'" 28.
126. Ibid.
127. Ibid., 201.

division of Western history: the pre-Christian, the Christian, and the post-Christian. He observed that the post-Christian period consisted of a radical change of worldview. "Christians and Pagans had much more in common with each other than either has with a post-Christian."[128] Lewis pointed out several important changes in political order, the arts, religion, and the perception of reality. He believed that a post-Christian is not relapsing into Paganism but is being steeped in naturalism. Also, the birth of the machines coupled with the myth of universal evolutionism imbedded in the human mind an image of progress. "It is the image of old machines being superseded by new and better ones."[129]

In another address, "Modern Man and his Categories of Thought," Lewis pointed out that modern evangelistic endeavor suffers because of the loss of the supernatural worldview as well as the consciousness of sin and divine judgment in the "Modern Man." He claimed that modern "Provincialism" cut people off from tradition. The concern for the practical has replaced the quest for truth. The "Developmentalist" view of history, disregarding human sin and corruption, defined good as "a state of flux." "Proletarianism" granted each individual the right to seek personal satisfaction without feelings of fear, guilt, or awe.

> They think from the very outset, of God's duties to them, not their duties to Him. And God's duties to them are conceived not in terms of salvation but in purely secular terms—social security, prevention of war, a higher standard of life. "Religion" is judged exclusively by its contribution to these ends.[130]

People are less concerned with what is objectively *true* but "only want to know if it will be comforting, or 'inspiring,' or socially useful." This concern for practicality results in "an indifference to, and contempt of, dogma," with a wide belief that "all religions really mean the same thing." Similarly, relativism sweeps all fronts, brewing skepticism about reason; increasingly, people accept "that reasoning proves nothing and that all thought is conditioned by irrational processes."[131]

Lewis was particularly alarmed by the conditioning of theology by modern categories of thought. In his representative address on this issue, "Modern Theology and Biblical Criticism," he landed a devastating attack on theological modernism, especially on biblical scholars, for their literary

---

128. Lewis, "*De Descriptione Temporum*," in *Selected Literary Essays*, 5.
129. Ibid., 10–11.
130. Lewis, "Modern Man and his Categories of Thought," in *Present Concerns*, 65.
131. Ibid.

insensitivity, groundless historical bias, naturalistic presupposition, and proud scholasticism.[132] He concluded of many modern theologians that "they speak simply as . . . men obviously influenced by, and perhaps insufficiently critical of, the spirit of the age they grew up in."[133] Elsewhere, he concluded, "[Their theology] may be so 'broad' or 'liberal' or 'modern' that it in fact excludes any real Supernaturalism and thus ceases to be Christian at all."[134]

Therefore, it is a fitting conclusion that Lewis's "mere Christianity" represents his corrective attempt against these tendencies. He called himself an "old Western man."[135] From what we can gather, he was a literary and religious historian with a sense of values; in other words, he had a clear preference for the worldview of an older historical period in contrast to the modern.[136] He preferred the characteristics of the "Christian era" of Western history over that of the "post-Christian era." His "mere Christianity" is a historically sensitive or tradition-sensitive formula, expressing the major characteristics of traditionally confessed Christianity as it stands directly against modern or "post-Christian" opinions.

THE MAIN DISTINCTIVE OF "MERE CHRISTIANITY"

Lewis's "mere Christianity" is essentially a reconstruction of a twin pillar perspective or worldview which the modern "Christianity-and-water" has rejected. Therefore, Lewis's theology is supernaturalistic and redemptocentric, in direct contrast to the naturalistic and ethicocentric religion of the

---

132. Lewis, "Modern Theology and Biblical Criticism," in *Christian Reflections*, 152–66.

133. Ibid., 158.

134. Lewis, "Christian Apologetics," in *God in the Dock*, 89.

135. Lewis, *"De Descriptione Temporum,"* in *Selected Literary Essays*, 14. Doris Myers argues, however, "[The] portrait of Lewis as a dinosaur, a surviving specimen, has been much exaggerated." She claims that in terms of Lewis's view of language, he "was very much a child of his own time," since "[the] twentieth-century preoccupation with language affected Lewis particularly in the areas of philosophy and literary criticism." Myers, *C. S. Lewis in Context*, xi. However, Lewis's professional up-to-dateness and his technical interest in language as a literary critic do not undermine the fact that he was largely a traditionalist as he claimed.

136. From a literary point of view Bruce Edwards calls Lewis's stance "rehabilitative." "At the heart of his criticism, as well as his apologetics and fiction, is a stance he would call *rehabilitative*. This rehabilitative stance manifested a reverence for the past, a principled skepticism of one's own period's mores and dogma, and a profound propensity for recovering and preserving lost values and ideals." Edwards, "Rehabilitating Reading: C. S. Lewis and Contemporary Critical Theory," in *Taste of the Pineapple*, 30.

modern or post-Christian era. These two pillar doctrines or perspectives were already spelled out by Lewis in a letter of November 8, 1939: "To me the real distinction [to be made regarding types of Christianity] is not between high and low but between religion with real supernaturalism and salvationism on the one hand and all watered-down and modernist versions on the other."[137] Lewis's dual emphasis of supernaturalism and salvationism is what formed his basic Christian presupposition or commitment.

Lewis used this presupposition as his criterion for evaluating diverse opinions about reality. For example, he incorporated some aspects of the Greek philosophy of Plato and Aristotle, also found in different shapes and forms in Augustine, Dante, Aquinas, and particularly in Boethius; however, he cannot be labeled, in the final analysis, as a consistent Platonist, Aristotelian, or Thomist. His thoroughly supernaturalistic and salvationistic worldview contrasts fundamentally with certain conclusions found in Hellenistic thought. Lewis did show some affinity with Romanticism. But in like manner, Lewis's "mere Christianity" functions as a criterion. For instance, the Romantic supernaturalist vision of nature is appreciated, but the same nature must be rejected as the source of the message of salvation. Lewis rejected both salvationism without supernaturalism and supernaturalism without salvationism. They must go together. And the climax of the Christian vision is found in Jesus Christ, the incarnate God (the "Myth Became Fact") who came to save the world.

Lewis's two pillar perspective does not seem arbitrary. First of all, as we have seen, they function as a corrective to the religious *Sitz im Leben* of his and our time. Second, they correspond to what traditional theology has maintained as the two pillar doctrines of Scripture, namely, God the Creator and God the Redeemer.

Lewis's idea of supernaturalism is not a vague or unidentifiable feeling or mood. Rather, it is a distinctive worldview standing in contrast to naturalism. Naturalism holds that reality consists entirely of the "natural." "The Natural is what springs up, or comes forth, or arrives, or goes on, of *its own accord*: the given, what is there already: the spontaneous, the unintended, and unsolicited."[138] The Supernaturalist, on the other hand, "thinks that things fall into two classes":

> In the first class we find either things or (more probably) One Thing which is basic and original, which exists on its own. In the second we find things which are merely derivative from that One Thing. The one basic Thing has caused all the other things

137. Lewis, *Letters of C. S. Lewis*, 327.
138. Lewis, *Miracles*, 6.

> to be. It exists on its own; they exist because it exists. They will cease to exist if it ever ceases to maintain them in existence; they will be altered if it ever alters them.[139]

For Lewis, then, supernaturalism is a term that embraces theism (most plausibly a belief in a personal Deity), creationism (that the self-existing being originated contingent beings), and the Creator-creature distinction (that there is a fundamental distinction between the two spheres of existence).

Salvationism, on the other hand, denies a developmental or evolutionary view of human history. Having recognized the fallen state of humanity, a catastrophic intervention of the Creator, both personal and cosmic, is deemed necessary. The solution to individual and social problems must be as radical as the problems themselves. The answer lies in the appearance of Christ and in people's willing acceptance of his person and redemptive work.

In the following chapters, we expound Lewis's "mere Christianity" and the corollary doctrines, tracing them in terms of the paradigm of pilgrimage, since the journey motif is dominant in his works. The motif is consistent with Lewis's supernaturalism and salvationism.

> We must simply accept it that we are spirits, free and rational beings, at present inhabiting an irrational universe, and must draw the conclusion that we are *not derived from it*. We are strangers here. We come from somewhere else. Nature is not the only thing that exists. There is "another world," and that is where we come from. And that explains why we do not feel at home here.[140]

The result will demonstrate that Lewis's "mere Christianity" challenged the spiritual laxity, doctrinal complacency, and scholastic irrelevancy of the Western church of his and our time. "Mere Christianity" is a *skandalon* to them. To the world, it is the *evangelium*.

---

139. Ibid., 7.
140. Lewis, "On Living in an Atomic Age," in *Present Concerns*, 78.

3

Away From Home

Restlessness and Wandering as Praeparatio Evangelica

Now we listen to Lewis the theologian, as he tell us what kind of spiritual journey characterizes Christian life. There are four stages to this pilgrimage: "Away from Home," "Homeward Turning," "Home Away from Home," and lastly, "The Final Home." This chapter focuses on what the "Away from Home" experience is like.

There are clearly two distinctive aspects Lewis wanted us to see about our inhabited world. First, the world offers its inhabitants perilous journeys. About the world Charles Williams depicts in his poems, Lewis said,

> [It] is a strong, strange, and consistent world. . . . It is certainly not a world I feel at home in. . . . It strikes me as a perilous world full of ecstasies and terrors, full of things that gleam and dart, lacking in quiet, empty spaces.[1]

For Lewis, this was not a poetic distortion of reality. The world according to Lewis, as with Williams, was teeming with living beings and full of rich contours, where strange and dangerous things await us. In it, human beings are restless wanderers from the beginning, feeling displaced and often left alone in solitude.

Second, however, it is the world of a Creator who has put sign-posts to himself in every corner so that his creatures would know him and, therefore, come to know where they truly belong. "Every created thing is, in its degree, an image of God, and the ordinate and faithful appreciation of that thing is a clue which, truly followed, will lead back to Him."[2] So, it is the

---

1. Williams and Lewis, *Taliessin through Logres*, 382.
2. Lewis, *Arthurian Torso*, 151.

world of splendor and awe to all, and especially to those who learn to see in nature the supernature, which sustains and gives meaning to it.³

In the world, people have all along discovered sign-posts. Some tried to describe them in mythologies; others tried to do it in various philosophies. Some managed to get very close to the truth, but many missed the point all together. For discovering them is one thing, but to correctly interpret them is a different matter. It is ultimately the Creator himself who gives us in time the right interpretation. When you accept his words, you must embark on a whole new journey. That is how the wandering stops and a journey begins.

Therefore, life in the world is both dangerous and mysterious. The recognition of the two-sided view of the world provided Lewis with an insight to assign proper meanings to both the quality of restlessness and of wonder. In theological language, Lewis as a Christian thinker incorporated both the concept of the Fall of humanity (and the whole creation along with it) and the enduring grace of God to sustain the creation despite its fallenness. In fact, a proper function of the latter is to provide a setting in which the redemption of humanity becomes possible. It is the common operation of God for his creation.⁴

---

3. For Lewis, supernature is the basis of nature, the ground upon which nature is made possible. Lewis's view clearly presupposes the supernatural creation of the world by God. The fact that Lewis often advocated the theistic evolutionary view of creation does not change the basic presupposition of God's supernatural presence and acts.

4. According to traditional theological categories, God's common operation is distinguished from his special (or redemptive) operation. Of the general operation of God in nature Louis Berkhof says, "It is the highest importance that the special operations of the Holy Spirit in the work of redemption should be seen against the background of his general operations in the sphere of nature and in the life of man.... In the sphere of nature it is the Holy Spirit that gives birth to all life, organic, intellectual, and moral, that maintains it amid all changes, and that leads it to its development and destiny.... The general operations of the Holy Spirit pertain to the established order of nature and of the life of man, as it is rooted in creation, and guarantees its development and completion.... Without the general operations of the Holy Spirit ... there would be no proper sphere for his special operations." (Berkhof, *Manual of Reformed Doctrine*, 223–24).

Furthermore, the general operations of God can be categorized into two distinctive modes: First, Natural or General Revelation, and second, Common Grace.

Natural or General Revelation provides an epistemological context for knowing the Creator and even allows an inescapable impression of his character so that unbelief is inexcusable. The Apostle Paul said, "[What] may be known about God is plain to [men], because God has made it plain to them. For since the creation of the world, God's invisible qualities—his eternal power and divine nature—have been clearly seen, being understood from what has been made, so that men are without excuse." (Rom 1:19–20 NIV). These remarkable claims are the basis for the conviction that God has not left his creatures without witnesses to his being.

Second, Common Grace refers to the existential and ethical context of people in general so that life in the fallen world remains possible. In the existential aspect, Common

SIGNS FROM "THE LANDLORD"

In *The Pilgrim's Regress*, Lewis's autobiographical allegory, he portrays the process of people's search for meaning in the light of his own intellectual journey. Basically, it is his own apology for his newly embraced Christian faith, its worldview and lifestyle. The book features two kinds of movement in the main character, John.

The first movement is a restless wandering as John sets out in search of a strange island seen in a vision, which produces in him an unquenched longing. It is a wandering because he knows not where to go. Unable to resist the longing, he leaves his home in the land of Puritania and, in swerving movements, travels from place to place, experiencing different stimuli, hearing different dogmas. The second movement is a journey or pilgrimage, a return to his spiritual birthplace that gives meaning to his existence, thus his true home.

Throughout the book, John contemplates the rumor of the Landlord. Who is he? What is he like? John is given conflicting pictures of his person and character. Lewis reminds us that John's restless wandering results from the signs the Landlord gives, but in such ways that John is not capable of understanding their significance. There is the vision of the island; there is the constant reminder of the set of rules, which is too large and ambiguous to follow. From Lewis's works in general, we can categorize the signs God gives to humanity as three: Joy, nature, and Tao (or natural moral law).

Lewis's discussion of these subjects does not strictly correspond with traditional natural theology, an attempt to understand God and his relationship with the world through reason apart from God's special revelation. As a study of various "sign-posts" from God, Lewis's work seems to resemble natural theology; however, his discussion sharply focuses on "theological psychology" characterized by a deep sense of anxiety and frustration. Each sign-post offers both pain and pleasure, bitter and sweet, fear and adoration. For Lewis, natural theology, taking the fallenness of humanity seriously, must accompany "theological psychology."

Grace points to the general blessings that God imparts to all people equally according to his pleasure so that life in the world can be sustained. In terms of the ethical aspect, it refers to the exertion of God's moral influence on humanity so that, without producing a redemptive effect in itself, sin is restrained, social order is maintained, and civility is promoted.

Therefore, the general operations of God establish for humanity the setting in which a life of awareness is possible. Humanity can sense their conscious existence, certain moral obligations, and have perceptions of nature to see inescapably the supernatural reality of God who created and sustains it. Lewis's major theological discourse presents his distinctive views in relation to the topic of the general operations of God.

Therefore, Lewis does not see the goal or purpose of natural theology as salvific in itself. It is best described as *Praeparatio Evangelica*, a preparation or context (which Lewis thought absolutely necessary) for the Gospel message. Through nature, Joy, and Tao, a real point of contact can be established for all people, since all experience the build-up of a tension or an anxiety of the heart, which is religious in nature. As Lewis entitled one of the chapters in *Mere Christianity*, "We have cause to be uneasy."[5]

The Observation of Nature

If Joy and Tao are examples of what traditional theology has called *cognitio dei insita*, this section deals with *cognitio dei acquisita*, or the knowledge of God acquired from the reality outside of oneself. Lewis affirmed that certain acquired and innate knowledge of God is objectively and universally apprehended. He discusses this in his address, "Is Theology Poetry?" "Theology, while saying that a *special illumination* has been vouchsafed to Christians and (earlier) to Jews, also says that there is some divine *illumination vouchsafed to all men*."[6] What is the content of the general "illumination"?

In *The Problem of Pain*, Lewis expressed his view of religious development. He identified the first stage as the experience of the numinous, which was followed by an awareness of some kind of morality. The next stage is accomplished when these two come together as an awareness that numinous power is actually the guardian of the morality to which they feel obligated.[7] The experience of the numinous is closely tied with the observation of nature.

Lewis described the experience of the numinous as one that excites "a special kind of fear . . . [that] may be called Dread." The numinous also induces "awe" as distinguished from "dread."[8] Humanity from early on ("that numinous awe" itself being "as old as humanity itself"[9]) came to sense a certain objective and universal reality that induced a two-fold response of fear and excitement (or dread and adoration). What is the origin of this experience of the Numious? "Now nothing is more certain than that man,

---

5. Lewis, *Mere Christianity*, fifth chapter of book 1, "Right and Wrong as a Clue to the Meaning of the Universe."

6. Lewis, "Is Theology Poetry?," in *Weight of Glory*, 83.

7. Lewis, *Problem of Pain*, 16–23. About the numinous, refer to the discussion of Rudolf Otto in the previous chapter.

8. Ibid., 17. Lewis thought that it is theoretically possible to think of a time when the perception of the numinous merely induced fear and dread before the humanity sensed anything like awe or adoration. This seems to be an unnecessary speculation.

9. Ibid., 19.

from a very early period, began to believe that the universe was haunted by spirits."[10] Lewis equated this uncanny notion of the universe with what Wordsworth described in *The Prelude* as the fear that was induced by the grandeur of nature when as a boy the poet rowed into a lake on a stolen boat. In other words, the apprehension of the numinous came by sensing a certain presence in nature (in reference to the whole universe).

The fear or awe of nature is not derived merely from perceived danger in the visible physical universe.

> When man passes from physical fear to dread and awe, he makes a sheer jump, and apprehends something which could never be *given*, as danger is, by the physical facts and logical deductions from them.[11]

Neither does the sense of awe arise out of the perceived orderliness of the physical universe. Something more mysterious or supernatural is in view. We may even call it a sort of mysticism.

> There seem, in fact, to be only two views we can hold about awe. Either it is a mere twist in the human mind, corresponding to nothing objective and serving no biological function, yet showing no tendency to disappear from that mind at its fullest development in poet, philosopher, or saint: or else it is a direct experience of the really supernatural, to which the name Revelation might properly be given.[12]

Lewis thought that there is a revelatory quality to this apprehension of the supernatural in nature. Lewis's vision of nature represents a supernaturalist view. Nature speaks. It commands us to look, listen, and attend.[13]

On the other hand, there is the danger of misconstruing the message of nature. The moods or spirits of nature can describe, in a sense, the context of humanity's wandering; but such cannot give an adequate illumination of the truth of God. Listen to Lewis's warning:

> The fact that this imperative [of nature] is so often misinterpreted and sets people making theologies and pantheologies and antitheologies—all of which can be debunked—does not really touch the central experience itself. What nature-lovers—whether they are Wordsworthians or people with "dark gods in their blood"—get from nature is an iconography, a language of

10. Ibid., 17.
11. Ibid., 20.
12. Ibid., 20–21.
13. Lewis, *Four Loves*, 36.

images. I do not mean simply visual images; it is the "moods" or "spirits" themselves—the powerful expositions of terror, gloom, jocundity, cruelty, lust, innocence, purity—that are the images. In them each man can clothe his own belief. We must learn our theology or philosophy elsewhere.[14]

Lewis's observation of the danger of creating one's own religion is quite consistent with Paul's analysis of humanity's natural religion.

> For although they knew God, they neither glorified him as God nor gave thanks to him, but their thinking became futile and their foolish hearts were darkened. Although they claimed to be wise, they became fools and exchanged the glory of the immortal God for images made to look like mortal man and birds and animals and reptiles. . . . They exchanged the truth of God for a lie, and worshipped and served created things rather than the Creator.[15]

Paul clearly pointed out two facts, which combined together make everyone deeply frustrated about the effect of sin: First, everyone clearly knows "God's invisible qualities" through the created world. The invisible qualities are described as "his eternal power and divine nature." Paul said that the knowledge is "plain" because "God has made it plain to them."[16] But in betrayal of this clear knowledge, people distort the truth of God. People are masterful icon-makers. And they are making counterfeit icons of God—in all cases grotesque misrepresentations of the power and the nature of God. On the other hand, Paul could not have affirmed more forcefully the integrity of the created world even under the original curse. There exists something wholesome; the very traces of God pervade the whole of his creation.

For Lewis, nature's role is not to convey a message but to set a proper context for perceiving God's qualities. "Nature will not verify any theological or metaphysical proposition. . . . She will help to show what it means."[17] Lewis said that for some the love of nature has been "an indispensable initiation" for knowing God. Yet, the limits are clearly established by Lewis. The role of nature is to arouse questions more than to give answers. Lewis put it this way:

---

14. Ibid.
15. Rom 1:21–23, 25 (NIV).
16. Rom 1:19–20 (NIV).
17. Lewis, *Four Loves*, 36.

> Nature cannot satisfy the desires she arouses nor answer theological questions nor sanctify us. Our real journey to God involves constantly turning our backs on her; passing from the dawn-lit fields into some poky little church, or (it might be) going to work in an East End parish.[18]

The role of nature is to awaken, with its terror and fascination-inducing presence, an unresolved tension in the heart of all people. It also affirms humanity's wanderer status. In this sense, nature functions as *praeparatio evangelica*.

The Experience of Joy

"[The] central story of my life," wrote Lewis, "is about nothing else" but the quality common to a series of his childhood experiences. He called it "Joy" or "an unsatisfied desire which is itself more desirable than any other satisfaction."[19] The quality of Joy is represented by the vision of an island in *The Pilgrim's Regress*. The vision accompanies a sweet sound of a musical instrument as John is led to a "green wood full of primrose." While John's mind swims in the sudden flood of childhood memory,

> there came to him from beyond the wood a sweetness and a pang so piercing that instantly he forgot his father's house, and his mother, and the fear of the Landlord, and the burden of the rules. All the furniture of his mind was taken away.... It seemed to him that a mist which hung at the far end of the wood had parted for a moment, and through the rift he had seen a calm sea, and in the sea an island, where the smooth turf sloped down unbroken to the bays, and out of the thickets peeped the pale, small-breasted Oreads, wise like gods.... He had no inclination yet to go into the wood: and presently he went home, with a sad excitement upon him, repeating to himself a thousand times, "I know now what I want."[20]

The story gives us some descriptions about the quality of Joy: (1) There is an element of sweetness. (2) There is a sense that something is drawing the subject towards an unknown object. (3) The moment when Joy attacks, there is a sharp sensation of a pang, a piercing of the soul. Lewis believed the experience of authentic Joy was "distinct not only from pleasure in general

---

18. Ibid., 39.
19. Lewis, *Surprised by Joy*, 17–18.
20. Lewis, *Pilgrim's Regress*, 8.

but even from aesthetic pleasure. It must have the stab, the pang, the inconsolable longing."[21] (4) The experience is so enrapturing that earthly things or pleasures are forgotten. (5) The experience is so overwhelming that the mind gets absorbed and acutely focused unto it. (6) The object to which it points is a reality quite outside of the subject himself. (7) It has a strong sensation of nostalgia. (8) It leaves behind a strong desire for more.

As a child, Lewis had experiences of the quality which he described in *The Pilgrim's Regress*. He recalls some "incurably romantic" sort of childhood experiences: One day, his brother Warnie brought into their nursery "the lid of a biscuit tin which he had covered with moss and garnished with twigs and flowers so as to make it a toy garden or a toy forest." The sight of it aroused a strange sense of "something cool, dewy, fresh, exuberant."[22] Also, there were the Castlereagh Hills a distance away but visible from his nursery windows. "They were not very far off but they were, to children, quite unattainable."[23] The hills triggered in him a sense of longing or *Sehnsucht*, the German word Lewis assigned to the quality. He was less than six years old when this experience first came to him.

There followed three distinctive episodes of Joy. The first took place when he "stood beside a flowering currant bush on a summer day." This moment of platitude turned into a moment of unusual rapture.

> [There] suddenly arose in me without warning, and as if from a depth not of years but of centuries, the memory of that earlier morning at the Old House when my brother had brought his toy garden into the nursery. It is difficult to find words strong enough for the sensation which came over me; Milton's "enormous bliss" of Eden (giving the full, ancient meaning of "enormous") comes somewhat near it. It was a sensation, of course, of desire. . . . [And] before I knew what I desired, the desire itself was gone, the whole glimpse withdrawn, the world turned commonplace again, or only stirred by a longing for the longing that had just ceased. It had taken only a moment of time; and in a certain sense everything else that had ever happened to me was insignificant in comparison.[24]

The second episode came when Lewis contemplated the "Idea of Autumn" while reading Beatrix Potter's book, *Squirrel Nutkin*. "It sounds fantastic to say that one can be enamored of a season, but that is something like

21. Lewis, *Surprised by Joy*, 72.
22. Ibid., 7.
23. Ibid.
24. Ibid., 16.

what happened; and, as before, the experience was one of intense desire."[25] The desire was obviously unattainable. How can the desire to possess Autumn be gratified? The experience, Lewis remembered, "was something quite different from ordinary life and even from ordinary pleasure; something . . . in another dimension."[26]

The third episode came through a poem, *Tegner's Drapa*. Lewis read,

> I heard a voice that cried,
> Balder the beautiful
> Is dead, is dead—

"Instantly I was uplifted into huge regions of northern sky, I desired with almost sickening intensity something never to be described (except that it is cold, spacious, severe, pale, and remote)."[27]

What is the role of this experience? Joy is by definition a sharp attack of awareness that one is displaced from the object desired. Thus, it awakens his/her sense of displacement and an intense desire for "home." Lewis said, "All joy (as distinct from mere pleasure, still more amusement) emphasizes our pilgrimage status; always reminds, beckons, awakens desire."[28]

Corbin Scott Carnell's *Bright Shadow of Reality* attempts to identify the meaning of Joy. According to him, it is "a sense of separation from what is desired, a ceaseless longing which always points beyond," and though it may have a variety of forms, "these are united in a common basis—a sense of displacement."[29]

Joy gives us a glimpse of our true happiness but leaves behind an even greater hunger and thirst. In fact, as an unsatisfied desire, it is "itself more desirable than any other satisfaction."[30] So in the case of Joy, wanting itself is the best having. On the other hand, this intensely desirable "desiring" also turns out to be "a particular kind of unhappiness or grief."[31] As in Wordsworth's sonnet, "Surprised by joy—impatient as the Wind," where "joy" turns out to be none other than a sudden rush of desire for his dead

---

25. Ibid., 16–17.
26. Ibid., 17.
27. Ibid.
28. Lewis, *Letters of C. S. Lewis*, 289. This letter to Dom Bede Griffiths, OSB, dated, November 5, 1959, is missing in the revised Harvest edition of 1993. The other citations for *Letters of C. S. Lewis* refer to the Harvest edition unless it is specifically noted otherwise.
29. Carnell, *Bright Shadow of Reality*, 23.
30. Lewis, *Surprised by Joy*, 18.
31. Ibid.

daughter, the experience really is "the worst pang that sorrow ever bore."[32] It is a paradoxical cross-section of emotions, leaving behind a bitter-sweet residue. As both a tremendously pleasing desire and an unfulfilled longing, Joy presents an unresolved tension, which constitutes a core human experience.

As a universal experience, it resembles Augustine's restless heart or Pascal's "God-shaped vacuum." "The human soul was made to enjoy some object that is never fully given—nay, cannot even be imagined as given—in our present mode of subject and spatio-temporal experience."[33] Many in vain look for satisfaction, without realizing that the real object of desire lies beyond what is humanly attainable.

The phenomenon of Joy appears in relation to all human desires. "There is something self-defeating about human desire, in that what is desired, when achieved, seems to leave the desire unsatisfied."[34] Such is the paradox of hedonism: the more one indulges in pleasure-seeking, the more unsatisfied one becomes. In fact, one is often overtaken by a sense of futility rather than of gratification. Lewis illustrates this in his celebrated sermon, "The Weight of Glory."

> The books or the music in which we thought the beauty was located will betray us if we trust to them; it was not in them, it only came through them, and what came through them was longing. These things—the beauty, the memory of our own past—are good images of what we really desire; but if they are mistaken for the thing itself they turn into dumb idols, breaking the hearts of their worshippers. For they are not the thing itself, they are only the scent of a flower we have not found, the echo of a tune we have not heard, news from a country we have not visited.[35]

This is what Lewis called "the inconsolable secret" in each and every one. Without the ultimate answer to our heart's desire, every little delight that comes our way will leave a trace of disappointment. Every Joy-inducing delight, when followed faithfully, will lead us outside of ourselves to the source.

> I am quite ready to describe "Sehnsucht" as "spilled religion," provided it is not forgotten that the spilled drops may be full of

---

32. Abrams et al., *Norton Anthology of English Literature*, 1441.
33. Lewis, "Afterword to Third Edition," in *Pilgrim's Regress*, 204–5.
34. McGrath, *Cloud of Witnesses*, 127.
35. Lewis, "The Weight of Glory," in *Weight of Glory*, 7.

blessing to the unconverted man who licks them up, and therefore begins to search for the cup whence they were spilled.[36]

Therefore, we have what apologists have called the "argument from desire" in Lewis's concept of Joy. Through his autobiography he was basically proclaiming to the world that he had not only argued an argument, but had lived it and proved it right. An early manuscript of *Surprised by Joy*, now in Walter Hooper's possession, is reported to begin with the statement:

> In this book I propose to describe the process by which I came back, like so many of my generation, from materialism to a belief in God. If that process had been a purely intellectual one, and if I were therefore simply giving a narrative form to a work of apologetic, there would be no place for my book. The defense of theism lies in abler hands than mine. What makes me bold to contribute my own story is the fact that I arrived where now I am, not by reflection alone, but by reflection on a particular recurrent experience. I am an empirical Theist. I have arrived at God by induction.[37]

We must not forget that this is only one perspective on Lewis's conversion story. The other perspective—seeing God besieging him, gradually but surely closing in until the moment of surrender—should not be ignored.

Nevertheless, Lewis saw real apologetic potential in the "argument from desire." It begins from the basic proposition that for every natural desire, there is an object that is meant to satisfy it. We feel hunger because there is such a thing as food; we feel thirst because water actually exists. The next stage is to honestly realize that there exists a desire, although often misunderstood, without material satisfaction. People try desperately to seek out gratification by creaturely means, only to end up with a greater hunger. This desire which no creaturely thing can satisfy is, then, is Joy; and interestingly, people find Joy itself more desirable than any other material satisfaction. Nevertheless, Joy must have a corresponding object that fulfills it: "This Desire was, in the soul, as the Siege Perilous in Arthur's castle—the chair in which only one could sit. And if nature makes nothing in vain, the One who can sit in this chair must exist."[38] What can satisfy Joy? Lewis concluded that Joy is a longing that points to the eternal world, and one that only God can satisfy.

---

36. Lewis, "Christianity and Culture," in *Christian Reflections*, 22.
37. Green and Hooper, *C. S. Lewis: A Biography*, 113.
38. Lewis, "Afterword to Third Edition," in *Pilgrim's Regress*, 205.

In *Mere Christianity,* Lewis attempted to show how people make mistakes about Joy. They commit one of two mistakes. (1) "The Fool's Way": They think something is not right with things themselves. They think that only if they find something better—a more beautiful woman, a more expensive holiday, a more luxurious automobile—will they find satisfaction. So "[they] spend their whole lives trotting from woman to woman . . . from continent to continent, from hobby to hobby, always thinking that the latest is 'the Real Thing' at last, and always disappointed."[39] (2) "The Way of the Disillusioned 'Sensible Man'": They soon decide that everything is really an adolescent dream. They learn not to question or seek. "This is, of course, a much better way than the first, and makes a man much happier, and less of a nuisance to society."[40] But, if there really is the object of Joy's desiring, this way ends up being as foolish as the first one.

Lewis said, therefore, we must seek "The Christian Way."

> Creatures are not born with desires unless satisfaction for those desires exists. A baby feels hunger: well, there is such a thing as food. A duckling wants to swim: well, there is such a thing as water. Men feel sexual desire: well, there is such a thing as sex. If I find in myself a desire which no experience in this world can satisfy, the most probable explanation is that I was made for another world. If none of my earthly pleasures satisfy it, that does not prove that the universe is a fraud. Probably earthly pleasures were never meant to satisfy it, but only to arouse it, to suggest the real thing. If that is so, I must take care, on the one hand, never to despise, or be unthankful for, these earthly blessings, and on the other, never to mistake them for the something else of which they are only a kind of copy, or echo, or mirage. I must keep alive in myself the desire for my true country. . . . I must make it the main objective of life to press on to that other country and to help others to do the same.[41]

Joy, then, is an incentive to turn people's restless wandering into a journey toward the other country for which they are made. This is Lewis's version of the "argument from desire."

As a conclusion to his autobiography, Lewis said that he had lost nearly all interest in the subject of Joy since he became a Christian, because desiring after "a desire" for God has no value when he had found God himself.[42]

---

39. Lewis, *Mere Christianity,* 119.
40. Ibid., 120.
41. Ibid.
42. Lewis, *Surprised by Joy,* 238.

Joy "was valuable only as a pointer," and "when we have found the road and are passing signposts every few miles, we shall not stop and stare."[43] For Christians, then, Joy is only an encouragement to continue to fix our eyes upon the object of our desire in our journey toward home.

The Recognition of Tao

As we have seen earlier, nature is for Lewis a pointer to its Creator. But in his view there is a superior testimony.

> We have two bits of evidence about the Somebody. One is the universe He has made. If we used that as our only clue, then I think we should have to conclude that He was a great artist (for the universe is a very beautiful place), but also that He is quite merciless and no friend to man (for the universe is a very dangerous and terrifying place). The other bit of evidence is that Moral Law which He has put into our minds. And this is a better bit of evidence than the other, because it is inside information. You find out more about God from the Moral Law than from the universe in general just as you find out more about a man by listening to his conversation than by looking at a house he has built.[44]

Consequently, Lewis spent a considerable amount of energy to prove the existence of a universal natural moral law.

We have seen in *The Problem of Pain* that Lewis suggested there are different stages of religious apprehension in human history. The first stage is the experience of the numinous, and this has been dealt with in the previous section. The second stage, however, is the acknowledgment of a universal sense of morality. "[They] feel towards certain proposed actions the experiences expressed by the words 'I ought' or 'I ought not.'"[45] In the third stage people began to identify the moral imperative with the Numious. "The Numinous Power for which they feel awe is made the guardian of the morality to which they feel obligation."[46]

Lewis argued that natural moral law exists as an absolutely objective reality pressing upon people's mind with a certain regularity. He used the term Tao to denote the natural moral law, and the term appears most

---

43. Ibid.
44. Lewis, *Mere Christianity*, 37.
45. Lewis, *Problem of Pain*, 21.
46. Ibid., 22.

representatively in *The Abolition of Man*. To Christians, Lewis's usage of the term can be rather confusing. As he incorporated the term as a part of his apologetic vocabulary, he described its original Chinese meaning this way:

> It is the reality beyond all predicates, the abyss that was before the Creator Himself. It is Nature, it is the Way, the Road. It is the Way in which the universe goes on, the Way in which things everlastingly emerge, stilly and tranquilly, into space and time. It is also the Way which every man should tread in imitation of that cosmic and supercosmic progression, conforming all activities to that great exemplar. "In ritual," say the Analects [of Confucius], "it is harmony with Nature that is prized."[47]

Most importantly, "It is the doctrine of objective value, the belief that certain attitudes are really true, and others really false, to the kind of thing the universe is and the kind of things we are."[48] Lewis argued that Tao, as a universal category, proves to be a common denominator in the ethical imperatives of "Platonic, Aristotelian, Stoic, Christian, and Oriental alike."[49]

Primarily, Lewis wanted to uphold a normative, objective, and universal moral principle. This is doubtless a major facet of his philosophy. Peter Kreeft, considering objectivity to be "the key to [Lewis's] mind and to his philosophy," comments, "He is a moral absolutist, and much of his anti-modern polemic is directed against moral relativism."[50] In favor of a Medieval concept of objective moral law, Lewis expressed his discontent with the new idea that entered into the European mind in the sixteenth century. This important discussion is found in his *English Literature of the Sixteenth Century*.

Lewis argued that Medieval Aristotelian ethics had the advantage of establishing natural law as something objective and absolute, to which even a king must stand accountable. "Aristotle (*Politics,* 1282) explicitly ruled that the highest power should hardly legislate at all. Its function was to administer a pre-existing law." Even in the process of producing concrete rules for concrete situations, "[the] main outlines of the law must be preserved. It creates, and is not created by, the State."[51] This law is the real sovereign. Lewis cited Bracton, "The King is under the Law for it is the Law that maketh him a King."[52] This Aristotelian principle coupled with the biblical no-

---

47. Lewis, *Abolition of Man*, 28.
48. Ibid., 29.
49. Ibid.
50. Kreeft, *C. S. Lewis: A Critical Essay*, 27, 41.
51. Lewis, *English Literature in the Sixteenth Century*, 47.
52. Ibid., 48.

tion of the natural law, found in Rom 2:15,[53] promoted a strong view of the natural moral law, which dominated the Medieval mind-set. So Aquinas could argue, "The civil law of this or that community is derived from the natural 'by way of particular determination.' If it is not, if it contains anything contrary to Natural Law, then it is unjust and we are not, in principle, obligated to obey it."[54] Lewis found an extension of this concept in Hooker, who asserted that though God is the author of the law, he is also a voluntary subject of the law. "They err who think that of the will of God to do this or that there is no reason besides his will." That is, in Lewis's words, "God does nothing except in pursuance of that 'constant Order and Law' of goodness which He has appointed to Himself."[55] One further step is left: Grotius in *De Jure Belli ac Pacis* (1625) asserted that "the Law of Nature, actually derived from God, would be equally binding even if we supposed that no God existed. It is another way of saying that good would still be good if stripped of all power."[56]

Lewis thought that this was the extreme opposite of Calvin's view which, in Lewis's words, "comes near to saying that omnipotence must be worshipped even if it is evil, that power is venerable when stripped of all good."[57] Lewis contended that the trend put in motion by Calvin's view, which he formulated as giving absolute legislative power to the civil magistrate as a divinely ordained institution, culminated in Machiavelli's *The Prince* as the farthest deviation from the Medieval principle.[58] It came to Machiavellian tyranny via "Rousseau, Hegel, and his twin offspring of the Left and the Right, for the view that each society is totally free to create its own 'ideology' and that its members, receiving all their moral standards from it."[59]

Lewis, here, seeing a historical trend in motion, quite unfairly places Calvin at the crossroads. In Calvin's *Institutes* there is an obvious effort to balance the extremes of usurping power on the one hand and tyranny on

---

53. Rom 1:15 is mistakenly given as the reference, but from the context it is clear that he was referring to Rom 2:15. Rom 2:14–15 (NIV) reads, "Indeed, when Gentiles, who do not have the law, do by nature things required by the law, they are a law for themselves, even though they do not have the law, since they show that the requirements of the law are written on their hearts, their consciences also bearing witness, and their thoughts now accusing, now even defending them."

54. Lewis, *English Literature in the Sixteenth Century*, 48.

55. Ibid., 49.

56. Ibid.

57. Ibid.

58. Ibid., 51.

59. Ibid., 50.

the other. Calvin wrote in 1559, six years following the translation of Machiavelli's *The Prince* into Latin, "[From] one side, insane and barbarous men furiously strive to overturn this divinely established order [of civil government]; while, on the other side, the flatterers of princes, immoderately praising their power, do not hesitate to set them against the rule of God himself. Unless both these evils are checked, purity of faith will perish."[60]

Peter Kreeft, in support of Lewis's assessment of Calvin's view, suggests that "Calvinism makes goodness arbitrary in making it depend solely on God's will (not his reason or his nature)."[61] Remarkably, it is assumed that Calvinism dissociates God's will or decree from his reason or nature, which would be a significant departure from Christian orthodoxy. While it is consistent to orthodox Christianity to claim that righteousness or truth derives its standard from the Word of God, the Word would never be detached from the being and the nature of God. Lewis's caricature of the theology under attack reveals the confusion.

> There were in the eighteenth century terrible theologians who held that "God did not command certain things because they are right, but certain things are right because God commanded them." To make the position perfectly clear, one of them even said that though God has, as it happens, commanded us to love Him and one another, He might equally well have commanded us to hate Him and one another, and hatred would then have been right. It was apparently a mere toss-up which He decided on. Such a view of course makes God a mere arbitrary tyrant. It would be better and less irreligious to believe in no God and to have no ethics than to have such an ethics and such a theology as this.[62]

Lewis appears to criticize the view that "right is right because God says it is right" and to consider such claim to be worse than having no religion. But were the theologians "terrible" because they tied righteousness with God's precepts or because they held an arbitrary view of God's nature? The answer is the latter.[63]

---

60. McNeill, *Calvin: Institutes of the Christian Religion*, vol. 2, book 4, ch. 10, sec. 1. About this comment of Calvin, McNeill noted, "These sentences (1559) evidently refer to the Anabaptists on the one hand, and on the other to Machiavelli, whose Italian *Il Principe* was only in 1553 translated into Latin. Calvin may also have in mind the emperor-cult of antiquity."

61. Kreeft, *C. S. Lewis for the Third Millennium*, 84.

62. Lewis, *Reflections on the Psalms*, 61.

63. The Orthodox Reformed or classical Calvinist position can hardly be accused of compromising the "goodness" of God in order to highlight his "sovereignty." God's

What was Lewis really intending to say? How did he understand the relationship between God's being (including both his will and nature) and the moral law or "goodness"? Did Lewis agree with Grotius's theory that the law of nature can stand outside the being of God? In other words, once God had established a standard for goodness, can that goodness stand outside the jurisdiction of God's power and still remain in effect?

In his 1943 article, "The Poison of Subjectivism," Lewis raised the question, "[How] is the relation between God and the moral law to be represented?"[64] He concluded that to say that "the moral law is God's law is no final solution." Why?

> Are these things right because God commands them or does God command them because they are right? If the first, if good is to be *defined* as what God commands, then the goodness of God Himself is emptied of meaning and the commands of an omnipotent fiend would have the same claim on us as those of the "righteous Lord." If the second, then we seem to be admitting a cosmic dyarchy, or even making God Himself the mere executor of a law somehow external and antecedent to His own being. Both views are intolerable.[65]

Having eliminated these two possibilities, he then appealed to the doctrine of the simplicity or unity of God (based on his deduced meaning of the Trinity, that God is not a person but commands a unity of Deity, being undivided "in the absolute being of the superpersonal God"). So he identified the problem to be that "when we attempt to think of a person and a law, we are compelled to think of this person either as obeying the law or as making it."[66] Therefore, he concludes,

> God neither *obeys* nor *creates* the moral law. The good is uncreated; it never could have been otherwise; it has in it no shadow of contingency; it lies, as Plato said, on the other side of existence. It is the *Rita* of the Hindus by which the gods themselves are divine, the *Tao* of the Chinese from which all realities proceed.

On the other hand, Christians formulate this differently from the Hindus and the Chinese.

---

sovereign will can certainly overrule subjective human judgments of what is good, but it does not and cannot contradict his own goodness.

64. Lewis, "The Poison of Subjectivism," in *Christian Reflections*, 79.
65. Ibid.
66. Ibid., 80.

> But we, favoured beyond the wisest pagans, know what lies beyond existence, what admits no contingency, what lends divinity to all else, what is the ground of all existence, is not simply a law but also a begetting love, a love begotten, and the love which, being between these two, is also imminent in all those who are caught up to share the unity of their self-caused life. God is not merely good, but goodness; goodness is not merely divine, but God.[67]

Lewis affirms that God does not *have* attributes as secondary expressions; rather, God's attributes are inherent to his Triune existence. He sustains the doctrine of God's simplicity. Therefore, the initial question, "Are things right because God command them or does God command them because they are right?" turns out to be faulty to begin with. Goodness (i.e., commanding of what is right) as God's attribute should never be considered in abstraction from his being. Goodness is not what God commands or that which pressures him to command itself. In this sense, his goodness is that which he is.

I wonder if there is a real difference between what Lewis *wanted* to establish and what the following statements entail:

> The moral standard which God constituted through both General and Special Revelation is an objective reality that stands outside each individual's subjective feelings or inclinations; this standard is absolutely consistent with the nature of God, therefore, manifesting divine goodness, justice, love, etc.; ultimately, as we stand before God's decrees, we are standing before the being of God who exercise His Lordship over us by his Word; the Hindu concept of *Rita* and the Chinese concept of *Tao* reflect something of the Natural Moral Law, which God has placed in the heart of people, but as concepts of impersonal absolutes, they fail to express adequately the reality which God has created.

I believe these statements are quite consistent to Lewis's thought. Peter Kreeft, on the other hand, asserts that Lewis followed George MacDonald's view that "God commands the good because it is good; it is not good

---

67. Ibid. Unfortunately, by making reference to *Rita* and *Tao* Lewis risked the danger of equating the Christian God with non-Christian notions of deity. Edmund Clowney well expressed the concern at this point: "Lewis lumps the Scriptural concept of the truth of the law with the *Rta* [sic] of Hinduism and the abyss of Taoism as evidence of a common consent to this code. . . . But can theism be set aside while natural law is defended from its attackers? Are not the principles of natural law twisted and deformed in ancient Paganism just as seriously as in modern relativism?" Clowney, "Review of *The Abolition of Man*," 80.

because he commands it,"⁶⁸ in opposition to Calvinism which, according to Kreeft, "reduces goodness to divine power and makes us ready to worship an omnipotent Fiend." But in fact it would seem that Lewis instead wanted to say, "God commands the good because He is good." That must be why Lewis commented in *Surprised by Joy,*

> God was to be obeyed simply because he was God. . . . God is to be obeyed because of what He is in Himself. If you ask why we should obey God, in the last resort the answer is, "I am." To know God is to know that our obedience is due to Him. In His nature His sovereignty *de jure* is revealed.⁶⁹

Having discussed the nature of the natural moral law, we should now go back to the main issue of understanding the role of the natural moral law in the life of wandering. In *Mere Christianity,* Lewis presented what is basically the moral argument for the existence of God. However, Lewis's point is not straightforward. Instead of simply arguing that there are values such as truth and goodness innate in humankind and which must have a cause, Lewis pointed out that a state of tension exists.

> These, then, are the two points I wanted to make. First, that human beings, all over the earth, have this curious idea that they ought to behave in a certain way, and cannot really get rid of it. Secondly, that they do not in fact behave in that way. They know the Law of Nature; they break it. These two facts are the foundation of all clear thinking about ourselves and the universe we live in.⁷⁰

Lewis sought to establish an epistemological condition which he thought was essential for a subsequent reception of the Gospel. It was to be a *praeparatio evangelica,* a recognition of the anxiety common to humanity at large. In his letter to the producer of his BBC broadcast (which was later edited into *Mere Christianity*), Lewis wrote,

> I think what I mainly want to talk about is the Law of Nature, or objective right and wrong. It seems to me that the New Testament, by preaching repentance and forgiveness, always assumes an audience who already believe in the Law of Nature and know they have disobeyed it. In modern England we cannot at present

---

68. Kreeft, *C. S. Lewis for the Third Millennium,* 85.
69. Lewis, *Surprised by Joy,* 231–32.
70. Lewis, *Mere Christianity,* 21.

assume this, and therefore most apologetic begins a stage too far on. The first step is to create, or recover, the sense of guilt.[71]

Lewis's evangelistic intent is clearly defined in the letter.

Lewis said that the natural moral law is peculiar and innate to the human nature. There are exceptions found among people, but they are at odds with nature in the same manner as being color-blind or tone-deaf. "But taking the race as a whole ... the human idea of decent behaviour was obvious to everyone"; the differences "have never amounted to anything like a total difference."[72] This natural moral law must be distinguished from our instincts or social conventions. There are different instincts at work and the moral law regulates the instincts. Instincts are like the keys on a piano: "The Moral Law tells us the tune we have to play.... Strictly speaking, there are no such things as good and bad impulses.... [A piano] has not got two kinds of notes on it, the 'right' notes and the 'wrong' ones. Every single note is right at one time and wrong at another."[73] There is a standard that stands above social conventions that becomes a basis for determining the moral qualities of each convention. The moral law is not only a way of living (a convention) but an imperative to live in a certain way (a moral "ought").

What then lies behind the moral law? If this something is real, is it then conscious or unconscious (a material view versus a religious view)? Since human beings are the highest form of life, we should expect the something to be more like a person than unconscious materials. "According to [the religious view], what is behind the universe is more like a mind than it is like anything else we know. That is to say, it is conscious, and has purposes, and prefers one thing to another."[74] We are then left with three choices: Pantheism, Dualism, and Christian Theism. Pantheism asserts that God is beyond good and evil, and therefore refuses to make any value judgments: "Confronted with a cancer or a slum the Pantheist can say, 'If you could only see it from the divine point of view, you would realize that this also is God.'"[75] To Christians this is sheer nonsense. According to Lewis, Christianity is a "fighting religion," which insists on putting things right again according to God's purpose. Dualism insists on believing in absolute good and absolute evil. But once you call anything good or bad, "you are putting into the universe a third thing in addition to the two Powers: some law or

---

71. Quoted in Green and Hooper, *C. S. Lewis: A Biography*, 202.
72. Lewis, *Mere Christianity*, 18–19.
73. Ibid., 22–23.
74. Ibid., 31–32.
75. Ibid., 44–45.

standard or rule of good which one of the powers conforms to and the other fails to conform it." He continues,

> But since the two powers are judged by this standard, then this standard, or the Being who made this standard, is farther back and higher up than either of them, and He will be the real God. In fact, what we meant by calling them good and bad turns out to be that one of them is in a right relation to the real ultimate God and the other in a wrong relation to Him.[76]

In *Mere Christianity*, Lewis moves on from the argument to the presentation of the message of Christ, his incarnation and atonement through death. Based on his recognition of the natural moral law, Lewis constructs an apologetic argument for the Christian worldview. Along with nature and Joy, the recognition of the natural moral law points to the "Landlord." The result is a sense of both obligation and of guilt.

Until now, our discussion has focused on the existential dimension of *praeparatio evangelica*: what each person experiences as a member of humanity. Next we move on to the historical dimension as we look into the dialectical relationship between the law and the prophets of the Hebrew people, and Pagan mythologies according to Lewis.

THE "SHEPHERD PEOPLE" AND THE PAGANS

A peculiarity of Lewis's interpretation of the history of Hebrews and Pagans provides us with important insights into his thinking. Hebrews are called "the Shepherd People," and were given written rules for life by God. The Pagans, on the other hand, were given "pictures" (a reference to Lewis's view of the function of Pagan mythologies), which in effectiveness are inferior to the law and the prophets which the Hebrews received. We must turn to Lewis's autobiographical allegory for expansion.

In *The Pilgrim's Regress*, John hears a fascinating story from a hermit whose name is History. History tells John that the Landlord has given two avenues to communicate his message to his tenants. To those who could read, he has given the rules. But not everyone can read. "What use are rules to people who cannot read?" Furthermore, since "[no] one is born able to read . . . the starting point for all . . . must be a picture and not the rules."[77] The pictures alone were dangerous, however, because people constantly made up stories about the pictures. The stories usually consisted of their

---

76. Ibid., 49.
77. Lewis, *Pilgrim's Regress*, 146.

mistaken opinions, equating the pictures with absurd and indecent ideas and acts. But the Landlord would occasionally give new pictures.

> Just when their own stories seemed to have completely overgrown the original messages and hidden them beyond recovery, suddenly the Landlord would send them a new message and all their stories would look stale. Or just when they seemed to be growing really contented with lust or mystery mongering, a new message would arrive and the old desire, the real one, would sting again, and they would say, "Once more it has escaped us."[78]

Then there were the Shepherd People who could read, and because they could read they were given not pictures but rules. "Now the Shepherds, because they were under the Landlord, were made to begin at the right end. Their feet were set on a road."[79] The Shepherds were given charge of the road. They put sign-posts on it; they kept it clean and diligently repaired it. But this was done in a very narrow and protective manner. It could not solve the mystery of the Landlord and his ways altogether.

So History points out the necessity of a convergence of the pictures and the rules by "a third thing." He says, "The truth is that a Shepherd is only a half a man, and a Pagan is only half a man, so that neither people was well without the other, nor could either be healed until the Landlord's Son came into the country."[80] From this suggestion of salvation history, Lewis turns now to a more personal dimension of how the rules and the pictures should work out in an individual's spiritual journey. He says,

> The pictures alone are dangerous, and the Rules alone are dangerous. That is why the best thing of all is to find Mother Kirk at the very beginning, and to live from infancy with a third thing which is neither the Rules nor the pictures and which was brought into the country by the Landlord's Son. That, I say, is the best: never to have known the quarrel between the Rules and the pictures. But it very rarely happens. The Enemy's agents are everywhere at work, spreading illiteracy in one district and blinding men to the pictures in another.[81]

The allegory is self-explanatory. The third thing is the Gospel, and the Landlord's Son is Jesus Christ who brings it. For those living after the Son's coming, it is best to be born in the church, seeing no conflict between the

78. Ibid., 148.
79. Ibid., 149.
80. Ibid.
81. Ibid., 147.

Law and the Myths. It is interesting to detect a similarity between Lewis's scheme and that of Chesterton in *The Everlasting Man*. The pattern is very similar, yet there is a significant difference: For Chesterton, the dialectic is between philosophies and mythologies which find consummation in Christ; for Lewis, it is between the religion of the Old Testament Israel and the mythologies of the Pagans which together find fulfillment in Christ, who is both the Messiah and "Myth Became Fact."

There are several significant concepts we must clarify in order to fully understand Lewis's scheme. First, something should be said about Lewis's view of the Hebrew people as the chosen ones; second, we must expand on the meaning of "myth" according to Lewis; and finally, we should see how Jesus Christ is the fulfillment, not only of the hope and expectations of the law and the prophets, but also of the Pagan myths.

The Shepherd People

Lewis clearly acknowledged the special place the Hebrews occupied in salvation history. He expressed the Hebrew people's distinctive status among all peoples of the world in at least three ways. First, he pointed out the revelatory significance of the Hebrew people. Their history demonstrates a unique religious development involving a special apprehension of the Creator God. Indeed, they were the chosen people who became guardians of God's special revelation. *The Problem of Pain* argued that the Hebrews made a most significant revelatory discovery when they stood before God at Sinai.

> [It] is most really and truly in Abraham that all people shall be blessed, for it was the Jews who fully and unambiguously identified the awful Presence haunting the black mountain tops and thunderclouds with "the *righteous* Lord" who "loveth righteousness."[82]

Mere Christianity presented the same reality from a different perspective; it was not the people who discovered God's revelatory presence but God who acted redemptively in the history of the people to reveal the sort of God he is.

> He selected one particular people and spent several centuries hammering into their heads the sort of God He was—that there was only one of Him and that He cared about right conduct. Those people were the Jews, and the Old Testament gives an account of the hammering process.[83]

---

82. Lewis, *Problem of Pain*, 23.
83. Lewis, *Mere Christianity*, 54.

An important point consistently made by Lewis is the content of the revelation. God revealed himself fully and unambiguously to the Hebrews as the one who is both powerful and righteous. This was a major step up in humankind's religious apprehension. The Hebrews, therefore, possessed the "special illumination" of God, which Christians later received in a fuller measure. Lewis pointed out that "theology . . . [says] that a special illumination has been vouchsafed to Christians and (earlier) to Jews."[84] Along with G. K. Chesterton, he highlights and affirms the validity of religious development among Pagan cultures; nevertheless, he acknowledges the unique place the Hebrew people occupied in the progressive process of God's revelation.

> The earliest stratum of the Old Testament contains many truths in a form which I take to be legendary, or even mythical—hanging in the clouds, but gradually the truth condenses, becomes more and more historical. From things like Noah's Ark or the sun standing still upon Ajalon, you come down to the court memoirs of King David. Finally you reach the New Testament and history reigns supreme, and the Truth is incarnate. And "incarnate" is here more than a metaphor.[85]

Lewis's view of Scripture is to be discussed in chapter 6. It is necessary to point out for now that there is a clear recognition in Lewis that the Hebrews uniquely received the revelation from God. Lewis, therefore, stated that Gentile Christians, "with their tendency to forget it easily enough and even flirt with anti-Semitism," should be reminded that "the Hebrews are spiritually *senior* to us, that God *did* entrust the descendants of Abraham with the first revelation of Himself."[86]

Second, Lewis believed that the Hebrews, entrusted with the revelation of God, were a people with a missiological call. Making the point that God's "selectiveness" does not denote "favoritism" but rather "responsibility," Lewis comments,

> The "chosen" people are chosen not for their own sake (certainly not for their own honour or pleasure) but for the sake of the unchosen. Abraham is told that "in his seed" (the chosen nation)[87] "all nations shall be blest." That nation has been chosen to bear

---

84. Lewis, "Is Theology Poetry?," in *Weight of Glory*, 83.

85. Ibid., 84.

86. Lewis, *Letters of C. S. Lewis*, 448–49.

87. Not addressed by Lewis here is the point that "the seed" not only refers to the nation of Israel but that it ultimately refers to Christ.

a heavy burden. Their sufferings are great: but, as Isaiah recognized, their sufferings heal others.[88]

Again, Lewis stated in his sermon, "The Grand Miracle," the very same point:

> The selectiveness in the Christian story is not quite like [other instances]. The people who are selected are, in a sense, unfairly selected for a supreme honour; but it is also a supreme burden. The people of Israel come to realize that it is their woes which are saving the world.[89]

A way to understand Lewis's assertion about Israel's suffering as that which saves the world is to see Israel's history, including their suffering, as leading toward the Messiah's entrance into the world. In the same sermon, Lewis mentioned the apparent process of narrowing in the Hebrew history until the last great obedience of a woman preceded the Messiah's birth.

> One people picked out of the whole earth; that people purged and proved again and again. Some are lost in the desert before they reach Palestine; some stay in Babylon; some becoming indifferent. The whole thing narrows and narrows, until at last it comes down to a little point, small as the point of a spear—a Jewish girl at her prayers. That is what the whole of human nature has narrowed down to before the Incarnation takes place.[90]

This naturally leads us to the final point.

Lewis acknowledged the Hebrew people as the indispensable context for the realization of Christian faith. Indeed, "[our] own religion begins," Lewis said, "among the Jews, a people squeezed between great warlike empires, continually defeated and led captive."[91] Lewis asserted that Christians ought to credit "the Jews" for being made "the vehicle of His own Incarnation"; thus we ought to feel "indebted to Israel beyond all possible repayment."[92] This means, although Lewis acknowledged a sort of parallel

---

88. Lewis, *Miracles*, 118. Lewis must be referring to Isa 53. It is interesting to note that Lewis followed a typical Rabbinical interpretation of the passage, seeing the suffering servant as the nation of Israel rather than a prophetic reference to the coming Messiah. While it is premature to conclude that Lewis was not mindful of the passage's Christological significance, the apparent assertion of the theory of Israel's vicarious suffering is interesting, to say the least.

89. Lewis, "The Grand Miracle," in *God in the Dock*, 85.

90. Ibid., 84.

91. Lewis, *Problem of Pain*, 16.

92. Lewis, *Reflections on the Psalms*, 28.

religious development between the Hebrews and Pagan cultures (an idea which spurred his conversion), he clearly gave a greater weight to the role of the chosen race. The Shepherd People had an important role to play in the coming of the Landlord's Son into the world. In an interview on the subject of Christianity, Lewis commented, "In reality, Christianity is primarily the fulfillment of the Jewish religion, but also the fulfillment of what was vaguely hinted in all the religions at their best. What was vaguely seen in them all comes into focus in Christianity—just as God Himself comes into focus by becoming a Man."[93] Humanity, wandering, and restlessness all found an important religious development in the Hebrew people. Their early history revealed the progressive coming-into-focus of God's saving intention.

Mythologies of the Pagans

The above reveals also that Lewis held a distinctive view of Pagan cultures. In short, Christianity represented the fulfillment of the best of the Pagan myths. Chesterton believed that ancient myths were not unrelated to the Christian stories. Lewis likewise highlighted an important revelatory role played by myths: the pictures in *The Pilgrim's Regress*. Lewis's view of myth is an important subject which requires our attention.

First of all, we must define what Lewis meant by myth. F. F. Bruce, in "Myth and History," provides a helpful analysis of the meaning of myth as it is used in academic literature, particularly in theology. Bruce points out that the meaning of the word is closely associated with its origin. The Greek word *mythos* originally meant "an utterance or a story which may be true or false."[94] In the earliest literature, *mythos* is used synonymously with *logos*, and only some of the later writers used them in contrast, "*mythos* being a fictional narrative whereas *logos* is the prosaic fact."[95] Our interest is particularly with its religious context; in this sense, "a *mythos* is a story about one or more of the gods, especially a story which was enacted in a sacred ritual." This enactment comprises of "the *legomena* (the things spoken) which accompany and interpret the *dromena* (the things done) or the *deiknymena* (the things shown)."[96] A phrase synonymous with *mythos* in this context is *hieros logos* (sacred story).[97] Sacred stories are very commonly found in all ancient cultures. Bruce has no hesitation in applying

---

93. Lewis, "Answers to Questions on Christianity," in *God in the Dock*, 54.
94. Bruce, "Myth and History," in Brown, *History, Criticism, and Faith*, 79.
95. Ibid.
96. Ibid.
97. Ibid., 80.

the notion of sacred story to the faith of Israel and even the New Testament Christian community. Applied to Israel and Christians, however, the notion is radically different. "[The] *mythos* in this instance is not the casting of a recurring fertility pattern in the form of a story thrown back to primeval times, but the recital of something that really happened in history, interpreted as the mighty, self-revealing act of Israel's God."[98]

Bruce's analysis sets the stage for our understanding of Lewis's approach to the issue. For Lewis, myth is an expression of universal truth in terms that human imagination can apprehend. In *Miracles,* Lewis said, "Myth in general is not merely misunderstood history (as Euhemerus thought) nor diabolical illusion (as some of the Fathers thought) nor priestly lying (as the philosophers of the Enlightenment thought) but, at its best a real though unfocused gleam of divine truth falling on human imagination."[99] In the context of the Christian message, Lewis formulated the idea of myth in a similar way to Bruce. "The Hebrews, like other people, had mythology: but as they were the chosen people so their mythology was the chosen mythology—the mythology chosen by God to be the vehicle of the earliest sacred truths, the first step in that process which ends in the New Testament where truth has become completely historical."[100] We must later consider the idea of "Myth Became Fact" in Jesus Christ. But first, we must grasp the meaning of myth in general as in Pagan cultures.

In the preface to his anthology drawn from the writings of George MacDonald, Lewis expressed his conviction that MacDonald was one of the greatest exponents of the art of myth-making. Lewis thought that myth is not essentially literary but extra-literary. "What really delights and nourishes me is a particular pattern of events, which would equally delight and nourish if it had reached me by some medium which involved no words at all—say by a mime, or a film."[101] The means of communication is only a vehicle through which the story (or the pattern of events) is "lodged in our imagination." "In poetry the words are the body and the 'theme' or 'content' is the soul. But in myth the imagined events are the body and something inexpressible is the soul: the words, or mime, or film, or pictorial series are not even clothes—they are not much more than a telephone."[102] That "something inexpressible" must be "the real though unfocused gleam of divine truth falling on human imagination." Lewis thought that most myths

98. Ibid.
99. Lewis, *Miracles,* 134n.
100. Ibid.
101. Lewis, "Preface," in *George MacDonald: An Anthology,* 15.
102. Ibid., 16.

were prehistoric in their origin, but that there are also some modern myth-makers. Lewis said, "MacDonald is the greatest genius of this kind whom I know."[103] Taking after MacDonald, Lewis's fictions generally have a mythopoeic quality to them. His works embody the "gleam of divine truth falling on human imagination."

In Lewis's main text on literary criticism, *An Experiment in Criticism*, he included a chapter entitled, "On Myth." In it, he tried to express succinctly the characteristics of myth, beginning with the assumption that there is a particular kind of story which has a value quite independent of its embodiment in any literary work. He thought that the only name that could possibly be given to such stories is myth.[104] But at this point, he issued an important caveat: "In the first place we must remember that Greek *muthos* does not mean this sort of story but any sort of story. Second, not all stories which an anthropologist would classify as myths have the quality I am here concerned with."[105] It is important to realize, then, Lewis was not concerned with a literary genre or a literary form but a particular *quality* which a particular sort of story evoked. He realized that the term, therefore, could be misleading. Nevertheless, he thought the use of the term, rather than an invention of a new one, involved a lesser evil. The fact that it is a certain quality apprehended by a subject, means that there is an inevitably subjective character about it even though Lewis tried to attribute a certain universal quality to it since it is a commonly held experience. He said, "Since I define myths by their effect on us, it is plain that for me the same story may be a myth to one man and not to another." Again he said, "[The] degree to which any story is a myth depends very largely on the person who hears or reads it."[106]

How did Lewis describe the characteristics of myth?

> 1. It is extra-literary. 2. The pleasure of myth depends on its introduction of a permanent object of contemplation (more like a thing than a narration) which works upon us by its peculiar flavour or quality, rather as a smell or a chord does. 3. Human sympathy is at a minimum. They are like shapes moving in another world. We see their relevance to our own life, but we do not imaginatively transport ourselves into theirs. 4. Myth is always, in one sense of that word, "fantastic." It deals with impossibles and preternaturals. 5. The experience may be sad or joyful but

---

103. Ibid.
104. Lewis, *An Experiment in Criticism*, 41–42.
105. Ibid., 42.
106. Ibid., 47–48.

> it is always grave. Comic myth is impossible. 6. The experience is not only grave but awe-inspiring. We feel it to be numinous. It is as if something of great moment had been communicated to us. The recurrent efforts of the mind to grasp—to conceptualize—this something, are seen in the persistent tendency of humanity to provide myths with allegorical explanations. And after all allegories have been tried, the myth itself continues to feel more important than they.[107]

The last point is particularly significant. Myth is not merely a pattern of events or a story but a certain happening, an event in itself which takes place at the time of its apprehension. A better way to put it is, taking into account the second characteristic, that experiencing myth is to subjectively encounter that permanent object of contemplation, which is more like a thing than narration. What is the meaning of this?

Roland Hein thinks that Lewis defines this particular understanding of myth with "greatest clarity and force." It is for Lewis "certainly one of the most basic elements in his thought."[108]

> Its presence is detected by an intuitive effect occurring in certain readers. Those who react with a pause and catch of breath, as though something "of great moment" has been conveyed, are encountering the dynamic of myth. They feel as though something numinous has confronted them. It is not so much that they receive a message, but rather they seem to have a fleeting contact with some remote unbroken world.[109]

Hein believes that the unbroken reality is a supernatural reality which myth, as a vehicle, communicates to people.[110] At this point, we should notice at least two important clues to understanding Lewis's idea of myth: First, myth communicates "reality" rather than merely true information; and second, this reality is lodged in human imagination rather than in reason.

Lewis explained this further in his brief but significant essay, "Myth Became Fact": "What flows into you from the myth is not truth but reality (truth is always *about* something, but reality is that *about which* truth is), and, therefore, every myth becomes the father of innumerable truths on the abstract level."[111] Here we have a clear distinction between truth and reality. Truth at best describes the reality but is not the reality itself. This obviously

---

107. Ibid., 43–44. This is a summary of Lewis's points.
108. Hein, "That Perilous Journey," 6.
109. Ibid.
110. Ibid., 211.
111. Lewis, "Myth Became Fact," in *God in the Dock*, 66.

poses an enormous epistemological problem, to which Lewis believed myth is a partial solution. First of all, Lewis presented the nature of the problem or dilemma.

> Human intellect is incurably abstract. . . . Yet the only realities we experience are concrete—this pain, this pleasure, this dog, this man. While we are loving the man, bearing the pain, enjoying the pleasure, we are not intellectually apprehending Pleasure, Pain, or Personality. When we begin to do so, on the other hand, the concrete realities sink to the level of mere instances or examples: we are no longer dealing with them, but with that which they exemplify. This is our dilemma—either to taste and not to know or to know and not to taste—or, more strictly, to lack one kind of knowledge because we are in an experience or to lack another kind because we are outside it. As thinkers we are cut off from what we think about; as tasting, touching, willing, loving, hating, we do not clearly understand. The more lucidly we think, the more we are cut off: the more deeply we enter into reality, the less we can think. You cannot *study* Pleasure in the moment of the nuptial embrace, nor repentance while repenting, nor analyse the nature of humour while roaring with laughter. But when else can you really know these things?[112]

There is, then, an important epistemological distinction between knowledge and experience, or, more technically, descriptive-analytical knowledge and participatory-experiential knowledge. We have earlier seen the very similar distinction Samuel Alexander makes between "Enjoyment" and "Contemplation," in which Lewis found an important solution to his problem of introspection.

Furthermore, Lewis highlighted the role of imagination above reason for receiving the quality of myth. Lewis said, "For me, reason is the natural organ of truth; but imagination is the organ of meaning. Imagination, producing new metaphors or revivifying old, is not the cause of truth, but its condition."[113] For Lewis, metaphors are indispensable tools for experiencing reality. Imagination is the way reality can be apprehended; and since reality, for Lewis, is the context for truth, imagination also must be the condition for truth, and the acquiring of truth in turn involves the function of reason. For Lewis, though reason was highly valued and effectively used, imagination seems to have a certain priority over reason. Especially in his view of

---

112. Ibid., 65–66.

113. Lewis, "Bluspels and Flalansferes: A Semantic Nightmare," in *Selected Literary Essays*, 265.

myth, the role of imagination is exalted. The impact of myth rests on human imagination rather than on reason.

Throughout his life, Lewis sought a harmonious union between reason and imagination. This was, in fact, his lifetime pursuit. He is often regarded as a romantic-rationalist or rational-romanticist. One of his earlier poems says something about this struggle in his thinking. The following poem is entitled "Reason":

> Set on the soul's acropolis the reason stands
> A virgin, arm'd, commercing with celestial light,
> And he who sins against her has defiled his own
> Virginity: no cleansing makes his garment white;
> So clear is reason. But how dark imagining,
> Warm, dark, obscure and infinite, daughter of Night:
> Dark is her brow, the beauty of her eyes with sleep
> Is loaded, and her pains are long, and her delight.
> Tempt not Athene. Wound not in her fertile pains
> Demeter, nor rebel against her mother-right.
> Oh who will reconcile in me both maid and mother,
> Who make imagination's dim exploring touch
> Ever report the same as intellectual sight?
> Then could I truly say, and not deceive,
> Then wholly say, that I BELIEVE.[114]

The nature of Lewis's struggle is clearly set before us. The clarity of reason and the relative obscurity but powerfully immediate experience of imagination are both necessary. Lewis decided not to abandon either, for to do so would be irresponsible and untruthful to the nature of human epistemology. So Lewis pursued some way of reconciliation. If the immediacy of imagination can be coupled with the clarity of reason, the greatest certainty would arise. Lewis, at least in the area of his Christian faith, found his answer in the incarnation of Jesus Christ, in whom myth (the quality lodged in imagination) became fact (the quality apprehended by reason). We should note how Lewis's use of reason is different from recent theological development highlighting the role of human imagination.

One of those recent thinkers is Garrett Green. His *Imagining God: Theology and the Religious Imagination*, begins with the remark:

---

114. Lewis, *Poems*, 81.

> The notion of imagination has emerged recently as a prominent focus of theological attention. It appears as the key term in the titles of two books that have attracted particular attention among academic theologians in the United States, David Tracy's *Analogical Imagination* and Gordon Kaufman's *Theological Imagination,* and it pops up in scores of other contexts, often incidentally but increasingly as a focal idea. A term that once flourished in theology among practitioners of "religion and literature," imagination is now attracting the attention of systematic and philosophical theologians.[115]

Green's supposition is that the possibility of the knowledge of God has been seriously challenged by the rise and dominance of empirical science. Imagination, then, turns out to be a key for religious epistemology which avoids both "extremes" of "the various traditionalists, literalists, and fundamentalists," and of "the straightforward skeptics, those doctrinaire atheists and agnostics who believe that nothing remains to be reconstructed after the destruction of the old supernaturalism."[116] Lewis, as an outspoken advocate of the old supernaturalism, did confront the skeptics and the atheists, but in a way different from Green and other recent thinkers.

Here is the key which sets Lewis apart from the modern scholars of imagination. Whereas the modern thinkers altogether give up the idea of religious "facts" and replace it with imaginative "ideas" of religion, Lewis stubbornly insisted upon reconciling "facts," "ideas," "truths," and "meanings" without abandoning either reason or imagination. Their distinctive functions were recognized; but neither was discarded as unnecessary. For him, Christian theism was the answer to overcoming the apparent conflict between the two avenues of knowledge. And in the incarnation of Jesus Christ, he found the main example of how the tension can be resolved.

We must now turn to that solution.

THE APPEARANCE OF "THE LANDLORD'S SON"

For Lewis, the appearance of the Son of God provides the occasion to crystallize the messages of both the rules and the pictures. Incarnation and redemption are fulfillment of the law and the prophets of the Hebrews. At the same time, they are "Myth Became Fact"; the pictures became realized in the realm of history. In theological terminology, Common Grace is made meaningful by the clear appearance of Saving Grace.

115. Green, *Imagining God,* 9.
116. Ibid., 11.

We should recall what Lewis points out in *The Pilgrim's Regress*: "The pictures alone are dangerous, and the rules alone are dangerous." So, one must focus on the "third thing which is neither the rules nor the pictures and which was brought into the country by the Landlord's Son."[117] The third thing is clearly a reference to the Gospel. Neither pictures nor rules can fully resolve the wandering. Only the third clearly directs them homeward. "The truth is that a Shepherd is only half a man, and a Pagan is only half a man, so that neither people was well without the other, nor could either be healed until the Landlord's Son came into the country."[118]

Such is the effect of the Gospel as described by Lewis. It is his way of stating what Paul says about the reconciliation of the Jews and the Gentiles.

> For [Christ] himself is our peace, who has made the two one and has destroyed the barrier, the dividing wall of hostility, by abolishing in his flesh the law with its commandments and regulations. His purpose was to create in himself one new man out of the two, thus making peace, and in this one body to reconcile both of them to God through the cross, by which he put to death their hostility.[119]

Now, Paul's purpose here is to establish the Gospel-induced unity of God's church as that which makes no essential distinction between the Jews and the Gentiles. They are together made into a new people, a community of believers, the body of Christ. Lewis, having hinted at this ecclesiological unity, attempted in the same stroke to make a case for an epistemological reconciliation. In the Gospel of Jesus Christ, both myth and history converge in a perfect union, and the marriage of imagination and reason takes place.

An elaboration of the point is found in his article "Myth Became Fact." In it, Lewis refuted an idea conveyed by his friend named Corineus. Corineus says, "[Historic] Christianity is something so barbarous that no modern man can really believe it: the moderns who claim to do so are in fact believing a modern system of thought which retains the vocabulary of Christianity and exploits the emotions inherited from it while quietly dropping its essential doctrines."[120] In other words, modern Christians have altogether abandoned the historical facts of Christianity and retained only its sentiment. This may indeed be said of many modern Christians. Lewis pointed out the strange fact that they, nevertheless, show no interest in cutting themselves away from "a system of names, ritual, formulae, and

---

117. Lewis, *Pilgrim's Regress*, 147.
118. Ibid., 149.
119. Eph 2:14–16 (NIV).
120. Lewis, "Myth Became Fact," in *God in the Dock*, 63.

metaphors," which seem to be mere shells of historic Christianity, and to retain them must be extremely inconvenient, bothersome, and even meaningless to be sure. That is precisely Corineus's point: "Why not cut the cord? ... Everything would be much easier if you would free your thought from this vestigial mythology."[121]

Lewis replies that this is a symptom of those who misunderstand the nature of religion. They want religion to move with the times, that is to move *away*. "But in religion," Lewis said, "we find something that does not move away," namely what Corineus calls "the myth."[122] Lewis pronounces victory for myth: "The myth ... has outlived the thoughts of all its defenders and of all its adversaries. It is the myth that gives life."[123]

Here we must not forget what was said earlier about Lewis's idea of myth. Otherwise, we face the danger of misunderstanding his article altogether. Yet in this article, it is Lewis who has instigated the potential danger by equating what Corineus means by myth and his own usage of myth. However, he minimizes the damage by briefly describing the epistemological tension between an abstract (descriptive) and concrete (experiential) knowledge in order to reinforce his idea of myth. The tension requires a resolution. Lewis insisted that myth is at least a partial solution. "In the enjoyment of a great myth we come nearest to experiencing as a concrete what can otherwise be understood only as an abstraction."[124] And what "flows into you from the myth is not truth but reality," and once again "truth is always *about* something, but reality is that *about which* truth is."[125] Reality has priority over truth, and likewise, myth is the mountain "whence all the different streams arise which become truths down here in the valley." In this sense, "myth transcends thought."[126] As a next step of his argument, Lewis took this concept of myth (which is the kernel of all religious thought) and applied it to Christianity.

At this point, while appreciating his acute analysis of human epistemology, some find Lewis's exalted view of myth troubling. Mark Edwards Freshwater, for example, concludes, "Lewis showed that the Christian story has a mythic power that is independent of the historical reality. Thus, both Lewis and Bultmann recognized the *kerygma* and radical obedience to it as the essence of Christianity."[127] Freshwater wants to argue that there is no

---

121. Ibid., 64.
122. Ibid., 65.
123. Ibid.
124. Ibid., 66.
125. Ibid.
126. Ibid.
127. Freshwater, *C. S. Lewis and the Truth of Myth*, 124. Freshwater shows as a

essential telic difference between Lewis and Bultmann; the difference is in what they consider to be "the *kerygma*" and their methodology for reaching it. So Freshwater says, "Although Lewis claimed Christianity to be 'myth become fact,' never in his writings did he provide the necessary basis for this assertion."[128] We may be sympathetic to Freshwater's argument, because Lewis gave myth priority over truths. However, Lewis's assertion must be considered within the larger context of his argument, and in particular his epistemological distinction between reality and truth. In essence, Lewis was not saying that myth itself has priority over truth, but it is reality (experienced through myth), which has priority over the truth. The objective is to approximate reality, that which truth points to. As we have seen, Lewis believed that myth is at least a partial means to the objective. What "flows into you from the myth is not truth but reality." Only in this sense, myth transcends truth. However, the slippery nature of Lewis's thought should be recognized. The most serious problem seems to be the lack of a clear criterion for determining which myth or which aspect of a myth conveys reality as it really is. In general, a convincing normative control or a basis for authoritative discernment seems to be missing.

However, Lewis asserted that the historical factuality of the Gospel of Christ specifically validates redemptive myths. Therefore, Lewis stated that incarnation transcends myth. Myth reached a higher level when it turned into a concrete historical fact in the incarnation of Jesus Christ. It is like imagination becoming clarified by its lodging in reason.

> The heart of Christianity is a myth which is also a fact. The myth of the Dying God, *without ceasing to be myth,* comes down from the heaven of legend and imagination to the earth of history. It *happens*—at a particular date, in a particular place, followed by definable historical consequences. We pass from a Balder or an Osiris, dying nobody knows when or where, to a historical Person crucified (it is all in order) *under Pontius Pilate.* By becoming fact it does not cease to be myth: that is the miracle.[129]

The "Myth Became Fact" incident provides the condition for a genuine profession of faith. Lewis indeed was able to say, "I believe." "To be truly

---

proof that Lewis was able to take the "myth of Christ" and transport it from the biblical setting to the imaginary land of Narnia, preserving its essential message. Freshwater, however, misses the point that the imaginary chronicles of Narnia serve only ectypally to the archtypal biblical narrative. Lewis would have certainly made this distinction according to his view of good literature (not creative originality but creative reflection of the objective truths and values).

128. Ibid., 126.
129. Lewis, "Myth Became Fact," in *God in the Dock,* 66.

Christian," Lewis said, "we must both assent to the historical fact and also receive the myth (fact though it has become) with the same imaginative embrace which we accord to all myths."[130] This "Myth Became Fact" is none other than a historical person whom we do not merely understand cognitively but upon whom we lay our trust. Christians are called to a relationship. The real clue to ending our wandering and turning it into a pilgrimage, a spiritual journey, is to be drawn to a person, not to an abstract truth. The incarnate Christ is the embodiment of "the way, the truth, and the life." He is the way we journey on; he is the truth we embrace; he is the life we live. The Christian journey, then, is not only a search for someone or something; it is a discovery of what we have become and are becoming in Jesus Christ. The mystical union with Christ is a notion that requires our imaginative welcome.

CONCLUSION

In this chapter, we have seen Lewis's theistic pointers which function as *praeparatio evangelica*, namely: (1) the discovery of the numinous in nature; (2) the experience of Joy; (3) the recognition of a universal natural moral law or *Tao*; (4) the special revelation in the history of Israel; and (5) the apprehension of Pagan redemption myths. The first three represent the existential dimension while the last two reflect the historical. The uniqueness of Lewis's theistic pointers, in contrast to traditional theistic arguments based on natural theology, is found in his consistent reference to what we have called "theological psychology." What serves as *praeparatio evangelica* is not a rationally derived set of theistic propositions but the state of tension inherent in each theistic pointer. Nature is not only orderly and delightful but dangerous and dreadful; Joy evokes both pleasure and sorrow; *Tao* awakens both the sense of obligation and inability; and neither the history of Israel nor Pagan redemption myth is complete in itself. All these remind us of our—and indeed humanity's—state of restless wandering. The awareness of the state of wandering, according to Lewis, is the precondition for the reception of the gospel of Christ. Lewis's insight into the fundamental state of tension found in humanity is a major accomplishment both theologically and apologetically. By pointing to the supernatural origin of the fundamental human experience, Lewis issues a significant challenge to a culture largely preoccupied with naturalistic solutions to human problems.

For Lewis, salvation must be as radical as the problem of alienation itself. To his understanding of this salvation we must now turn.

130. Ibid., 67.

4

Homeward Turning

The Doctrine of Conversion

In the previous chapter, we surveyed humanity's restless wandering and how, according to Lewis, this situation serves as a preparation for the Gospel. Lewis's conviction is well demonstrated in a statement he made about his BBC series which became the basis for *Mere Christianity*.

> [These talks] are *praeparatio evangelica* rather than *evangelium*, an attempt to convince people that there is a moral law, that we disobey it, and that the existence of a Lawgiver is at least very probable and also (*unless* you add the Christian doctrine of the Atonement) imparts despair rather than comfort.[1]

The reason behind Lewis's emphasis on pre-evangelism is, obviously, his concern for what is to follow, that is evangelism proper; and the purpose of evangelism is to lead people to Christian conversion. Pre-evangelism serves to promote a conscious awareness of the transcendental reality or at least the acceptance of its possibility. The Gospel presentation, on the other hand, reveals the immanence of that transcendental reality as it became an objective historical fact by the incarnation of Christ as we have seen in the discussion of "Myth Became Fact." Pre-evangelism promotes a sense of discomfort, a conscious awareness of both existential and historical tension. The Gospel in turn presents itself as the solution to the reality of frustration and fragmentation: God, who revealed himself most concretely in Christ, is the centerpiece, the corner stone, which makes life whole according to its creaturely *telos*. It follows that conversion is the consciously experienced

---

1. Lewis, *Letters of C. S. Lewis*, 359.

process of being brought into a relationship with God in which the saving knowledge of the Gospel transforms a person.

Lewis's deep concern for promoting Christian conversion is more than evident. Revealing his evangelistic intent quite frankly, he wrote, "Most of my books are evangelistic, addressed to *tous exo*."[2] This suggests that his books on Christian subjects are primarily addressed to "those outside" rather than those in the Christian community. In other words, he aimed, first of all, at bringing those outside into the experience of Christian conversion, and the edification of those within the Christian community naturally took a secondary place. Furthermore, Lewis clearly identified his desire to reach a popular audience rather than religious professionals. Defending his style and content, Lewis said, "I was writing *ad populum*, not *ad clerum*," and "[this] is relevant to my manner as well as my matter."[3]

In short, Lewis's understanding of the process of conversion can be summarized as an apprehension of the Creator God and his supernatural reality, which prompts a person to turn to the eternal object of delight, embarking on a journey toward him, and in the process gaining true personal identity in the context of an eternal relationship with him. Therefore, conversion consists of a change of direction in a person's spiritual journey. One turns away from the "journey homeward to habitual self"[4] and turns to God, the eternal object of delight.

Traditionally, theologians have identified repentance and faith as the two basic elements of which the process of conversion consists. As we turn to the discussion of Lewis's view of conversion, we will therefore examine his understanding of repentance and faith. A further important theological issue, which arises as we deal with the process of conversion, is that of the active and passive dimensions of conversion.

REPENTANCE AS "DYING TO SELF"

Despite Lewis's emphasis on the need of Christian conversion, he stood at a distance from the revivalistic movements of his time. He said,

2. Lewis, *God in the Dock*, 181. The quote comes from Lewis's response to W. Norman Pittenger's "A Critique of C. S. Lewis" (1958). William Luther White objects to authors who have used this quote out of context to build the case that all Lewis's books, regardless of their genres, are evangelistically motivated. See White, *Image of Man in C. S. Lewis*, 79. I agree with White on this point and think that Lewis was referring mostly to his works on Christian subjects. This is not to say that other books do not reveal Lewis's Christian commitment.

3. Lewis, *God in the Dock*, 182.

4. Lewis, *Weight of Glory*, 14. The phrase Lewis enjoyed quoting belongs to Keats.

> When I began, Christianity came before the great mass of my unbelieving fellow-countrymen, either in the highly emotional form offered by revivalists or in the unintelligible language of highly cultured clergymen. Most men were reached by neither. My task was therefore simply that of a *translator*—one turning Christian doctrine, or what he believed to be such, into the vernacular, into language that unscholarly people would attend to and could understand.[5]

His desire to reach the "unscholarly" by avoiding intellectualism has already been documented.[6] In addition, Lewis, as we can see in the quotation above, thought that emotionalism, as well as intellectualism, renders the message of the gospel unintelligible to the average audience. His view of conversion is, therefore, quite distinct.

What Conversion Does Not Entail

Apparently, Lewis distanced himself from any emotionalistic or decisionistic view of conversion. Instead, he maintained a steady emphasis on the *process* that leads into the moment of spiritual awakening and that which follows. There is something decisive about the conversion experience; at the same time, it is a part of the continuum of one's spiritual journey which begins from the plain fact that an individual is a creation of God placed in his created world. Lewis's own conversion story, for instance, is really a story of his early life leading to the time of conversion. His conversion, though dramatized to highlight his inner struggle,[7] was not characterized by an emotional upheaval.[8]

Nevertheless, conversion is a decisive turn from a life of restless wandering, apart from God, into a pilgrimage toward one's true home.

---

5. Lewis, *God in the Dock*, 183.

6. I refer to Lewis's statement, "I was writing *ad populum*, not *ad clerum*." Quoted earlier in Lewis, *God in the Dock*, 182.

7. Lewis especially emphasized the fact that his theistic conversion was not a wish-fulfillment but something quite contrary to his inclination. He was overcome by "the steady, unrelenting approach" of God which at last made him surrender. "In the Trinity Term of 1929 I gave in, and admitted that God was God, and knelt and prayed: perhaps, that night, the most dejected and reluctant convert in all England." Lewis described his inner condition as "kicking, struggling, resentful, and darting his eyes in every direction for a chance to escape." Lewis, *Surprised by Joy*, 228–29.

8. His conversion to Christianity (which followed his theistic conversion) is characterized by a noticeable lack of drama. Lewis recalled, "I was driven to Whipsnade one sunny morning. When we set out I did not believe that Jesus Christ is the Son of God, and when we reached the zoo I did." Ibid., 237.

Therefore, the key attitude toward conversion is a solemn commitment to a new course of life.

Lewis thought that triumphalistic emotional highs tend to interfere with the journey rather than assist it. In his reply to a woman's victorious report of her conversion, Lewis issued words of caution.

> The only (possibly, not necessarily) unfavourable symptom is that you are just a trifle too excited. It is quite right that you should feel that "something terrific" has happened to you. . . . Accept these sensations with thankfulness as birthday cards from God, but remember that they are only greetings, not the real gift. I mean that it is not the sensations that are the real thing. The real thing is the gift of the Holy Spirit which can't usually be—perhaps not ever—experienced as a sensation or emotion. The sensations are merely the response of your nervous system. Don't depend on them. Otherwise when they go and you are once more emotionally flat (as you certainly will be quite soon), you might think that the real thing had gone too. But it won't. It will be there when you can't feel it. May even be operative when you can feel it least.
>
> Don't imagine it is all "going to be an exciting adventure from now on." It won't. Excitement of whatever sort, never lasts. This is the push to start you off on your first bicycle: you'll be left to [do] lots of dogged pedalling later on.[9]

Lewis guarded himself and others from being overly concerned or dependent upon the emotional state accompanying the process of conversion. There are moments of triumph but they are mixed with distresses. In fact, he considered the presence of distress the very sign of a true conversion.[10]

Why does the process of conversion involve distress? The answer lies in the fact that conversion first of all means to repent, and repentance means a surrender or the death of self in order to take on a new life. This is highlighted more than any other concerns in Lewis's view of salvation. For Lewis, conversion essentially involves a kind of death; it is a good death since it leads to life. Nevertheless, since it is a death it involves a deeply felt sense of anxiety and loss. For human beings who are symptomatically egocentric, death to self is a radical demand God lays down on those who desire to embark on a Christian journey.

Why did Lewis advocate such a radical view of conversion? Why does an act of repentance involve a death rather than a commitment to reform

---

9. Lewis, *Letters of C. S. Lewis*, 421.
10. Ibid., 419.

one's way? It is because Lewis had a radical view of sin. Sin, for Lewis, was not simply an ethical matter. Lewis's "mere Christianity," with its view of sin and human corruption, challenged the modernist version of naturalistic and ethicocentric theology.

Lewis's View of Sin

In *The Pilgrim's Regress*, the pilgrims must travel beyond the giant chasm called *Peccatum Adae* through a baptismal death. The name of the chasm is a clear reference to Adam's original sin and the consequential corruption of human nature. It is a reminder of the seriousness of the problem at hand, requiring a radical remedy. It takes a death to get across the chasm.

Repentance does not arise out of a person's "vague, though uneasy, feeling that he hasn't been doing very well lately."[11] The awareness of one's sin must be the starting point: "[Christianity] therefore has nothing . . . to say to people who do not know they have done anything to repent of and who do not feel that they need any forgiveness."[12] For this reason, Lewis claimed, "A recovery of the old sense of sin is essential to Christianity."[13]

In fact, Lewis's awareness of human sinfulness apparently deepened with time. *Letters to Malcolm*, published immediately following his death, contains a discussion of the Puritan view of sin. He said that the reading of Alexander Whyte[14] brought him "violently face to face with a characteristic of Puritanism." "[One] essential symptom of the regenerate life is a permanent, and permanently horrified, perception of one's natural and (it seems) unalterable corruption."[15] Lewis realized that this recognition of inner corruption is a regular feature of "the old conversion stories." He particularly recalled Bunyan's words: "But my inward and original corruption . . . that I had the guilt of, to amazement. . . . I was more loathsome in mine own eyes than was a toad. . . . Sin and corruption, I said, would as naturally bubble out of my heart, as water would bubble out of a fountain."[16] Lewis also reminded the reader of the words of an unnamed Puritan author who observed in his own heart that it was "as if I had in the heat of summer lookt down into the

---

11. Lewis, *Screwtape Letters*, 65.
12. Lewis, *Mere Christianity*, 38.
13. Lewis, *Problem of Pain*, 57.
14. Alexander Whyte (1836–1921), a Scottish minister, was a remarkable preacher who also taught New Testament literature at New College, Edinburgh. He was called the "last of the Puritans."
15. Lewis, *Letters to Malcolm*, 98.
16. Ibid.

Filth of a Dungeon, where I discerned Millions of crawling living things in the midst of that Sink and liquid Corruption."[17]

While deeply aware of the paradoxical danger of introspection, which "breeds its own perverse pride," Lewis nevertheless showed considerable sympathy with the Puritan concern. "I won't listen to those who describe that vision as merely pathological. I have seen the 'slimy things that crawled with legs' in my own dungeon." He lamented, "[In] solitude, and also in confession, I have found (to my regret) that the degrees of shame and disgust which I actually feel at my own sins do not at all correspond to what my reason tells me about their comparative gravity."[18] Lewis's mature struggle with his own sinful disposition seems to be a reflection of his own earlier observation. "[We] actually are, at present, creatures whose character must be, in some respects, a horror to God, as it is, when we really see it, a horror to ourselves. This I believe to be a fact: and I notice that the holier a man is, the more fully he is aware of that fact."[19]

Like Charles Williams, Lewis characterized the ultimate end of sin as "self-love" or "self-preservation." The doctrine of the Fall requires us, according to Lewis, to "look for the great sin on a deeper and more timeless level than that of social morality." What then is this great sin? Lewis answered,

> This sin has been described by Saint Augustine as the result of Pride, of the movement whereby a creature (that is, an essentially dependent being whose principle of existence lies not in itself but in another) tries to set up on its own, to exist for itself. . . . This sin is committed daily by young children and ignorant peasants as well as by sophisticated persons, by solitaries no less than by those who live in society: it is the Fall in every individual life, and in each day of each individual life, the basic sin behind all particular sins: at this very moment you and I are either committing it, or about to commit it, or repenting it.[20]

The sin of "self-love" is not a mere act or series of acts but a permanent tendency imbedded in humanity's fallenness. "The gravitation away from God, 'the journey homeward to habitual self,' must, we think, be a product of the Fall."[21] The tragedy of this tendency is that it radically disorients man and woman's true creaturely position. In other words, Lewis's view of sin is radical because it stems from a radical view of the Fall.

17. Ibid.
18. Ibid., 98–99.
19. Lewis, *Problem of Pain*, 68.
20. Ibid., 75.
21. Ibid., 76.

Lewis's View of the Fall

Lewis observed the state of the fallen humanity as a radical change from the state of the initial creation. "According to [the doctrine of the Fall], man is now a horror to God and to himself and a creature ill-adapted to the universe."[22] In *The Problem of Pain*, Lewis outlined the story of the Fall of humanity as a journey away from God toward self, but qualified this story as "a myth in the Socratic sense," meaning "an account of what *may have been* the historical fact."[23] Lewis engaged in this speculation, because he could not accept the Genesis account of Adam and Eve as historical but as a mythic account, which may contain historical elements.

In a personal letter, Lewis speculated about the emergence of Adam.

> I . . . had pictured Adam as being, physically, the son of two anthropoids, on whom, after birth, God worked the miracle which made him Man: said, in fact, "Come out—and forget thine own people and thy father's house." The Call of Abraham wd. [sic] be a far smaller instance of the same sort of thing, and regeneration in each one of us wd. [sic] be an instance too, tho' [sic] not smaller one. That all seems to me to fit in both historically and spiritually.[24]

The "theistic evolutionary" paradigm, which features Darwinian theory of human origins modified by the notion of divine oversight of the process, appears to be one he adopted to interpret the *meaning* of the "myth" presented in the early chapters of Genesis.

The idea of the Fall, nevertheless, is central to Lewis's theology. Following is the summary of Lewis's story of the Fall of humanity:

> (1) "For long centuries God perfected the animal form which was to become the vehicle of humanity and the image of Himself." The making of the perfect animal form with "a brain sufficiently complex" could have taken ages. But for this animal form to become a human being, a radical step was necessary.
>
> (2) "Then, in the fullness of time, God caused to descend upon this organism, both on its psychology and physiology, a new kind of consciousness which could say 'I' and 'me,' which could look upon itself as an object, which knew God, which could make judgments of truth, beauty, and goodness, and which was so far above time that it could perceive time flowing past." This

---

22. Ibid., 69.
23. Ibid., 77, 77n.
24. Lewis, *Letters of C. S. Lewis*, 417.

"first man" had a quality which surpasses ours. "Man was then all consciousness." That is even his "organic processes obeyed the law of his own will, not the law of nature." Even appetites and desires were under the disposal of his will. Even "the processes of decay and repair in his tissues were conscious and obedient." This being, wholly in command of himself, also commanded all lower lives he came in contact with. This "paradisal man" was "made to be the priest and even, in one sense, the Christ, of the animals—the mediator through whom they apprehended so much of the Divine splendour as their irrational nature allows." The new consciousness God endowed upon this man made him fully oriented towards God. "God came first in his love and in his thought, and that without painful effort." Upon him "being, power and joy descended from God" in the form of gift; man on the other hand returned to God "obedient love and ecstatic adoration." Man was then "truly the son of God, the prototype of Christ," in whom filial self-surrender came naturally with "joy and ease." Interestingly, however, judging from archeological artifacts, this creature was an underdeveloped "savage," more like a child than a fully mature adult. However, the learned and the adult would have no advantage over this "naked, shaggy-bearded, slow-spoken creature."

(3) "We do not know how many of these creatures God made, nor how long they continued in the paradisal state. But sooner or later they fell." This meant that they "ceased directing their lives to their Creator," desiring to be on their own, "to take care of their own future, to plan for pleasure and for security." Even taking "time, attention, and love" for God was out of their own resources, with the stamp of their own ownership. "They wanted . . . to 'call their souls their own.' But that means to live a lie, for our souls are not, in fact, our own." This must be the first sin which fulfills the two conditions: "that it must be very heinous" and "that it must be something which a being free from the temptations of fallen man could conceivably have committed." This sin was possible even to paradisal man because God apparently thought worth taking the risk of giving him the consciousness of self. Such awareness always carried the danger of "self-idolatry." Nevertheless, the sin is heinous because he was wholly conscious and able to willfully control all aspects of his life with ease. Furthermore, he had no inclination to resist self-surrender to God. In the truest sense he enjoyed being himself, fully capable of perfectly willing surrender and obedience, without evil passion or inclination controlling over him. And with

this, to have chosen self-idolatry over self-surrender was the sin of the most heinous nature.

(4) Though man expected to retain the full control of the human organism by ceasing to obey God, he ended up losing that authority. "[Its] authority over the organism was a delegated authority which it lost when it ceased to be God's delegate. Having cut itself off, as far as it could, from the source of its being, it had cut itself off from the source of power." Therefore, God chose no longer to rule the human organism by the rebellious human spirit; instead "he began to rule the organism in a more external way, not by the laws of spirit, but by those of nature." The status of man fell in such a way that he now must obey one of God's lower laws rather than the higher law God made fitting for a human being.[25]

(5) The new human species emerged, with its characteristic very different from the specification of God, and its condition was "transmitted by heredity to all later generations." This change of man was a radical kind that cannot be a process of mere natural change or evolutionary variation: "[It] was the emergence of a new kind of man—a new species, never made by God, had sinned itself into existence."[26]

Lewis's account suggests that human beings emerged from a lower animal form, clearly rejecting the biblical account of the Creation. However, Lewis ironically asserted that the first human "savage" was in "the paradisal state," commanding a perfect psycho-physical unity, unlike fallen humanity. We have here an interesting mixture of Darwinian evolutionism and the Christian notion of the Fall. Lewis accepted Darwinian evolutionism, apparently with some tension in his mind, as a biological theory but rejected the popular evolutionism as a view of history or reality in general.[27] Lewis

---

25. The idea contained in this sentence, Lewis said, is consistent to a development of Hooker's conception of law: "To disobey your *proper* law (i.e., the law God makes for a being such as you) means to find yourself obeying one of God's lower laws." Lewis gave an illuminating illustration: "[If], when walking on a slippery pavement, you neglect the law of Prudence, you suddenly find yourself obeying the law of gravitation." Lewis, *Problem of Pain*, 82n.

26. This is a summary of Lewis's presentation found in Lewis, *Problem of Pain*, 77–84.

27. Lewis was somewhat inconsistent in his evaluation of Darwinian theory. In 1946, he wrote, "With Darwinianism as a theorem in Biology I do not think a Christian need have any quarrel." (Lewis, "Modern Man and his Categories of Thought," in *Present Concerns*, 63). However, a few years earlier (in 1944), Lewis already raised a serious question about the theory. "'Evolution itself,' [D. M. S. Watson] wrote, 'is accepted by zoologists not because it has been observed to occur or . . . can be proved by logically

thought the "myth" of progress or developmentalism directly contradicted the notion of the Fall.

However, Lewis's notion of the Fall is derived from a "myth" since his interpretation of the early chapters of Genesis is clearly mythic rather than historic. One may raise the question of authority: Why should Lewis choose to accept the "myth" of the Fall rather than that of popular evolutionism? Lewis attributed an authoritative status to the Genesis "myth," calling it a myth which God raised above itself to serve his purpose.[28] Lewis's view of Scripture, which we elaborate in chapter 5, seems rather obscure.

Despite his ambivalence toward the historicity of the Genesis account, Lewis's story contains basic biblical themes about the Fall: it stemmed from man's willful rejection of the life of submission and obedience to God, it radically altered man's state of being, and its effect is somehow transmitted to all subsequent generations.

---

coherent evidence to be true, but because the only alternative, special creation, is clearly incredible.' Has it come to that? Does the whole vast structure of modern naturalism depend not on positive evidence but simply on an *a priori* metaphysical prejudice? Was it devised not to get in facts but to keep out God?" (Lewis, "Is Theology Poetry?," in *Weight of Glory*, 89). However, in an essay published in 1952, Lewis clearly acknowledged weakening status of the theory without refuting it. "I am not in the least concerned to refute Darwinism as a theorem in biology. There may be flaws in that theorem, but I have here nothing to do with them. There may be signs that biologists are already contemplating a withdrawal from the whole Darwinian position, but I claim to be no judge of such signs." (Lewis, "The World's Last Night," in *World's Last Night*, 101).

On the other hand, Lewis was clearly hostile to the developmental view of history, which he called "the great myth of progress." "[We] must sharply distinguish between Evolution as a biological theorem and popular Evolutionism or Developmentalism which is certainly a Myth. . . . I call it a Myth because it is . . . the imaginative and not the logical result of what is vaguely called 'modern science.'" (Lewis, "The Funeral of a Great Myth," in *Christian Reflections*, 82–83). Again he said, "[In] my opinion, the modern conception of Progress or Evolution (as popularly imagined) is simply a myth, supported by no evidence whatever." (Lewis, "The World's Last Night," in *World's Last Night*, 101).

28. Lewis stated, "I have . . . no difficulty in accepting, say, the view of those scholars who tell us that the account of Creation in *Genesis* is derived from earlier Semitic stories which were Pagan and mythical. . . . When a series of . . . retellings turns a creation story which at first had almost no religious or metaphysical significance into a story which achieves the idea of true Creation and of a transcendent Creator (as *Genesis* does), then nothing will make me believe that some of the retellers, or some one of them, has not been guided by God. Thus something originally merely natural—the kind of myth that is found among most nations—will have been raised by God above itself, qualified by Him and compelled by Him to serve purposes which of itself it would not have served." (Lewis, *Reflections on the Psalms*, 111). Lewis's idea of turning non-religious myth into religiously significant story seems theologically naive. Pagan myth can hardly be considered non-religious. The process logically requires a radical reinterpretation rather than an "evolution" or a transmission.

In order to understand conversion as the reversal of the process, Lewis's psychology of fallen man must be carefully delineated, for it forms the context for understanding his notion of dying to self or self-surrender. Fallen man, now subject to God's lower laws, is no longer governed by his will but "fell under the control of ordinary biochemical laws and suffered whatever the inner-workings of those laws might bring about in the way of pain, senility, and death."[29] The resulting tragedy was the uncontrolled invasion of various desires, unwilled by human reason, but "just as the biochemical and environmental facts happened to cause them."[30] The mind, having lost its God-given liberty, "fell under the psychological laws of association," and the will, unable to control the rushing thoughts and desires, at best managed to force them into a hidden domain which became "the subconscious."[31] The result of this radical change in human psychology was that the "human spirit from being the master of human nature became a mere lodger in its own house, or even a prisoner; rational consciousness became what it now is—a fitful spot-light resting on a small part of the cerebral motions."[32] One may detect the influence of Thomistic thought in Lewis's separation of spirit and nature, especially if he should consider the change to mean the limitation of the spirit's power rather than the corruption of the spirit itself. Lewis clearly thought the latter.

Lewis recognized the radical depth of the Fall. He held that, following it, the integrity of human spirit could not be left intact. In fact, the real problem went far deeper than a mere disorientation or "a disturbance of the relation between his component parts" by the limitation laid upon the regulative faculties (which Lewis collectively called "the human spirit"). Not only was the spirit's power relatively weakened, the spirit itself was subjected to "the corruption" or "an internal perversion." "It had turned from God and become its own idol, so that though it could still turn back to God, it could do so only by painful effort, and its inclination was selfward."[33] What follows is Lewis's powerful statement of the inclination of the corrupted human spirit.

---

29. Lewis, *Problem of Pain*, 82.

30. Ibid.

31. Ibid. Apparently, Lewis, being antagonistic to the presuppositions of the psychoanalytic theories of his time, accepted some of their diagnoses of human psychology with ease.

32. Ibid., 83.

33. Ibid., 83–84. Lewis here warned the readers not to make judgments about his posture on the Pelagian-Augustinian controversy. He wanted to make no particular contribution to it. He said, "I mean only that such return to God was not, even now, an impossibility. Where the initiative lies in any instance of such return is a question on which I am saying nothing." (83n).

Hence pride and ambition, the desire to be lovely in its own eyes and to depress and humiliate all rivals, envy, and restless search for more, and still more, security, were now the attitudes that came easiest to it. It was not only a weak king over its own nature, but a bad one: it sent down into the psycho-physical organism desires far worse than the organism sent up into it.[34]

Therefore, the conversion of a person requires a turn about, a repentance or a surrender of self-will to the Creator. This process is described as the death of the old self. The idea of "death" is more than just symbolism; the true humanity as God's cherished creation died with the Fall, and we need a new kind of death in order to be revived. Repentance, therefore, is not a sort of self-improvement but a kind of death.

Now repentance is no fun at all. It is something much harder than merely eating humble pie. It means unlearning all the self-conceit and self-will that we have been training ourselves into for thousands of years. It means killing part of yourself, undergoing a kind of death.[35]

If this is so, while sinners ought to repent, they really cannot. There is a tragic inability that all sinners must face. "The worse you are the more you need it and the less you can do it. The only person who could do it perfectly would be a perfect person—and he would not need it."[36] Therefore, repentance is not something a person can initiate.

The Theory of Christ's Substitutionary "Repentance"

What we need, therefore, is God himself, who is perfect, operating in us to do and will what we, left on our own, are incapable of doing. "[We] now need God's help in order to do something which God, in His own nature, never does at all—to surrender, to suffer, to submit, to die."[37] Here we find the key that opens the door of salvation. The key is God becoming a man, the incarnation of God in Christ. "He could surrender His will, and suffer and die, because He was man; and He could do it perfectly because He was God."[38]

---

34. Ibid., 83.
35. Lewis, *Mere Christianity*, 59.
36. Ibid.
37. Ibid., 60.
  38. Ibid. Lewis's good rhetoric is misleading: Christ's perfect surrender was possible not necessarily because he was God but also because he was a perfect man.

In order to understand the situation more clearly, we need to identify the view of atonement that he embraced. From the initial appearance, Lewis thought it unnecessary to hold to a specific historical theory of atonement. "[Neither] this theory nor any other is Christianity. The central Christian belief is that Christ's death has somehow put us right with God and given us a fresh start. Theories as to how it did this are another matter."[39] However, Lewis pointed out that there is a certain "reality" of atonement or "the thing itself" that accomplished salvation for us. Like nutrients working behind the food we eat, the "reality" works as long as we believe "that Christ was killed for us, that His death has washed out our sins, and that by dying He disabled death itself."[40] Theories are like counting the nutritional values; we do not need to engage ourselves in them in order to benefit from the "reality" itself.

However, from the very creed Lewis presented, one theory is eliminated: A strictly Aberlardian example or moral influence theory is excluded in favor of a substitutionary theory. The death of Christ is not just a supreme example of God's love which moves our heart. Edgar W. Boss's assessment proves to be off the mark. "[Lewis] claims to have no theory of the Atonement, but he does. It is the Example Theory with a very important modification."[41] Boss's argument is based on Lewis's comments in *The Problem of Pain*, where he mentioned the possibility that the glorified saints would not celebrate the cancellation of their sins and having them forever erased. Since "all times are eternally present to God," Lewis thought it plausible to assume that the acts of sin are caught in the eternal moment. Therefore, the saints would possess "the perfected humility that bears the shame forever, rejoicing in the occasion which it furnished to God's compassion and glad that it should be common knowledge to the universe."[42] However, this comment seems to highlight the result or the effect rather than a theory of atonement.

In fact, Lewis did provide a discussion on theories of atonement. In effect, he introduced three substitutionary theories: (1) The penal substitution (forensic) theory; (2) the commercial (ransom) theory; and (3) the substitutionary repentance theory. He clearly disliked the first.

---

39. Lewis, *Mere Christianity*, 57.

40. Ibid., 58.

41. Boss, "The Theology of C. S. Lewis," 190. By "a very important modification," Boss means the supernaturalist emphasis Lewis made, whereas he believes "the Example Theory is usually held by Naturalists."

42. Lewis, *Problem of Pain*, 61.

> Christ had volunteered to bear a punishment instead of us. . . .
> And what possible point could there be in punishing an innocent person instead? None at all that I can see, if you are thinking of punishment in the police-court sense.[43]

Lewis thought that the idea of penal substitution hardly communicates anything meaningful to a modern person. "Legal fiction, adoption, and transference or imputation of merit and guilt . . . could never have played the part they did play in theology if they had always been felt to be so artificial as we now feel them to be."[44]

However, Lewis felt that a commercial notion still speaks to a modern mind.

> On the other hand, if you think of a debt, there is plenty of point in a person who has some assets paying it on behalf of someone who has not. . . . [It] is a matter of common experience that, when one person has got himself into a hole, the trouble of getting him out usually falls on a kind friend.[45]

Apparently, Lewis's reason for rejecting the forensic notion, in favor of the commercial one, is an evangelistic one, that is, to highlight a more communicable metaphor for the contemporary mind. However, with the rejection of the forensic notion, a powerful dimension of the biblical doctrine of justification disappears, namely the seriousness of sin and the enormous task of justifying a sinner condemned to death. In this sense, abandoning a biblically supported notion based on the criterion of its communicability in the modern culture has enormous dangers.

On the other hand, Lewis's modified ransom theory[46] appears powerfully in *The Lion, the Witch and the Wardrobe*. It is clear that Lewis intentionally avoided describing the death of Aslan in the place of Edmund as a penal substitution; nevertheless, the effect of Aslan's substitutionary sacrifice is to make possible Edmund's escape from death that he deserves. One could say Edmund is justified to live his life because Aslan dies *in his place*. The death appeases the demand of the "deep magic" that every traitor

---

43. Lewis, *Mere Christianity*, 59.
44. Lewis, *Problem of Pain*, 88.
45. Lewis, *Mere Christianity*, 59.
46. Charles Taliaferro argues, "Aslan's ransoming Edmund and his subsequent resurrection fits the classic ransom theory of the atonement." Taliaferro, "A Narnian Theory of the Atonement," 75. I call it a *modified* ransom theory, because it apparently overcomes the major weakness of the classical formula, namely the idea that the Evil One is entitled to an appeasement. In Narnian theory, the appeasement is directed to the law of the "Emperor-beyond-the-Sea," not to the Witch.

belongs to the Witch and is her "lawful prey and that for every treachery [she has] a right to kill."[47] The sacrifice is not aimed at "appeasing" the Witch but the law of the "Emperor-beyond-the-Sea," which says that unless blood is shed for the act of treachery, "all Narnia will be overturned and perish in fire and water."[48] However, the death of Aslan in place of Edmund accomplishes more than merely appeasing the law. It goes far beyond the significance of Edmund's treachery, because it fulfills a "deeper magic" that is rooted in "the incantation" from "the stillness and the darkness before Time dawned," which promises "that when a willing victim who had committed no treachery was killed *in a traitor's stead*, the Table would crack and Death itself would start working backward."[49] Lewis apparently recognized the powerful mystery of Christ's atoning sacrifice, which far exceeds the idea of Christ's moral example or moral influence. A certain objective requirement has been appeased and fulfilled by the substitutionary death of Jesus Christ.

However, we must go a step further into Lewis's view of the atonement. At heart, Lewis was deeply concerned about the subjective transformation of the offender through the inner working of the atonement as well as the objective substitutionary accomplishment of the work of Christ. The sinner's need is not to "improve" but to "surrender." The atonement is the reality that enables sinners to repent or surrender to God, which they are unable to do on their own. The theory of Lewis's choice hinges upon the notion of repentance, and this is the third theory he presents in *Mere Christianity*.

In the substitutionary repentance theory of the atonement, the work of Christ is not so much to bear the consequence of our sins but to release us from our inability to turn to God in self-surrender. Christ as the perfect man surrendered himself willingly to God.

> In fact, it needs a good man to repent. And here comes the catch. Only a bad person needs to repent: only a good person can repent perfectly. The worse you are the more you need it and the less you can do it. The only person who can do it perfectly would be a perfect person—and he would not need it. . . . But the same badness which makes us need [repentance] makes us unable to do it. . . . But supposing God became a man—suppose our human nature which can suffer and die was amalgamated with God's nature in one person—then that person could help us. He could surrender His will, and suffer and die. . . . That is

---

47. Lewis, *The Lion, the Witch and the Wardrobe*, 155.
48. Ibid., 156.
49. Ibid., 178–79 (emphasis mine).

the sense in which He pays our debt, and suffers for us what He Himself need not suffer at all.[50]

The suffering of Christ, culminating in his death, was in fact an act of repentance or self-surrender undertaken on behalf of the sinners who are themselves unable to repent. The sinners can succeed in "dying" by sharing in God's dying in Christ.

In an illuminating article, Christian Kettler traces a line of theological influence from John McLeod Campbell to R. C. Moberly, then to C. S. Lewis. Kettler believes that Campbell (1800–1872), a Scottish pastor-theologian and the author of *The Nature of the Atonement* (1867), was the one who provided the basic structure to Moberly's (1845–1903) theory of the atonement, which in turn shaped Lewis's view expressed in *Mere Christianity*.[51] Campbell's theory appeals to Jonathan Edwards's description of God's two possible alternatives to deal with human sin, namely a vicarious punishment or a vicarious repentance. Contrary to Edwards, however, Campbell explored the latter option, which he thought was "the higher and more excellent" view of the atonement. According to him, the vicarious repentance of Christ points to his perfect confession of the sins of humanity following the acceptance of the condemnation upon himself through vicarious humanity. Therefore, he addressed "the total need of humanity" as well as "the total inability of humanity to repent." "It is a 'perfect repentance,' a 'perfect sorrow,' a 'perfect contrition,' with all the elements of repentance 'excepting the personal consciousness of sin.'"[52]

Moberly, an Anglican theologian, followed Campbell's view in his book, *Atonement and Personality* (1917). Having accepted much of Campbell's teaching about the "perfect penitent," Moberly viewed Christ as "the inclusive total of true Humanity" while each person is only potentially a part of that humanity. Therefore, the penitence of Christ opened the "true possibility of repentance" for all people.[53] His opening-of-the-possibility view, Moberly thought, could remove the misunderstanding of the vicariousness of Christ's repentance to mean that individuals have no need to repent since Christ has already done so for them.

Kettler argues that C. S. Lewis's version of "the Perfect Penitent"[54] is "the echo of Moberly"; however, Lewis's distinct contribution centers on

---

50. Lewis, *Mere Christianity*, 59–60.
51. Kettler, "Vicarious Repentance of Christ," 529.
52. Ibid., 530–31.
53. Ibid., 534.
54. This is the title of the chapter in *Mere Christianity* which deals with Lewis's view of the atonement.

"his teaching on our need to participate in the dying and rising of Christ."[55] Nevertheless, the notion of "participation" was very important in both Campbell and Moberly as well.[56] The apparent theological dependence is surprising only on the account that Lewis made no known reference to either Campbell or Moberly. We can suspect that the exposure to Moberly's theology came through Anglican pulpits rather than the literature bearing his name.[57] Regardless, Lewis declared, "Such is my way of looking at what Christians call the Atonement."[58]

To summarize, we find in Lewis an acknowledgment that the radical degree of human corruption caused by the Fall, needing a radical remedy which is found in Christ's substitutionary death. In essence, Christ, as a representative of humankind, accomplished the life of perfect self-surrender (or perfect repentance). In Christ, a certain reversal of the Fall began to take place. People are called to participate in this great reversal by committing themselves to Christ and by undergoing true repentance in Christ.

> The perfect surrender and humiliation were undergone by Christ.... Now the Christian belief is that if we somehow share the humility and suffering of Christ we shall also share in His conquest of death and find a new life after we have died and in it become perfect, and perfectly happy creatures. This means something much more than our trying to follow His teaching.... In Christ a new kind of man appeared: and the new kind of life which began in Him is to be put into us.[59]

What is the new kind of life that is put into us? Lewis contended that the new kind of life is none other than the "begotten" life of Christ, *Zoe*, which is fundamentally different from the "created" life in the natural order, *Bios*.

---

55. Kettler, "Vicarious Repentance of Christ," 538.

56. Ibid., 539–40; Torrance, "Contribution of John McLeod Campbell," 310.

57. Lewis's frequent theological dependence on George MacDonald, who may have known the work of John McLeod Campbell, a fellow Scot (MacDonald being twenty-four years junior to Campbell), makes us suspect the route of influence. MacDonald and Campbell both rejected penal substitutionary theory of atonement and sought to highlight the forgiving love of God, which requires no penal appeasement. While the phrase "substitutionary repentance" or "perfect penitence" is rather foreign to MacDonald, he nevertheless described the death of Christ as the supreme instance of "dying to self." "[Christ] died that we might live—but live as He lives, by dying as He died who died to Himself." (Lewis, *George MacDonald: An Anthology*, 85). For Lewis, "dying to self" is the fundamental meaning of "repentance."

58. Lewis, *Mere Christianity*, 61.

59. Ibid., 62.

The metaphysical distinction between the two kinds of life is described in two ways: (1) A sort of Creator-creature distinction. "What God begets is God; just as what man begets is man. What God creates is not God; just as what man makes is not man."[60] (2) A sort of Platonic distinction between form and matter. "*Bios* has, to be sure, a certain shadowy or symbolic resemblance to *Zoe*: but only the sort of resemblance there is between a photo and a place, or a statue and a man."[61] Amazingly, God's identification with humanity in Christ opened the flood-gate to pour *Zoe* into humankind. Thus, "a man who changed from having *Bios* to having *Zoe* would have gone through as big a change as a statue which changed from being a carved stone to being a real man."[62] We have a theology of radical immanence in Lewis. In Christ, the two horizons crash in, and the life of God is infused into humankind; the Creator's life is implanted into the creaturely existence.[63] As a result, we are made into "little Christs." "Every Christian is to become a little Christ. The whole purpose of becoming a Christian is simply nothing else."[64]

How can this new kind of life be infused in us? Lewis names three ordinary means: baptism, belief, and the Lord's supper; but he confesses, "I cannot myself see why these things should be the conductors of the new kind of life," but "I believe it on His authority."[65] However, this is not the end of the discussion. They are expressions of what must happen in each person.[66] Lewis said that we must consciously "dress up as Christ" as "he has ordered us to do."[67] This, however, differs from ordinary ideas of "morality" and "being good."

> The Christian way is different: harder, and easier. Christ says "Give me All. I don't want so much of your time and so much of your money and so much of your work: I want You. I have not

---

60. Ibid., 138.
61. Ibid., 140.
62. Ibid.
63. The theology of radical immanence reminds of the theological movement often called "neo-orthodoxy." The radically Christocentric theology fails to maintain the Creator-creature distinction, which is an essential Christian worldview. In Christ, believers are not made divine but truly the image of God by the renewing work of the Holy Spirit. The regenerated life is not a divine life but a life obedient to the indwelling Spirit of God.
64. Lewis, *Mere Christianity*, 153.
65. Ibid., 62–63.
66. "Belief," on the other hand, must be something more internal. Our discussion on Lewis's view of faith will soon follow.
67. Lewis, *Mere Christianity*, 161.

come to torment your natural self, but to kill it. No half-measures are any good. . . . Hand over the whole natural self, all the desires which you think innocent as well as the ones you think wicked—the whole outfit. I will give you a new self instead. In fact, I will give you Myself: my own will shall become yours."[68]

What is demanded of us is a surrender, a sort of death so that a new life can be given.

"Dying to Self"

In *The Pilgrim's Regress*, John the pilgrim's conversion involves his plunge into the baptismal water. He hears an exhortation, *Securus Te Projice*, or throw yourself away without care. Having first of all become naked, John is told to dive into the water. He is taken over by fear and says, "I have never learned to dive." Mother Kirk responds, "There is nothing to learn. The art of diving is not to do anything new but simply to cease doing something. You have only to let yourself go." Vertue, who stands naked beside John, utters, "It is only necessary to abandon all efforts at self-preservation." Even jumping into the water is discouraged, because it represents a certain human struggle. Mother Kirk warns,

> If you jump, you will be trying to save yourself and you may be hurt. As well, you would not go deep enough. You must dive so that you can go right down to the bottom of the pool: for you are not to come up again on this side. There is a tunnel in the cliff, far beneath the surface of the water, and it is through that that you must pass so that you may come up on the far side.[69]

What is narrated is the meaning of baptism, not merely the sacramental act but what must actually take place in the spiritual life of a person. Rather than struggling against the leading of God, one must give in. One must be confronted by the powerful paradox of conversion: "The cure of death is dying. He who lays down his liberty in that act receives it back."[70]

Therefore, repentance is not a mere reform; the problem is much too deep for a superficial fix-up. It is a radical way, and therefore it is both harder and easier than the ordinary idea of self-improvement. The total dependence is in view, but not in Schleiermacherian *Gefühl* of absolute

---

68. Ibid., 167.
69. Lewis, *Pilgrim's Regress*, 166–67.
70. Ibid., 164.

dependence.[71] Lewis did not advocate a religious feeling or consciousness of dependence as the essence. Rather, Lewis demanded a willful turn about based on the acceptance of Christ's substitutionary atonement, which results in a constant yielding of oneself to God. The surrender does not arise out of one's naturally embedded religiosity; instead, the surrender goes against the fallen human nature. Repentance requires a death to personal comfort and objectives; selfward journey must be turned into a Godward commitment. But, for human beings, as creatures of God, this is the way to the true home.

We are reminded of George Herbert's portrait of a penitent heart.[72] One must approach the altar of God's mercy and lay down one's hardened heart; the hardened heart must be broken down and itself be made into an altar. And one must cry, "Oh let thy blessed SACRIFICE be mine / And sanctify this ALTAR to be thine."[73] This is the beginning of the soul's journey into the sanctuary of God's presence.

But a more striking reminder is George MacDonald's fantasy stories, filled with the message of good death. I have earlier mentioned the short story, "The Golden Key," and, of course, *Phantastes*. In MacDonald's stories, Lewis found "a sort of cool, morning innocence, and also, quite unmistakably, a certain quality of Death, *good* Death."[74] Among MacDonald's stories, the notion of good death appears most clearly in *Lilith*, a deeply theological fantasy written almost thirty-five years after *Phantastes*. The character Lilith, Adam's first wife, is presented as an epitome of selfishness and self-idolization. The central message of the story is that salvation accompanies the process of abandoning old selves and being renewed by God's grace. MacDonald declares, "You will be dead so long as you refuse to die."[75]

Because God intends to carry out a full treatment, the self-surrender of repentance is profoundly uncomfortable to the fallen inclination of the human heart. Christ, in this sense, is unsafe. Mr. Beaver, responding to young Lucy who asks whether Aslan was "safe," says, "Who said anything

---

71. Friedrich D. E. Schleiermacher (1768-1834), a German theologian considered the father of liberal Protestantism, made piety central to Christian theology. Attempting to construct an essentially nonconceptual theology, in response to Kantian critique of speculative theology, Schleiermacher defined the essence of religion as "*gefühl* (often translated as feeling) of absolute dependence." Apparently, he had in mind a preconceptual, pre-emotional awareness or consciousness of being utterly dependent. The result seems to be subjectivistic and obscure.

72. Lewis noted that he was deeply influenced by George Herbert's (1593-1633) poems, especially *The Temple*. The work was listed as one of the ten most influential books for shaping his view of life. Fey, *Christian Century*, 719.

73. Herbert, *The Country Parson*, 139.

74. Lewis, "Preface," in *George MacDonald: An Anthology*, 21.

75. Lewis, *George MacDonald: An Anthology*, 127.

about safe? 'Course he isn't safe. But he's good. He's the King, I tell you."[76] Therefore, Christian life operates by the principle of faith, and it is not a mere assent to a set of information; on the contrary, it is a personal trust in God in Christ who is *good*. This personal trust is none other than a dimension of self-surrender to the loving and caring God.

FAITH AS TRUST

On more than one occasion, Lewis attempted to define his understanding of the meaning of faith. He lived and taught at a time when the intellectual integrity of religious faith was under severe attack from the academic community. For instance, in the 1948 Oxford University symposium on the topic of faith and reason, Antony Flew, who has ever since been a representative critic of Christian faith, attempted to invalidate the reasonableness of Christian belief in the form of a "falsification principle." He claimed that believers, by continually modifying and qualifying their belief system, do not allow counter arguments to ever falsify it. He contended that to know the meaning of an assertion is to know the negation of that assertion and that if there is no possibility of negation, it is not really an assertion.[77] Lewis himself raised the question whether faith ought to be regarded as a sort of virtue, "an intention to believe what you want to believe in the face of evidence to the contrary,"[78] and argued that to define faith as "the power of believing what we know to be untrue"[79] is inadequate and misleading. Instead, he defined faith as "the power of continuing to believe what we once honestly thought to be true until cogent reasons for honestly changing our minds are brought before us."[80] To clarify his point, Lewis made distinctions between two senses of the word "faith" as well as two functions of faith.

Lewis distinguished (1) "a settled intellectual assent," and (2) "a trust, or confidence, in the God whose existence is [first] assented to."[81] The first sense of faith or belief is properly called a "notional" or "intellectual" faith. It requires a sufficient usage of a reasoning process. Lewis noted, "Nearly everyone I know who has embraced Christianity in adult life has been influenced by what seemed to him to be at least probable arguments for

---

76. Lewis, *The Lion, the Witch and the Wardrobe*, 86.
77. Flew and MacIntyre, *New Essays in Philosophical Theology*, 96–97.
78. Lewis, "Religion: Reality or Substitute?," in *Christian Reflections*, 42.
79. Ibid.
80. Ibid.
81. Lewis, "Is Theism Important?," in *God in the Dock*, 172–73.

theism."[82] This, perhaps, is the observation of a man uniquely situated in an academic setting; other settings probably demonstrate a reverse tendency, that is, *fides quaerens intellectum,* which would be getting to Faith-1 from Faith-2. However, Lewis's own conversion manifests a Faith-1 to Faith-2 pattern of progress, and he thought all along that this was quite natural. At any rate, he believed that like all other forms of knowledge, Faith-1 is acquired through necessary reasoning. By the process of reasoning, he did not mean merely an exercise of reason. He held that knowledge generally came through three avenues: authority, reason, and experience. "[On] these three, mixed in varying proportions all our knowledge depends."[83] However, a person arriving at Faith-1 has not yet come into a religious state and is no different from the devils who "believe and tremble" according to Jas 2:19. Lewis thought that philosophical arguments for the existence of God have their aim at producing Faith-1.[84]

Faith-2, on the other hand, is of a different quality. It is distinguished from Faith-1, *Credere Deum esse* (faith that God is), and refers to a relational status, *Credere in Deum* (faith in God).[85] Even though Lewis believed that Faith-2 is naturally preceded by Faith-1, he never supposed the procession to be automatic. Rather, Faith-2 is a gift or a special grace.[86] This gift is like being given a new perception or "the seeing eye." He said, "To some, God is discoverable everywhere; to others, nowhere. . . . Much depends on the seeing eye."[87]

According to Lewis's system, Antony Flew's criticism fails sufficiently to distinguish between the two senses of faith.[88] For Lewis, Faith-1 should rightfully feel quite uncommitted and move according to either positive or negative assertions. With enough accumulation of the positive assertions, Faith-1 functions as a potential religion. Therefore, we can conclude that in terms of Faith-1, Antony Flew's demand ought to stand, because Faith-1 takes into account empirical observations which *logical positivists,* such as Anthony Flew, base the meaningfulness of discourse. On the other hand, Faith-2 functions quite differently. There is a certain obstinacy in this sort of faith, and it is rightfully there. Lewis's definition of faith as "the power

---

82. Ibid., 173.

83. Lewis, "Religion: Reality or Substitute?," in *Christian Reflections,* 41.

84. Lewis, "Is Theism Important?," in *God in the Dock,* 173.

85. Lewis, "On Obstinacy in Belief," in *World's Last Night,* 30.

86. Lewis, "Is Theism Important?," in *God in the Dock,* 174. Lewis gave 1 Cor 12:1–11 and Eph 2:8 as proof texts.

87. Lewis, "The Seeing Eye," in *Christian Reflections,* 171.

88. Lewis's challenges are implied and not explicitly stated in his published works.

of continuing to believe" holds true in this sense. As a gift-faith, Faith-2 transcends natural observation of facts; a certain settled conviction or properly basic commitment in the personal God shapes the believer's perspective. Lewis, in essence, declares Flew's view of the Christian faith too simplistic and that, in reality, his "falsification principle" must be applied to two separate categories. At one level, Lewis challenges Flew by saying that faith *is* falsifiable (Faith-1), contrary to his assertion. At another level, however, Lewis challenges Flew by saying that by definition faith (Faith-2) means *the power to "continue believing,"* and in this sense transcends the demand of falsification based on empirical evidences. In constructing the two-level meaning of faith, Lewis (1) places Christian faith on a rational ground (Faith-1 pre-conditions and may lead to Faith-2), and (2) raises Christian faith above the level of "positivistic" verification demands (Faith-2 is qualitatively different from Faith-1).[89]

Christian faith is more than an assent to a set of propositions. It is not only a belief in an objective set of facts but a subjective apprehension of it, thus inducing a participatory or relational knowledge. It is not only a belief but a trust in a personal being. "We trust not because 'a God' exists, but because *this* God exists. . . . We believe that His intention is to create a certain personal relation between Himself and us."[90] A complete trust is a necessary condition of that relationship, and that relationship being a "love-relationship" must involve "trusting the beloved beyond the evidence, even against much evidence."

> No man is our friend who believes in our good intentions only
> when they are proved. No man is our friend who will not be very

---

89. Lewis's two-level view of faith is still not adequate to refute Flew's argument. At the core, Flew is challenging the validity of Christian claims as a whole regardless of it being Faith-1 or Faith-2. The real problem with Flew is his own presuppositional bias, which makes him unable to see from the Christian perspective. This can be addressed in two ways: First, his positivistic bias demands that only empirical observations can be the proper ground of meaningful discourse, thus excluding religious language in general. It clearly manifests Flew's naturalistic bias. Second, his "presumption of atheism" reveals his bias that atheism is more basic to the natural human cognition than theism. For him, an atheist is "not someone who positively asserts the non-existence of God; but someone who is simply not a theist." He argues, therefore, "the onus of proof must lie upon the theist." (Flew, *Presumption of Atheism*, 14). The biblical worldview of Christian faith challenges both of Flew's biases. The Christian worldview presupposes supernaturalism and the assumption of theism. The very first verse of Scripture, "In the beginning, God created the heavens and the earth," clearly demonstrates these two biblical presuppositions: The supernatural reality of God precedes the creation of the natural; and the existence of God is the condition of all things, including human cognition.

90. Lewis, "On Obstinacy in Belief," in *World's Last Night*, 25.

slow to accept evidence against them. Such confidence, between one man and another, is in fact almost universally praised as a moral beauty, not blamed as a logical error. And the suspicious man is blamed for a meanness of character, not admired for the excellence of his logic.[91]

Lewis's exposition of faith as trust is extremely helpful and convincing. He had clearly distinguished between an intellectual faith and a saving faith and provided a sound exposition of the often misunderstood faith discussion in the Epistle of James. He wrote with conviction, "To believe that God—at least *this* God—exists is to believe that you as a person now stand in the presence of God as a Person. . . . You are no longer faced with an argument which demands your assent, but with a Person who demands your confidence."[92]

With this faith, it is possible and plausible to live out the life of self-surrender. What Christianity demands makes sense only in the category of such a trust. "We ask them to believe that what is painful will relieve their pain and that what looks dangerous is their only safety."[93] Conversion requires this change of the heart, and it indeed is a gift of God. Repentance, as already affirmed, is not a comfortable matter. Turning away from ourselves to turn toward God with an utter self-surrender is a fearful thing. The Christian journey, from its earliest stages, is not without pain. The bait is not coated with sweet things. People who come in with such expectations too quickly lose their zeal. Like "seed sown on rocky places, [they] hear the word and at once receive it with joy," but "when trouble or persecution comes because of the word, they quickly fall away."[94] It requires the "root" of a firm trust in the person of God in order to yield much crop. Lewis was not romantic about the Christian outlook of life.

> If human life is in fact ordered by a beneficent being whose knowledge of our real needs and of the way in which they can be satisfied infinitely exceeds our own, we must expect *a priori* that His operations will often appear to us far from beneficent and far from wise, and that it will be our highest prudence to give Him our confidence in spite of this.[95]

---

91. Ibid., 26.
92. Ibid.
93. Ibid., 23.
94. Mark 4:16–17 (NIV).
95. Lewis, "On Obstinacy of Belief," in *World's Last Night*, 24–25.

This precisely was the point Lewis repeatedly made in his novels. The way of God is different from our way; to grasp this truth and to turn to him is wisdom.

Lewis's complex novel, *Till We Have Faces*, manifests this profound theme. All Orual's complaints amount to her vain opinions, and her high-spirited love for her beautiful sister Psyche is but a selfish obsession. Having heard the voice of god [sic] saying, "Die before you die. There is no chance after," Orual contemplates the meaning of this death. Thus comes the moment of her initial enlightenment. She says,

> But by the death which is wisdom I suppose he meant the death of our passions and desires and vain opinions. And immediately (it is terrible to be a fool) I thought I saw my way clear and not impossible. To say that I was Ungit meant that I was as ugly in soul as she; greedy, blood-gorged.[96]

Unfortunately, her initial approach is to willfully improve herself. She says, "But if I practised true philosophy, as Socrates meant it, I should change my ugly soul into a fair one. And this, the gods helping me, I would do. I would set about it at once."[97] Not until she enters into the great vision of the court of god, does she see her real self.

As she stands pouring out her complaints against the gods, she begins to reveal her heart filled with her dreadful obsession with self. She utters,

> That there should be gods at all, there's our misery and bitter wrong. There's no room for you and us in the same world. You're a tree in whose shadow we can't thrive. We want to be our own. I was my own and Psyche was mine and no one else had any right to her.[98]

Even Psyche's happiness, if it stands outside of Orual's possession of her, is condemned to be evil. This "horrible, new happiness" is but evil because it separated Orual from her. Orual's frantic words follow: "She was mine. *Mine*. Do you not know what the word means? Mine! You're thieves, seducers. That's my wrong."[99] To her amazement, she realizes that the complaint is the answer she needs. That is her wrong! Having found her face, the true face, she confronts the god who comes to judge Orual.

Hand in hand with Psyche, who has already passed the utmost death, Orual stands at the edge of a pool and experiences a kind of death she has

---

96. Lewis, *Till We Have Faces*, 279, 281–82.
97. Ibid., 282.
98. Ibid., 292.
99. Ibid.

not understood before. "The air was growing brighter and brighter about us; as if something had set it on fire. Each breath I drew let into me new terror, joy, overpowering sweetness. I was pierced through and through with the arrows of it. I was being unmade. I was no one."[100] Soon she sees two women reflected on the water, both beautiful "beyond all imagining, yet not exactly the same."[101] She experiences the real conversion. The book ends with her great new insight. "I know now, Lord, why you utter no answer. You are yourself the answer. Before your face questions die away."[102] The self-surrender comes when she encounters the person, not merely intellectual statements or assertions. Coming into the trusting relationship with the Lord turns all the questions about the perceived misery, hardship, loss, and pain into meaningless words. When a naked heart stands before God who is a person, a new life emerges through a kind of death, a good death.

ACTIVE AND PASSIVE DIMENSIONS OF CONVERSION

A difficult theological issue must be addressed at this point. Theologians have traditionally differentiated between the secret work of God in regenerating a person (thus the passive dimension of salvation) and the conscious experience of turning toward God through repentance and faith in conversion (thus an active dimension of salvation). However, it must be recognized that even in the process of conversion, there is an immediate work of the Holy Spirit taking place; therefore, it is not sound to think that conversion is merely a voluntary act of the person involved. It is, therefore, often stated that, distinct from regeneration (in which God alone works and a person is entirely passive), in conversion the person cooperates with the work of God within him/her. However, the term "cooperate" must not be understood according to the modern meaning of "partnership" or "synergy." Rather, it means that by nature conversion requires a human responsiveness to God's work in the inner person. Thus, we must say that conversion has two dimensions: active and passive.

Lewis often raised the question of the initiative, although he seemingly was skeptical about discovering an answer. How then does he reconcile the passive and active dimensions of conversion? Which is prior, divine or human initiative? The question of the initiative is set within a larger question: How is the sovereign operation of God in redemption (the doctrine of election and predestination) reconciled with the notion of human freedom (the

---

100. Ibid., 307.
101. Ibid., 308.
102. Ibid.

doctrine of free will)? Lewis, being a lay person, felt justified not to hold a clear theological commitment to a particular strand of thought. In this sense, he could not be labeled as a strict Arminian or a Calvinist.

On the other hand, Lewis was not an academic charlatan. It is unreasonable to assume that Lewis constructed his theological and philosophical reasoning without a certain system or logic. Since the issue is such a central one for one's theological and philosophical reasoning, we have a warrant to believe that Lewis must have thought through the issue.

To deal with the issue at hand, it is important to understand Lewis's anthropological thought. Lewis held to the traditional Christian teaching that the human being is a bearer of the image of God. He understood this in two ways: first, a person is a reflection of God's power and glory, and second, a person is like clay upon which God's impression has been laid. This means that a person is at the same time free to will and dependent upon God for wholeness, meaning, and contentment. In fact, his best possible will is to submit his will to God's will. Clarence Francis Dye offers a good exposition of Lewis's view of a person's relationship with God. He rightly points out two major "ingredients of Lewis's anthropology," which are "his concept of free will and his concept of man as contingent—of man as always being in a relationship to God."[103] Dye seeks to establish Lewis's dual emphases on a person's independence as a free moral agent, which is the state desired and instituted by God himself in creation, and on his or her dependence on God as creaturely and contingent beings, the state equally desired and instituted by God in creation.

In our earlier discussion of the psychology of fallen humanity, we noted Lewis's assertion that the paradisal man had no conflict between his moral agency and contingency. He used his free will to assume his subordinate posture before God, with ease and no conflict of inclination. However, the Fall brought about a major change in the situation. The fall resulted in the corruption of human spirit. Although Lewis desired not to agree with what the doctrine of total depravity seems to suggest,[104] there is no ques-

---

103. Dye, "The Evolving Eschaton in C. S. Lewis," 69.

104. Lewis's position ought not to be understood as ignoring human depravity as a whole. He affirmed the radical depravity of human beings but expressed his discontentment with the term, "total depravity." "I disbelieve that doctrine, partly on the logical ground that if our depravity were total we should not know ourselves to be depraved, and partly because experience shows us much goodness in human nature." (Lewis, *Problem of Pain*, 66.) If "total depravity" simply meant that man and woman are absolutely unable to save themselves on their own ability, Lewis would have agreed. But if it means (and apparently this is how Lewis understood the doctrine) that there is absolutely nothing good in man, though created by God, having lost all sound knowledge and moral imperatives, Lewis would reject it, as he clearly did in the above statement.

tion that Lewis held to the view of radical depravity, that something drastic and decisive happened in the Fall of man to his being as a whole. As we have seen already, to Lewis, the Fall did not result in merely a disorientation of relatively functional faculties, requiring merely a better management. Rather, he identified the state of corruption as that which ran deep into the spirit of man itself. It would be redundant to expand this point any further.

The question is, then, how does a person turn back to God, his true home? It was the free will that introduced evil into the world in the first place; if so, do people as fallen beings still retain the power to willingly turn back to God? Do they have an inherent power to will and carry out such a tremendous spiritual accomplishment? Lewis apparently believed that though people's selfward inclination makes it painfully difficult, it is still possible for them to turn back to God.[105] At the same time, he did not want to address the question, "Where does the initiative lie?" Lewis wanted to take seriously the biblical texts about human responsibility such as the parable of the sheep and the goats (Matt 25:30–46); at the same time, he could not discount the Pauline assertions of Divine sovereignty in the matters of redemption. He felt that "[no] one can make these two views consistent." Even though the reality "must be self-consistent," until "we can see the consistency it is better to hold two inconsistent views than to ignore one side of the evidence."[106] Thus he concluded, "The real inter-relation between God's omnipotence and man's freedom is something we can't find out." But as a subjective experience, in retrospect, the Pauline account seems to fit.

> Everyone looking back on *his own* conversion must feel—and I am sure the feeling is in some sense true—"It is not I who have done this. I did not choose Christ: He chose me. It is all free grace, which I have done nothing to earn." That is the Pauline account: and I am sure it is the only true account of every conversion *from the inside*.[107]

This certainly was true of Lewis's own conversion.

He, "the most dejected and reluctant convert in all England,"[108] did not assume himself to be the initiator. It was in every way God closing in on him, like a cat trapping a mouse until there is no escape. Furthermore, it seemed logical to him to think that "if Shakespeare and Hamlet could ever meet, it must be Shakespeare's doing. Hamlet could initiate nothing."[109] At

---

105. Lewis, *Problem of Pain*, 83.
106. Lewis, *Letters of C. S. Lewis*, 433.
107. Ibid.
108. Lewis, *Surprised by Joy*, 228–29.
109. Ibid., 227.

the same time, Lewis with amazement recalled his personal willingness to open himself up to God at which moment he felt wholly free to act.

> The choice appeared to be momentous but it was also strangely unemotional. I was moved by no desires or fears. In a sense I was not moved by anything. I chose to open, to unbuckle, to loosen the rein. . . . You could argue that I was not a free agent, but I am more inclined to think that this came nearer to being a perfectly free act than most that I have ever done.[110]

If the testimony seems paradoxical, it was probably intended to be so by Lewis himself. It is a mystery. It was God who freed Lewis's will to act freely.

Lewis considered "strictly causal thinking" to be very inadequate "when applied to the relationship between God and man." Lewis thought that "[we] profanely assume that divine and human action exclude one another like the actions of two fellow-creatures so that 'God did this' and 'I did this' cannot both be true of the same act except in the sense that each contributed a share."[111] He appealed to Phil 2:12–13. He said,

> You will notice that Scripture just sails over the problem. "Work out your own salvation in fear and trembling"—pure Pelagianism. But why? "For it is God who worketh in you"—pure Augustinianism. It is presumably only our presuppositions that make this appear nonsensical.[112]

On the other hand, Lewis thought that there was a very practical problem in regard to this issue. How about our prayers? Do they have any meaning if God foresees all things? He felt compelled to reconcile human actions and God's providence in order to make sense out of our duty to pray. "His providential and creative act (for they are all one) takes into account

---

110. Ibid., 224.

111. Lewis, *Letters to Malcolm*, 49–50.

112. Ibid., 49. However, "work *out* your salvation" should not be seen as a Pelagian exhortation (contrary to "work *for*" or "work *up to* your salvation"). While it clearly emphasize our conscious effort, it is not to produce salvation but to work out its consequences (i.e., sanctification). Furthermore, the verse may be better interpreted as a communal exhortation rather than a reference to the outworking of personal salvation. A contextual reading of the verses reveals a more corporate dynamic at work. Thus, Ralph Martin comments, "[The] true exegesis must begin with the definition of *salvation*, not in personal terms, but in regard to the corporate life of the Philippian church. The readers are being encouraged to concentrate upon reforming their church life, 'working at' this matter until the spiritual health of the community, diseased by strife and bad feelings, is restored." And, "the much-needed restoration of harmonious relationships within the church, its corporate 'salvation,' can only be produced in dependence upon God's power." (Martin, *Epistle of Paul to the Philippians*, 115–16).

all the situations produced by the acts of His creatures. And if He takes our sins into account, why not our petitions?"[113] To give a further explanation to this matter, Lewis appealed to the Boethian concept of time and eternity, that God beholds from his high tower of *providentia* in his eternal, timeless present, and dispenses his rewards and punishments to us living in time.

> There remaineth also a beholder of all things which is God, who foreseeth all things, and the eternity of His vision, which is always present, concurreth with the future quality of our actions, distributing rewards to the good and punishments to the evil. Neither do we in vain put our hope in God or pray to Him; for if we do this well and as we ought, we shall not lose our labour or be without effect.[114]

Lewis's discussion of time and eternity is found in *Mere Christianity*, where he affirms the supratemporal quality of God, that he is not subjected to "the Time-stream of this universe any more than an author is hurried along in the imaginary time of his own novel."[115] Lewis believed that God "does not live in a Time-series at all," and that with him "it is, so to speak, still 1920 and already 1960. For His life is Himself."[116] The issue of prayer will get a thorough treatment in the following chapter.

CONCLUSION

We have seen in this chapter that Lewis's view of the doctrine of conversion portrays the beginning of a homeward journey. In the moment of conversion, the pilgrim is confronted by the voice, "Which you choose: Jump, or be thrown.... Give in or struggle."[117] It takes God's grace to cease struggling and freely give in. For the moment of death to self is indescribable to mere natural ears; and the other side is a whole new world though it is the same place where the pilgrim traveled before.

We have clear statements about Lewis's supernaturalist view of salvation or "salvationism," which characterizes his "mere Christianity." He rejected developmentalist notions of salvation, which only amount to religions of self-improvement. Lewis recognized the radical human problem of sin stemming from the fallen state, and pointed to Christ's atonement as the

113. Ibid., 50.
114. Boethius, *Theological Tractates*, 347, 411.
115. Lewis, *Mere Christianity*, 147.
116. Ibid.
117. Lewis, *Pilgrim's Regress*, 164.

only remedy. The theory of substitutionary atonement he espoused is an unorthodox kind, as we have seen, and the description of the new life in Christ falls short of adequately maintaining the Creator-creature distinction. Nevertheless, these theological "innovations" do not critically undermine the salvationistic distinctives of his "mere Christianity."

Lewis's repeated appeals to two-level reality at times contribute to unnecessary concession to non-Christian thought. First, Lewis accepted Darwinism as a biological theory while rejecting its implications as a larger worldview. Second, Lewis allowed the presupposition of *logical positivists* to exercise its naturalistic criterion in the domain of Faith-1 while largely guarding it from the domain of Faith-2. A thoroughly consistent application of the Christian presupposition, distinctively present in Lewis's "mere Christianity" in the form of supernaturalism and salvationism, could have avoided unnecessary confusion.

In the next chapter, we turn to the shape of new life in the fallen world, or "home away from home."

5

Home Away From Home
The New Life in the Fallen World

The new life acquired through the dying-to-self process of conversion is a radically different life from what preceded it. The restless wandering is now turned into a purposeful and hopeful journey. Nevertheless, it is important to understand that Lewis's view of salvation is not naively triumphalistic. It is true that the wandering has come to an end with the *good death*; still, the remaining life is a journey. The new life has already begun, but the pilgrims are not yet at the final home. Perhaps, in the spirit of Lewis's journey motif, the best way to describe the life following "homeward turning" is "home away from home." The old tendency of the selfward journey has been transformed into a journey out of self back to the Creator who initiated this renewed relationship of love. The people of God are now placed in a world that is rightfully their home, because it is the world of their Father. On the other hand, it is still the fallen world. They must continue to struggle to live out their new life in a hostile context. The final eschatological consummation, when the dramatic divorce of heaven and hell will take place, is yet to come. Until the personal eschaton draws upon us through the physical death and/or the universal eschaton comes upon the world, "[when] the author walks on to the stage,"[1] the journey must continue.

In the homeward journey, unlike the earlier stage of wandering, certain conditions allow the pilgrims to be steadfast through the trials they must face. These conditions make the "home away from home" experience bearable and even joyful. *The Pilgrim's Regress* presents them as (1) Mother Kirk and the company of the fellow pilgrims, (2) the accompaniment of the

---

1. Lewis, *Mere Christianity*, 66.

appointed guide named Slikisteinsauga, and (3) the songs that give courage to the pilgrim's heart.

At the same time, the threat present in the world is real; it is a dangerous place to journey through. The pilgrims in *The Pilgrim's Regress* must face dragons and battle against them. Lewis, more successfully than many other Christian writers, presented a practical demonology in his celebrated masterpiece, *The Screwtape Letters*. Lewis's insightful observation of the psychology of temptation has proved itself as an invaluable assistance to Christians.

In this chapter, I will address the topics that are relevant to the state of "home away from home." The first three will deal with the conditions or means through which the pilgrims find strength to make the journey: the church, the guide, and prayer. In the final section, I will discuss the topic of the tempter and temptations in the light of Lewis's practical demonology. These issues emerge as Lewis's central concerns in his portrait of the journey through the world, "the home away from home."

THE CHURCH

It is none other than Mother Kirk who stands by the "baptismal" water into which the pilgrim is told to dive. Mother Kirk is described as "crowned and sceptred," standing in the midst of the silent people whose "faces were turned towards her."[2] She is the one who teaches John and other pilgrims how to dive properly and what must be done once submerged under water. Lewis later tried to clarify that Mother Kirk ought not to be paralleled to any specific ecclesiastical position; rather, the title ought to be thought of as a reference in the broadest sense to the Christian church, which stands against unbelief. "The book," Lewis said, "is concerned solely with Christianity as against unbelief. 'Denominational' questions do not come in."[3] The symbolism, then, points us to what traditionally has been called the universal church, which binds together all those who belong to the body of Christ who is the head of the church.

Lewis presented a distinction between the church, which to the natural eye seems deficient, and the true spiritual church. Previously, Mother Kirk appears as a poorly attired aged woman of whom John says, "She looks to me much more like a witch."[4] The country people talk of her as being "second-sighted" or even crazy. Although she claims to have "the power that

---

2. Lewis, *Pilgrim's Regress*, 166.
3. Lewis, "Afterword to Third Edition," in *Pilgrim's Regress*, 209.
4. Lewis, *Pilgrim's Regress*, 70–71.

the Landlord has given" to carry the pilgrim down the cliff into the canyon, John can only respond reasonably: "And how could you carry us down, mother? We would be more fit to carry you."[5]

In one sense, this shows much about the inability of the natural man and woman to see through the humble appearance of the Christian church. On the other hand, the appearance of Mother Kirk must be contrasted with her later appearance as one who is "crowned and sceptred." Once again, Lewis could be referring to our need to see through the mundane appearance of the Christian church and notice her God-given authority and power. Yet, at the same time, Lewis must be saying something quite objectively true: the church is imperfect, but it is the vessel in which the true church operates with its divinely instituted authority and power. She is the church militant who must stand against the scheme of the enemy.

The Sacraments

Having plunged into the "baptismal" water, the pilgrim experiences "dying many deaths."[6] The pilgrim must learn the meaning of "the dying" through a mysterious voice, which tells him that this is not just a figurative motion but a participation in the true mythology, not of human invention. Consistent with Lewis's epistemological paradigm for reason and imagination, the voice tells him the real power of this participation. "[This] is My inventing, this is the veil under which I have chosen to appear even from the first until now. For this end I made your senses and for this end your imagination, that you might see My face and live."[7] Lewis believed that human faculties of reason and imagination together are meant to collaborate, yielding the knowledge of the content of divine revelation. The imagination is necessary because the revelation itself contains a certain veil-like character (an inescapable breach between the Creator and the creature). Only in the incarnation of Christ, has the veil been lifted and the "Myth Became Fact," without losing its mythic power. The fact that the pilgrim's "baptism" involves this dynamic reveals something about Lewis's view of the sacraments.

Lewis had a high view of the sacraments. He said, "Our life as Christians begins by being baptised into a death; our most joyous festivals begin with, and centre upon, the broken body and the shed blood."[8] These sacraments point to the rich depth of Christianity as that which places Joy in the

---

5. Ibid., 71.
6. Ibid., 168–69.
7. Ibid., 169.
8. Lewis, *Reflections on the Psalms*, 52.

context of Christ's suffering and death. They reveal the essential elements of Christianity. G. P. Kingsley observes that according to the Anglican view the sacraments do not impart "saving grace," which is limited to the work of Christ alone, but "sanctifying grace," and that Lewis adhered to this position.[9] However, Lewis did not sharply distinguish between "saving grace" (or better "justifying grace") and "sanctifying grace." In *Mere Christianity*, Lewis merged "belief" (coterminous with "trust" in this case), a decidedly internal action, with baptism and Holy Communion, necessarily outward actions, as three ordinary means of "[spreading] the Christ life to us."[10] He chose not to say which of these three things are more essential. Rather, he recognized a certain inherent (or even mystical) spiritual significance (or potency) of baptism and the Communion. This must be expanded.

Lewis considered the meaning of the sacraments to extend beyond the physical elements; the spiritual meaning directs us to something far deeper than the bloody animal rituals of the Old Testament Judaism. On the other hand, the actual materials and outward actions involved in these sacraments are not accidental or nonessential.

> And let me make it quite clear that when Christians say that Christ-life is in them, they do not mean simply something mental or moral. When they speak of being "in Christ" or of Christ being "in them," this is not simply a way of saying that they are thinking about Christ or copying Him. They mean that Christ is actually operating through them; that the whole mass of Christians are the physical organism through which Christ acts.... It explains why this new life is spread not only by purely mental acts like belief, but by bodily acts like baptism and Holy Communion. It is not merely the spreading of an idea; it is more like evolution—a biological or superbiological fact. There is no good trying to be more spiritual than God. God never meant man to be a purely spiritual creature. That is why He uses material things like bread and wine to put the new life into us.[11]

Whatever we make of Lewis's allusions, his key point comes across quite clearly. The acts are not merely figurative, but certain true benefits are mysteriously (or more consistent with Lewis's choice of terms, mythologically) transferred to us through the sacraments.

---

9. Kingsley, "The Doctrine of Soteriology in the Writings of C. S. Lewis," 39.
10. Lewis, *Mere Christianity*, 62.
11. Ibid., 65.

The Company of Pilgrims

Having thus experienced the baptismal death, John, along with his companion Vertue, emerges out on the other side. It is the green forests "full of the sounds of birds and the rustle of leaves." There he witnesses a remarkable sight.

> [They] were received into a great company of other pilgrims who had all descended like them into the water and the earth and again come up, and now took their march westward along the banks of a clear river. All kinds of men were among them.... It was a wonder to John to find so many companions: nor could he conceive how he had failed to run across them in the earlier parts of his journey.[12]

Thus, the pilgrim's journey homeward is set in the context of a larger body of believers.

This corporate aspect of Christian life is something Lewis had to learn to enjoy against his nature. It was an aspect of the commitment he had made to Christ and obviously entailed some elements disagreeable to his natural disposition. Lewis said, "As soon as I became a Theist I started attending my parish church on Sundays and my college chapel on weekdays . . . because I thought one ought to 'fly one's flag' by some unmistakable overt sign." But internally he was struggling with this new facet of his life: "The idea of churchmanship was to me wholly unattractive. I was not in the least anticlerical, but I was deeply antiecclesiastical."[13] He disliked intensely the collective and ceremonious aspect of church life; it was just a "wearisome 'get-together' affair."

> I couldn't yet see how a concern of that sort should have anything to do with one's spiritual life. To me, religion ought to have been a matter of good men praying alone and meeting by twos or threes to talk of spiritual matters. . . . I have, too, a sort of spiritual *gaucherie* which makes me unapt to participate in any rite.[14]

Did Lewis ever come to agree with this corporate aspect of Christian faith? First of all, Lewis became acutely aware of its danger. Perhaps it is a common characteristic of an adult convert to notice something negative about church-life, to which those who never left the company from

12. Lewis, *Pilgrim's Regress*, 169.
13. Lewis, *Surprised by Joy*, 233–34.
14. Ibid., 234.

childhood might be immune. At any rate, the ability to give warning about real problems cannot be a disadvantage. Lewis warned of the serious danger of ritualism. He noticed how possible it is to reduce our Christian life to "the merely dutiful 'church-going' and laborious 'saying our prayers.'"[15] Church life, as the part of a compartmentalized life assigned to religious matters, can be extremely dangerous, even verging on idolatry:

> Religion . . . appears to exist as a department, and, in some ages, to thrive as such. It thrives partly because there exists in many people a "love of religious observances." . . . There exists also . . . the delight in religious (as in any other) organisation. Then all sorts of aesthetic, sentimental, historical, political interests are drawn in. Finally sales of work, the parish magazine, the bell-ringing, and Santa Claus. . . . The department of life, labelled "sacred," can become an end in itself; an idol that hides both God and my neighbors.[16]

Lewis firmly believed in the holistic demands of Christian faith. Church life should not become an end in itself but only an outward sign of a deeper sense of belonging. All of life must fall under the reign of God. "Either it is an illusion or else our whole life falls under it." All the spheres of our lives belong properly connected to our relationship with God. "We have no nonreligious activities, only religious and irreligious."[17]

Then, why should church exist at all? "[The] Church exists for nothing else but to draw men into Christ, to make them little Christs. If they are not doing that, all the cathedrals, clergy, missions, sermons, even the Bible itself, are simply a waste of time."[18] Lewis went even further to say that the whole universe is created probably for the same purpose. We have a clear statement of Lewis's salvationist thrust: everything belongs within this grand purpose of God to save the world according to his eternal and wise plan. Unless the purpose is carried out in the church, it not only turns out to be ineffective but even diabolical in its effect. Screwtape claims, "One of our great allies at present is the Church itself." The sheer human, almost entrepreneurial factors can detract people from coming to Christ.

> All your patient sees is the half-finished, sham Gothic erection on the new building estate. When he goes inside, he sees the local barber with rather an oily expression on his face bustling

---

15. Lewis, *Reflections on the Psalms*, 46.
16. Lewis, *Letters to Malcolm*, 30.
17. Ibid.
18. Lewis, *Mere Christianity*, 170.

up to offer him one shiny little book containing a liturgy which neither of them understands, and one shabby little book containing corrupt texts of a number of religious lyrics, mostly bad, and in very small print.[19]

Screwtape describes how the picture above contrasts with the reality of the divinely instituted authority of the church, "[spreading] out through all time and space and rooted in eternity, terrible as an army with banners."[20] Unfortunately, the latter is invisible to human eyes, so they often merely focus on what visibly takes place. The danger of misunderstanding the church is real.

Nevertheless, the church, with its often unimpressive presence in the world, belongs to the matter of the highest spiritual priorities, because the Holy Spirit works through her to proclaim salvation. What nature cannot give, God instituted the church to provide. "Our real journey to God involves constantly turning our backs on [nature]; passing from the dawn-lit fields into some poky little church, or (it might be) going to work in an East End parish."[21] The church exists in order to proclaim the message of salvation to the world.

Furthermore, the church is the setting for communal worship and communal discovery of who God is. The church, by definition, is a worshipping community; Lewis acknowledged that worship or adoration should be public or communal and that this character is of the utmost importance. He added that in the act of adoration even private worship naturally turns into a communal one "with angels and archangels and all the company" in the "transparent publicity of Heaven."[22]

Lewis felt that he had nothing authoritative to say about the matters of liturgy. He simply desired to abolish from worship anything that distracts from the act of worship. "I assume from the outset that nothing should be done or sung or said in church which does not aim directly or indirectly either at glorifying God or edifying the people or both. A good service may of course have a cultural value as well, but that is not what it exists for."[23]

In the matters of music, for example, a mere excellence of music simply as music does not accomplish the aim of worship. "The excellence proves 'keenness'; but men can be 'keen' for natural, or even wicked, motives."[24] Lewis clearly saw the danger of church life set in the context

19. Lewis, *Screwtape Letters*, 25.
20. Ibid.
21. Lewis, *Four Loves*, 39.
22. Lewis, *Letters to Malcolm*, 100.
23. Lewis, *Christian Reflections*, 94.
24. Ibid., 98.

of its mere cultural significance; a symptom has become more evident in the post-Christian West, which has lost much of its supernatural outlook. Lewis deeply grieved over this spiritual decline in his own cultural context. A church gathering is not a cultural experience; it must be a worshipful company of believers who, as the body of Christ, celebrate the gathering's supernatural significance and glorify the Lord of their salvation.

Furthermore, the church is a uniquely effective channel of conveying God's word. In fact, Lewis considered the church, as a community of believers, to be a particularly effective instrument for the "science of knowing God."

> God can show Himself as He really is only to real men. And that means not simply to men who are individually good, but to men who are united together in a body, loving one another, helping one another, showing Him to one another. For that is what God meant humanity to be like; like players in one band, or organs in one body. Consequently, the one really adequate instrument for learning about God is the whole Christian community, waiting for Him together. Christian brotherhood is, so to speak, the technical equipment for this science—the laboratory outfit.[25]

The Christian community, if focused right and kept clean and bright according to its proper aim, turns out to be a uniquely qualified instrument for God to reveal Himself to his people.

The Meaning of Membership

One address given by Lewis stands out as the best representation of his mature view of the Christian community. It is entitled "membership" and was given to a society meeting[26] in Oxford in 1945. In it, Lewis rejected the idea that religion should be defined as "what a man does with his solitude."[27] He asserted that the idea of private religion is "paradoxical, dangerous and natural."

It is paradoxical because "this exaltation of the individual in the religious field springs up in an age when collectivism is ruthlessly defeating the individual in every other field."[28] Modern life is characterized by being in a crowd, noise, and bustle. "We live, in fact, in a world starved for

---

25. Lewis, *Mere Christianity*, 144.
26. The Society of St. Alban and St. Sergius, Oxford.
27. Lewis, "Membership," in *Weight of Glory*, 106.
28. Ibid.

solitude, silence, and privacy, and therefore starved for meditation and true friendship."[29]

This paradoxical situation poses two great dangers, which naturally reflect the danger of the idea of private religion. First, to make Christianity a private affair and at the same time banish all privacy turns out to be a clever strategy of the enemy. The end result is to push out Christianity altogether in a person's life. Second, an error can be committed by those who know that Christianity is not a solitary affair "by simply transporting into our spiritual life that same collectivism which has already conquered our secular life."[30] This is another of the enemy's strategies. Modern collectivism is "an outrage upon human nature." As a result, we can end up vacillating between the ideas of private religion, which we conceive to be wrong yet feel natural in, and the collective one; and we are uneasy in both.[31]

Lewis, therefore, proposed a new paradigm for understanding the communal notion of Christian faith since the church is the Bride and Body of Christ. Lewis suggested a three level structure to this reality: Participation in the Body of Christ stands at the highest level; personal and private life occupy the second level; and the collective life of the secular community is at the lowest level. The lower level's role is to support and promote the higher level. "The secular community, since it exists for our natural good and not for our supernatural, has no higher end than to facilitate and safeguard the family, and friendship, and solitude."[32] This is the picture of a sound society according to Lewis:

> As long as we are thinking only of natural values we must say that the sun looks down on nothing half so good as a household laughing together over a meal, or two friends talking over a pint of beer, or a man alone reading a book that interests him; and that all economic, politics, laws, armies, and institutions, save insofar as they prolong and multiply such scenes, are a mere ploughing the sand and sowing the ocean, a meaningless vanity and vexation of spirit.[33]

Collective matters ought not to become the center of attention in the society, just as a healthy person should not constantly be reminded of his or her digestive system. However, Lewis realized that it is natural to be consumed by the means and lose sight of the end. "I think it probable that the collectivism

29. Ibid., 107.
30. Ibid., 108.
31. Ibid.
32. Ibid.
33. Ibid., 108–9.

of our life is necessary and will increase, and I think that our only safeguard against its deathly properties is in a Christian life."[34]

In what sense can a Christian life be our safeguard against collectivism? It is a misunderstanding that the cure of collectivism is found in solitude and, therefore, to assume that Christianity ought to consider itself a private religion in order to oppose collectivism. "The Christian is called not to individualism but to membership in the mystical body."[35] How, then, is the mystical body different from secular collectivism? Lewis suggested that the very term "membership" must be redefined in its original Christian context. While the contemporary meaning of membership denotes a homogeneous class of people belonging together in a social structure, the original meaning of member, from its Greek root, is "organ." Members, therefore, refer to "things essentially different from, and complementary to, one another," and they could differ "not only in structure and function but also in dignity."[36] This kind of unity Lewis called "the extreme differentiation of persons in harmonious union," is therefore "our true refuge both from solitude and from the collective."[37]

A Christian, through baptism, is called into a body, which is not merely a massing together of persons, but a dynamic and spiritual union between those who have different functions and duties. We learn this also from *The Pilgrim's Regress*: the pilgrims, though many, are assigned different paths all leading to the same end. John and Vertue, having arrived at the baptismal death at the same time, must travel on different roads, facing different manifestations of the enemy. Christians are called into the body of Christ as one; but, at the same time, everyone is given a journey that is distinct from others. God gives each his or her own story.

This theme is also featured in *The Horse and His Boy*. When Shasta finds out that Aslan the great lion is the one who wounded his companion Aravis, he cannot hold back his bewilderment.

> "Then it was you who wounded Aravis?"
> "It was I."
> "But what for?"
> "Child," said the Voice, "I am telling you your story, not hers. I tell no one any story but his own."

---

34. Ibid., 109.
35. Ibid., 110.
36. Ibid.
37. Ibid., 111.

When the boy Shasta asks in puzzlement who this Aslan is that he should address each one as an individual, the response is wholly divine:

> "Who are you?" asked Shasta.
> "Myself," said the Voice, very deep and low so that the earth shook: and again "Myself," loud and clear and gay: and then the third time "Myself," whispered so softly you could hardly hear it, and yet it seemed to come from all round you as if the leaves rustled with it.[38]

This is a profound theme: God, in his grandeur, leads each individual through a journey of his or her own. He does this because he is the great I AM. No one can question it. No one is entitled to an answer unrelated to him. It is Paul who heard the voice, "My grace is sufficient for you, for my power is made perfect in weakness." The same Paul wrote to those who object to God's sovereign grace and judgment: "But who are you, O man, to talk back to God? Shall what is formed say to him who formed it, 'Why did you make me like this?' Does not the potter have the right to make out of the same lump of clay some pottery for noble purposes and some for common use?"[39]

In the community of believers, the differences are pointers to the richness of God's ways. Lewis observed, "That is why the worldlings are so monotonously alike compared with the almost fantastic variety of the saints." In the same breath, Lewis exclaimed, "Obedience is the road to freedom, humility the road to pleasure, unity the road to personality."[40] Of course, the profound unity of the body of Christ results from its common goal: "His presence, the interaction between Him and us, must always be the overwhelmingly dominant factor in the life we are to lead within the Body, and any conception of Christian fellowship which does not mean primarily fellowship with Him is out of court."[41] These words are consistent with Lewis's "mere Christianity." The core objective is very clearly salvationistic, which is to restore and continue to enjoy our relationship with God. This can never be compromised, or it is no longer a Christian community. Once this unity is established, we can celebrate a fascinating variety of authentic lives standing before God. None is forced to wear a uniform of artificial equality (which "is necessary in the life of the State"). "In the Church we

---

38. Lewis, *Horse and His Boy*, 176.
39. 2 Cor 12:9 and Rom 9:20–21 (NIV).
40. Lewis, "Membership," in *Weight of Glory*, 113.
41. Ibid., 112.

strip off this disguise, we recover our real inequalities, and are thereby refreshed and quickened."[42]

Lewis believed that the notion of equality is both a result of the Fall and the remedy for it. This means that the function of equality is protective but not definitive. The real meaning behind the notion of equality is not the idea that all people are good but that all fallen people are wicked. A democracy is not a system of mutual self-assertion but of mutual checks and balances, because fallen beings cannot handle power. "[All] power corrupts, and absolute power corrupts absolutely."[43] Lewis thought it meaningless to say that people are of equal value, because "[the] value of each human soul considered simply in itself, out of relation to God, is zero." God loves us "not because we were lovable, but because He is Love." So Lewis concluded, "If there is equality, it is in His love, not in us."[44] Once again,

> Authority exercised with humility and obedience accepted with delight are the very lines along which our spirits live. Even in the life of the affections, much more in the Body of Christ, we step outside that world which says "I am as good as you." It is like turning from a march to a dance.[45]

On the other hand, this should never give away to a misunderstanding that it is mere individuality that is exalted in the body of Christ. It is, most clearly, the *body* consisting of many different members. Each believer is joined to the immortal Head and partakes in his everlasting life. "It was not for societies or states that Christ died, but for men."[46] Yet to partake in Christ's death, believers are called to "the crucifixion of the natural self." We share the victory by being in the victor, who died by giving himself completely to the will of God. Marveling at the profound paradox of Christian faith, Lewis noted, "There lies the maddening ambiguity of our faith as it must appear to outsiders. It sets its face relentlessly against our natural individualism; on the other hand, it gives back to those who abandon individualism an eternal possession of their own personal being, even of their bodies."[47] Amazingly, in Christ, our self-identity is eternally preserved.

In fact, true personality lies still ahead. Yet this true personality does not grow from our inner potential. Lewis's "mere Christianity" consciously

---

42. Ibid., 113.
43. Ibid., 114. The axiom is from Lord Acton.
44. Ibid., 115.
45. Ibid., 115–16.
46. Ibid., 117.
47. Ibid.

departed from Aristotelian thought at this point. The true personality will come to us "when we occupy those places in the structure of the eternal cosmos for which we were designed or invented" by the Creator himself.[48] Even in his retelling of the Greek mythology of Psyche in *Till We Have Faces*, Orual's transformation does not stem from a Socratic self-improvement, but only through a "divine judgment," the coming of "[the] most dreadful, the most beautiful, the only dread and beauty there is."[49] Lewis rejected the idea of salvation as "the development from seed to flower." He believed that Christian salvation involves something much more catastrophic. "The very words *repentance, regeneration, the New Man,* suggest something very different."[50] The true value of each individual is received only by union with Christ. In fact, one is not himself or herself until he/she is united with Christ by being in the body of Christ. This body of Christ is one's real home. The remaining course of the journey does not prevent him/her from spiritually being at home. In the light of the eschatological fulfillment, it is "the home away from home"; nevertheless, it is his or her true home indeed.

In "Membership," Lewis successfully handled a two-fold objective: First, he "wanted to try to expel that quite un-Christian worship of the human individual simply as such." He rejected what he called the "Pelagian" error that "each of us starts with a treasure called 'personality' locked up inside him, and that to expand and express this, to guard it from interference, to be 'original,' is the main end of life."[51] Second, Lewis "wanted to show that Christianity is not, in the long run, concerned either with individuals or communities . . . but a new creature."[52] Lewis has given us helpful ecclesiological insights: the meaning of the church as the body of Christ and its supernatural and salvific objective, which clearly delineate its boundaries.

THE GUIDE

Having emerged out of the baptismal water, John and Vertue are taken aside by "a comely person" who told them that "he had been appointed to be their Guide." The Guide was born in the mountains where the Landlord dwells,

48. Ibid., 118.

49. Lewis, *Till We Have Faces*, 307. Orual earlier makes a self-conscious resolution to change: "I was as ugly in soul as [Ungit]; greedy, blood-gorged. But if I practiced true philosophy, as Socrates meant it, I should change my ugly soul into a fair one. And this, the gods helping me, I would do. I would set about it at once" (281–82). But this turns out to be in vain.

50. Lewis, "Membership," in *Weight of Glory*, 118.

51. Ibid., 119.

52. Ibid., 120.

as his agent to lead the pilgrims in their "regress." In the 1943 Geoffrey Bles edition of *The Pilgrim's Regress*, Lewis included headlines on each page, and in one of them the Guide is identified as an angel.[53] In Christian theology generally, the Guide who leads the pilgrims through this journey would be identified as the Holy Spirit, the third person of the Trinity. The constant communication between the pilgrims and the Guide in Lewis's allegory might naturally point in this direction. However, this was not his intention. In fact, the doctrine of the Holy Spirit seems to be the least developed or specified aspect of Lewis's theology. The weight of our concern, however, should be on his role rather than his identity. Beside leading and directing the pilgrims, the Guide effects two important endowments upon the pilgrims. First, he "sharpens" their eyes, and second, he "arms" them "at all points."

The Guide was born in the mountains where the Landlord dwells, and he was given a name Slikisteinsauga, because "his sight was so sharp that the sight of any other who travelled with him would be sharpened by his company."[54] Kathryn Lindskoog thinks that the name is derived from "sleekstone," a stone used for polishing things.[55] The first effect of Slikisteinsauga is to polish and sharpen the eyes of John and Vertue to see clearly the Landlord's castle in the Eastern Mountains, which is in fact the island John has been looking for all his life. Not only are their eyes sharpened to see the objective clearly, but they begin to see the things very differently on their post-conversion "regress" or pilgrimage through the old country traveled in their previous wandering.[56] The Guide reminds them that these renewed eyes are not playing a trick on them. In fact, now at last they see the land as it really is. The Guide says, "[Your] eyes are altered. You see nothing now but realities."[57]

The Seeing Eye

This alteration of perception is the main theme of Lewis's article, "The Seeing Eye," which was originally published in 1963 under the title "Onward, Christian Spacemen."[58] Lewis declared, "To some, God is discoverable

---

53. Lewis, *Pilgrim's Regress*, 199. The same text was published by Eerdmans Publishing Company in 1958 and 1981 editions. Our references are based on the 1981 edition.
54. Lewis, *Pilgrim's Regress*, 170.
55. Lindskoog, *Finding the Landlord*, 99.
56. Lewis, *Pilgrim's Regress*, 171.
57. Ibid., 177.
58. The initial title was given by the editors of the periodical, *Show*, published in

everywhere; to others, nowhere. . . . Much depends on the seeing eye."[59] "The seeing eye" is understood in two different ways: (1) A certain way of seeing reality by contrast with the scientific method of seeing matters; it is a supernatural worldview in opposition to a mere naturalistic worldview; and (2) a gaining of a certain "faculty of recognition" that incorporates an ability to recognize God as God. Violations of the first thought include assuming that one can see God, if he exists, by merely traveling to outer space, and it resembles "trying to verify or falsify the divinity of Christ by taking specimens of His blood or dissecting Him."[60] It is futile: "If God created the universe, He created space-time, which is to the universe as the metre is to a poem or the key is to music. To look for Him as one item within the framework which He Himself invented is nonsensical."[61] A person may get over this initial misunderstanding and instead begin to look elsewhere, into the realm of mystery such as oneself or the conscience; even so, without the faculty of recognition (the second point above), one cannot recognize the work of God as such.

Lewis retold his conversion story in metaphorical language to get this point communicated. He claimed that he had not tried to search for God; on the other hand, he was making a serious effort to be honest before his conscience. In the process, he recognized the God who was pursuing him. "He was the hunter (or so it seemed to me) and I was the deer." Lewis continued, "He stalked me like a redskin, took unerring aim, and fired."[62] As a result, Lewis began to recognize a voice (he spoke "symbolically").

> [That] voice which speaks in your conscience and in some of your intensest joys, which is sometimes so obstinately silent, sometimes so easily silenced, and then at other times so loud and emphatic, is in fact the closest contact you have with the mystery; and therefore finally to be trusted, obeyed, feared and desired more than all other things.[63]

America. Walter Hooper, who gave the second title, recalled that Lewis "heartily disliked" it. Hooper, "Preface," in Lewis, *Christian Reflections,* xiv. The article was published in 1963 following the first manned space-travel of Sputnik. The article begins, "The Russians, I am told, report that they have not found God in outer space." (Lewis, "The Seeing Eye," in *Christian Reflections,* 167).

59. Ibid., 171.
60. Ibid., 172.
61. Ibid., 168.
62. Ibid., 169.
63. Ibid., 170.

Lewis experienced it and responded accordingly—that is, he gave in to the overwhelming multifaceted pursuit of him by God—because he was given "a seeing eye." It is important to note the two-fold emphasis: you come to know God through the proper avenue of that knowledge and even when you come to the right avenue, you still need the right apparatus, the proper faculty of recognition. In other words, first, you must come to the right place, and second, you must make a certain "jump" or a "change."

It is quite clear that Lewis not only emphasized the objectivity of reality, but the need for an internal (i.e., subjective), spiritual change in order to see reality as it really is. This is consistent with Lewis's view of the Fall and the corruption of humanity. That is not to say that Lewis thought religion is merely psychological; nothing could be further from the truth.[64] Nevertheless, we must understand Lewis's dual recognition, that the supernatural world is objectively real and that a person must go through a certain spiritual and psychological change in order to see that reality as it really is. Lewis's "mere Christianity" incorporates the noetic effect of sin as a matter of great importance.

The second important action of the Guide to highlight is the arming of the pilgrims. In the allegory, the Guide "armed John and Vertue at all points and led them back through the country they had just been travelling."[65] With the armor, especially the sword, they must slay the dragons. Facing the Northern dragon, John keeps "his grip steady on the sword hilt, his eyes strained into the darkness, and his feet ready to spring." When the freezing cold breath of the dragon touches his face, instead of panic, "[his] strength was multiplied." With laughter, John makes "thrust after thrust into the brute's throat."[66] Lewis's portrait of the pilgrim is an obvious reference to the Pauline exhortation.

> [Be] strong in the Lord and in his mighty power. Put on the full armor of God so that you can take your stand against the devil's schemes. . . . Stand firm then, with the belt of truth buckled around your waist, with the breastplate of righteousness in

---

64. Peter Kreeft (in *C. S. Lewis: A Critical Essay*) and Scott Oury (in "'The Thing Itself': C. S. Lewis and the Value of Something Other," in Schakel, *The Longing for a Form*) treat "objectivity" as the key concept to understanding Lewis's mind and his philosophy. They are certainly correct in identifying this emphasis in Lewis. He expressed his distress over the subjectivistic tendency of his time. Nevertheless, I find in Lewis's balanced understanding of "mere Christianity" a clear recognition of the noetic effect of the Fall and corruption. It is unfortunate, therefore, that scholars who emphasize Lewis's idea of "objectivity" often make little effort to recognize this other aspect of his thought.

65. Lewis, *Pilgrim's Regress*, 175.

66. Ibid., 194.

place, and with your feet fitted with the readiness that comes from the gospel of peace. . . . Take . . . the *sword* of the Spirit, which is *the word of God.*[67]

The full armor readies the pilgrims to stand against the devil's scheme in the spiritual warfare. In Lewis's allegory, the sword is of special importance. The Guide asks, "Have you any practice with a sword?" "None, sir," answers John. To this, the Guide's unexpected answer is, "None is better than a smattering."[68] Could this be another incident of Lewis's clever warning against undiscerning biblical scholars who "claim to see fern-seed and can't see the elephant ten yards away in broad daylight"?[69]

Both as a literary scholar and a theologian Lewis devoted a significant amount of discussion to the topic of Scripture and the Word of God. Scripture was indeed "written for our learning" in the life of pilgrimage; however, it was considered a "leaky vehicle" to carry the Word of God.[70] Now we must turn to the subject.

Scripture and the Word of God

Lewis's view of Scripture has been a matter of contention, especially in the United States where the doctrine of Scripture for long has served as a litmus test, providing "theological party" identification. An in-depth exploration would distract us from our central theme, and there are works available dealing directly with the topic.[71] This is not to say that further study is not necessary. However, for our purpose, we will focus on Lewis's understanding of the relationship between the Bible and the Word of God, and the place of the Bible in Christian pilgrimage.

Lewis did not equate the Bible with the Word of God and was little interested in the issues of inerrancy and infallibility. He was content to say that the Bible, as an imperfect vessel, "carries the Word of God," so that "we (under grace, with attention to tradition and to interpreters wiser than

---

67. Eph 6:10–11, 6:14–15, 6:18 (NIV) (emphasis mine).

68. Lewis, *Pilgrim's Regress*, 191.

69. Lewis, "Modern Theology and Biblical Criticism," in *Christian Reflections*, 157. The article contains Lewis's attack on literary and spiritual incompetence he perceived in modern critical scholarship of the Bible.

70. Lewis, *Reflections on the Psalms*, 22, 112.

71. Some helpful works on the topics are: Friesen, "Scripture in the Writings of C. S. Lewis"; Christensen, *C. S. Lewis on Scripture*; Freshwater, "C. S. Lewis and the Quest for the Historical Jesus"; Alasdair I. C. Heron, "What is Wrong with Biblical Exegesis? Reflection upon C. S. Lewis' Criticism," in Walker, *Different Gospels*; Boss, "The Theology of C. S. Lewis."

ourselves, and with the use of such intelligence and learning as we may have) receive that word from it not by using it as an encyclopedia or an encyclical but by steeping ourselves in its tone and temper and so learning its overall message."[72] He wanted his readers to be mindful of the fact that the Bible consists of human literature, some of it written initially without religious purpose in mind. Christensen is right to conclude that the Bible according to Lewis is "human literature carrying a divine message," that it is as if "God's Word is the 'treasure' revealed through 'earthen vessels.'"[73] Nevertheless, Lewis held that "God must have done what is best, this is best, therefore God has done this."[74]

Lewis's rejection of the doctrine of inerrancy or infallibility was not based on his distrust of supernatural elements in the Bible as in the liberal biblical scholarship.[75] In fact, in his "Modern Theology and Biblical Criticism" (known earlier as "Fern-seed and Elephants"), Lewis relentlessly attacked modern biblical scholars, represented by Rudolf Bultmann, for their lack of literary, historical, and spiritual judgment. Hence, he accused, "These men ask me to believe they can read between the lines of the old texts; the evidence is their obvious inability to read (in any sense worth discussing) the lines themselves.[76]

We are faced with a rather interesting complexity in Lewis's view of the Bible. While not a conservative in this matter, he obviously distrusted the liberal biblical scholarship of his time. He approached the Bible as literature and thought its inspiration was not unlike that of other good literature. How, then, is the Bible set apart as the "vessel" of God's eternal Word? Lewis's idea of transposition provides the answer.

Transposition

The idea of transposition is Lewis's solution to the problem "of the obvious continuity between things which are admittedly natural and things which,

---

72. Ibid., 112.

73. Christensen, *C. S. Lewis on Scripture*, 96.

74. Ibid.

75. In his letter to Corbin Carnell, dated April 4, 1953, Lewis defended his ground for thinking Book of Jonah as unhistorical. He said to deny the historicity of the Jonah story is not the same as denying New Testament miracles. He clarified, "Where I doubt the historicity of an Old Testament narrative I never do so on the ground that the miraculous as such is incredible." The letter is included in Christensen's book as an appendix, 97–98.

76. Lewis, "Modern Theology and Biblical Criticism," in *Christian Reflections*, 157.

it is claimed, are spiritual."⁷⁷ Transposition is, in short, an "adaptation from a richer to a poorer medium."⁷⁸ When a higher reality is reproduced in the lower reality, the limitation of the lower medium necessarily imposes certain difficulties. Nevertheless, the difficulties do not make it impossible to transpose the meaning.

Lewis illustrated this principle from the phenomenon of *glossolalia*. Speaking in tongues in the Bible is clearly the manifestation of the supernatural act of the Holy Spirit. However, as it is experienced in the human subject, it necessarily involves natural phenomena; it is, in fact, "an affair of the nerves," or merely speaking of human languages. The same phenomenon could be seen in other circumstances to be pathological; it is not difficult to guess why the crowd in Jerusalem at Pentecost thought the disciples were drunk!⁷⁹

Lewis gave other examples: Moments of intense aesthetic rapture are reducible to a series of physical sensations. Detached from the meaning of those moments, "[i]ntrospection can discover no difference at all between my neural response to very bad news and my neural response to the overture of *The Magic Flute*."⁸⁰ In this sense, Lewis took "our emotional life to be 'higher' than the life of our sensations—not, of course, morally higher, but richer, more varied, more subtle."⁸¹ A further example is found in the process of taking a photograph of a real scene. What is, in fact, a three-dimensional reality is reduced to the two. Nevertheless, the identity or continuity between the two realities cannot be denied. To bridge the distance between the two, we must exercise perspective, that is "we must give more than one value to a two-dimensional shape."⁸² The same is true of playing an orchestral music piece on a piano. The lower medium, due to its limitation or lack of rich variety, must resort to assigning more than one function to its elements; for example, the same piano notes must represent violins in one passage and flutes in another.

Lewis drew two important conclusions about the principle of transposition: (1) "[In] each case what is happening in the lower medium can be understood only if we know the higher medium."⁸³ We can understand pictures only because we know and live in the three-dimensional world.

77. Lewis, "Transposition," in *Weight of Glory*, 56.
78. Ibid., 60.
79. Acts 2:13.
80. Ibid., 58.
81. Ibid., 59.
82. Ibid., 60.
83. Ibid., 61.

The same analogy applies to Lewis's apprehension of the Word of God in the Bible. The Bible, though it consists of human literature, is unique because it is the chosen vessel for transposing the Word of God into a medium communicable to humans. If the first principle is correct, the transposition is possible only if the Holy Spirit allows our participation in the higher reality. In this sense, what is taking place in the process of transposition is not merely a conversion of the higher reality into a lower medium, but the taking up of the lower medium as the vehicle of the higher reality.

The second conclusion naturally follows from the first one: (2) "[The] word *symbolism* is not adequate in all cases to cover the relation between the higher medium and its transposition in the lower."[84] Lewis explained,

> Pictures are part of the visible world themselves and represent it only by being part of it. Their visibility has the same source. The suns and lamps in pictures seem to shine only because real suns and lamps shine on them; that is, they seem to shine a great deal because they really shine a little in reflecting their archetypes. The sunlight in a picture is therefore not related to real sunlight simply as written words are to spoken. It is a sign, but also something more than a sign, and only a sign because it is also more than a sign, because in it the thing signified is really in a certain mode present. If I had to name the relation I should call it not *symbolical* but *sacramental*.[85]

In other words, the higher reality descends, penetrates, and transforms the lower reality in the act of transposition. In this sense, the relationship between the Bible and the Word of God could be described as sacramental. Therefore, it is meaningless to discuss whether the Bible is a "true" or "false" representation of the Word of God. Whether the Bible is correct or incorrect is not the issue. Instead, it is a matter of a proper reception of it. The one who approaches the Bible purely from the point of view of the lower medium inevitably makes the mistake of saying that it is merely human literature.

In his address, "Transposition," Lewis applied the concept of transposition to doctrines of heaven, incarnation, and the resurrection of the body, but not explicitly to the doctrine of the Scripture, but only as an indicator of how the natural and the supernatural coexist as a coherent whole. It is, however, clear that for Lewis the Bible, as the inscripturated Word of God, is a transposition of the supernatural message of God. Thus, Lewis introduced his understanding of the nature of Scripture as a parallel reality to the incarnation.

84. Ibid., 62.
85. Ibid., 62–63 (emphasis mine).

For we are taught that the Incarnation itself proceeded "not by the conversion of the godhead into flesh, but by taking of (the) manhood into God"; in it human life becomes the vehicle of Divine life. If the Scriptures proceed not by conversion of God's word into a literature but by taking up of a literature to be the vehicle of God's word, this is not anomalous.[86]

We have here a clear instance of the application of the concept of transposition.

The Nature of Religious Language

Lewis's view of Scripture is conditioned by the nature of religious language, another of his major concerns in conjunction with the concept of transposition. A concise discussion is in order. Apparently, Lewis's theory of language is tied to Owen Barfield's *Poetic Diction*, which emerged during a period of active intellectual interaction between the two.[87] Lewis said, "Much of the thought which [Barfield] put into *Poetic Diction* had already become mine before that important little book appeared."[88] Doris Myers observes that both Barfield's and Lewis's concern for language rose out of a specific context in the early twentieth century.

> Certainly the postwar period was very much dominated by the low evaluation of language.... In the intellectual realm it is easy to point to the twentieth-century fruition of nineteenth-century Darwinian naturalism; to the development of twentieth-century philology; to Bertrand Russell's logical atomism, which contributed to twentieth-century logical positivism, and Ludwig Wittgenstein's *Tractatus Logico-Philosopicus* (1918), which led to the whole movement known as linguistic philosophy with its credo, "All philosophy is a critic of language."[89]

A representative study of language in this direction, *The Meaning of Meaning* by C. K. Ogden and I. A. Richards, attacked "language superstition" characterized by the view "that words . . . always imply things corresponding

---

86. Lewis, *Reflections on the Psalms*, 116.

87. Barfield, *Poetic Diction*. It was first published in 1928. Barfield began the work shortly before he engaged in the "Great War" with Lewis (1925–27). Adey, *C. S. Lewis's "Great War,"* 12–13.

88. Lewis, *Surprised by Joy*, 200.

89. Myers, *C. S. Lewis in Context*, 2. Myers argues that the shift in attitude was largely due to the abuse of language through the communications media during World War I (the case was worse with World War II) for propaganda and the mobilization of public opinions.

to them." Instead, a word functions as a "symbol" to a "referent" (object) connected by sensations inducing behavioristic conditioning. The concept rejects "the primitive idea that Words and Things are related by some magic bond."[90]

Barfield, on the other hand, held that the human mind is an active participant in the intelligence inherent to the nature of the universe. This is consistent to his anthroposophic belief that the world is in essence mental rather than material. Human cognition of the external world becomes possible when the percept of the "pure sense-datum," meaningless in itself, is processed by and synthesized with the concept or "what I bring to the sense-datum from within."[91] Myers summarizes Barfield's view of language:

> [In] order to know something, a person must recognize it, and to recognize it, he must be able to relate it to other things. Such relationships are concepts, and concepts must be expressed as resemblances and analogies—metaphors. Since Barfield defines knowledge as "the ability to recognize significant resemblances and analogies," it follows that our knowledge of the universe depends on metaphor. And since human intelligence is a participation in the cosmic Intelligence, the knowledge that human beings gain through metaphor corresponds with the way the universe really is.[92]

Having concluded that the essential quality of language is metaphorical, Barfield denied the existence of perfectly literal language. Thus, it is not valid to separate scientific knowledge from poetic language. Rather, science incorporates "the poetic diction of science."[93]

Lewis, as Barfield, accepted that there is "a kind of psycho-physical parallelism (or more) in the universe" which makes metaphorical language possible and meaningful.[94] He acknowledged the significance of metaphors in language, but he modified Barfield's view by introducing two additional dimensions to the topic: (1) The distinction between truth and meaning; and (2) The distinction between a quantity-informative language (scientific improvement of the ordinary language) and the quality-informative language (poetic improvement of the ordinary language).

---

90. Ogden and Richards, *Meaning of Meaning*, 31, 47, 53.
91. Barfield, *Poetic Diction*, 55.
92. Myers, *C. S. Lewis in Context*, 8.
93. Barfield, *Poetic Diction*, 138.
94. Lewis, "Bluspels and Flalansferes: A Semantic Nightmare," in *Selected Literary Essays*, 265.

First, truth (opposed to falsehood) is something one derives through the function of reason. Lewis as "a rationalist" struggled to identify truth (or objective facts). However, rational effort for truth-finding can be conducted only on the condition of meaning (opposed to "nonsense"). Meaning, therefore, "is the antecedent condition both of truth and falsehood."[95] Meaning, however, arises out of the function of imagination to produce new metaphors or revive old ones. To put it differently, an assignment of truth-value is only possible within the sphere of conceptual meaning. There is no point in saying something nonsensical is false. "The relation between meaning and truth seems to be this. A thing can't be true or false unless it means something; but to find out what it means is not to find out whether it is true or false."[96] On the other hand, since meaning must arise out of "true" or "right" imagination, there is a sense of mutual dependency between truth and meaning. "[The] truth we won by metaphor could not be greater than the truth of the metaphor itself; and . . . all our truth, or all but a few fragments, is won by metaphor."[97] Nevertheless, we should notice how the issue of meaning can be detached from the issue of verification or falsification in Lewis's theory, becoming vulnerable to dangerous theological implications arising from a dualistic view of reality.

Second, Lewis distinguished three types of language: ordinary, scientific, and poetic. The first is the basis for the other two; the other two are skillful improvements of the first.[98] Scientific language improves ordinary language to convey more precise information about the *quantity*. To illustrate, ordinary language says, "It was very cold"; while scientific language informs us, "There were 13 degrees of frost."[99] Poetic language improves ordinary language to convey not only emotions but *qualitative* information "with a great many more adjectives." In terms of the same illustration, poetic language utters,

> Ah, bitter chill it was!
> The owl, for all his feathers was a-cold;
> The hare limped trembling through the frozen grass,
> And silent was the flock in woolly fold:
> Numb'd were the Beadsman's fingers.[100]

---

95. Ibid.

96. Lewis, unpublished letter to Owen Barfield, n.d., cited in Holyer, "C. S. Lewis on the Epistemic Significance of the Imagination," 217–18.

97. Lewis, "Bluspels and Flalansferes: A Semantic Nightmare," in *Selected Literary Essays*, 265.

98. Lewis, "The Language of Religion," in *Christian Reflections*, 129.

99. Ibid., 129–30.

100. Ibid., 129, 131.

Lewis thought that a remarkable power of poetic language is "to convey to us the quality of experiences which we have not had, or perhaps can never have, to use factors within our experience so that they become pointers to something outside our experience."[101] However, he felt that poetic language "suffers two disabilities in comparison with scientific": (1) "It is verifiable or falsifiable only to a limited degree and with a certain fringe of vagueness"; and (2) "such information as poetic language has to give can be received only if you are ready to meet it half-way." A reader must trust the poet, and "[only] by so doing will you find out whether he is trustworthy or not."[102]

Lewis thought the language of religion, as distinguished from theological language (which, along with apologetics, states "religious matter in a form more like that we use for scientific matter"), is "something that ranges between the ordinary and the poetical."[103] As in Lewis's description of poetic language, religious language communicates information, but its verifiability or falsifiability can be limited, and the recipient must be committed to an assumption of belief. About his own discourse on religious language, Lewis said,

> I have not tried to prove that the religious sayings are true, only that they are significant: if you meet them with a certain good will, a certain readiness to find meaning. For if they should happen to contain information about real things, you will not get it on any other terms.[104]

We notice how Lewis slipped in the earlier-mentioned distinction between truth and meaning. He contends that religious language (leaning to the poetical) is primarily a conveyor of meaning to those who approach it with readiness to accept. Accordingly, Scripture should be approached as the language of religion. A certain perspective is necessary:

> The Cartesians read animal life as mechanism. Just in the same way Scripture can be read as merely human literature.... [But] what is required ... is not merely knowledge but a certain insight; getting the focus right.... One who contended that a poem was nothing but black marks on white paper would be unanswerable if he addressed an audience who couldn't read. Look at it through microscopes, analyse the printer's ink and the paper, study it (in that way) as long as you like; you will never find something over and above all the products of analysis

---

101. Ibid., 133.
102. Ibid., 135.
103. Ibid.
104. Ibid., 141.

whereof you can say, "This is the poem." Those who can read, however, will continue to say the poem exists.[105]

The Shape of the Text

What did Lewis say about the shape of the Scriptural text so that it requires a right focus? In short, it looks unimpressive and obscure under ordinary scrutiny. In general, the human qualities are clearly visible: Lewis asserted, "Naivety, error, contradiction, even (as in the cursing Psalms) wickedness are not removed."[106] Again, about the Old Testament, he said,

> Thus something originally merely natural—the kind of myth that is found among most nations—will have been raised by God above itself, qualified by Him and compelled by Him to serve purposes which of itself it would not have served. Generalising this, I take it that the whole Old Testament consists of the same sort of material as any other literature—chronicle (some of it obviously pretty accurate), poems, moral and political diatribes, romances, and what not; but all taken into the service of God's word.[107]

The New Testament, though much more historically accurate, still suffers obscurity. The teaching of Jesus, "in which there is no imperfection," nevertheless contains "paradox, proverb, exaggeration, parable, irony; even . . . the 'wisecrack'. He utters maxims which, like popular proverbs, if rigorously taken, may seem to contradict one another."[108] Paul lacked the gift of "lucidity and orderly exposition," and his letters contain "[the] crabbedness, the appearance of inconsequence and even of sophistry, the turbulent mixture of petty detail, personal complaint, practical advice, and lyrical rapture."[109] Moreover, there seem to be inconsistent accounts of same matter or event such as the genealogies in Matt 1 and Luke 3 and the death of Judas in Matt 27:5 and Acts 1:18 and 19.[110]

---

105. Lewis, *Reflections on the Psalms*, 116–17.
106. Ibid., 111.
107. Ibid.
108. Ibid., 113.
109. Ibid., 113–14.
110. In Lewis's response to Professor Clyde Kilby of Wheaton College, who requested his opinion on the college's statement about its position on biblical inspiration. Lewis, *Letters of C. S. Lewis*, 480.

Lewis's Hermeneutical Principles

How should we read and interpret the Bible then? (1) Scripture must be seen from the perspective of the higher medium (namely God's Word) rather than the lower medium (Scripture itself as human literature), according to the principle of transposition, even though "the lower nature, in being taken up and loaded with a new burden and advanced to a new privilege, remains, and is not annihilated."[111] (2) Scripture must not be used as an encyclopedia or an encyclical written in "cut-and-dried, fool-proof, systematic fashion," something "we could have . . . relied on like the multiplication table."[112] The utmost importance is the meaning not facts. (3) Lewis encouraged a "spiritual reading" of Scripture, requiring a certain "spiritual insight," which discovers even multiple meanings in scriptural passages.[113] The fact that Lewis thought a multiplicity of meanings could be laid on a single passage is consistent with his view of transposition. (4) The literalistic reading in general can be misleading. "There is almost no 'letter' in the words of Jesus. Taken by a literalist, He will always prove the most elusive of teachers."[114] One must not treat it as scientific language but as religious language, focusing on the conveyed meaning rather than the truthfulness or correctness of each detail. (5) What is required is "our total response" of "the whole man" by reliving "the whole Jewish experience of God's gradual and graded self-revelation," by "steeping ourselves in a Personality [of Our Lord], acquiring a new outlook and temper, breathing a new atmosphere, suffering Him, in His own way, to rebuild in us the defaced image of Himself," and by witnessing "a whole Christian life in operation" in Paul or "Christ Himself operating in a man's life."[115] In other words, one must not dissect the text as in scientific research but willingly participate in the supernatural and saving presence of God in the text. In sum, we may refer to Lewis's hermeneutics as a *sacramental* use of Scripture.

Nevertheless, Lewis encouraged both "repeated leisurely reading" and discriminating reading using "our conscience and our critical faculties."[116] Those who study the pattern of Lewis's spiritual life never fail to notice "the

---

111. Lewis, *Reflections on the Psalms*, 116.

112. Ibid., 112.

113. Lewis said, "If the Old Testament is a literature thus 'taken up,' made the vehicle of what is more than human, we can of course set no limit to the weight or multiplicity of meanings which may have been laid upon it." Ibid., 117.

114. Ibid., 119.

115. Ibid., 114.

116. Ibid.

quiet regularity of his Bible-reading."[117] His numerous letters encourage his fellow pilgrims to take note of the Bible's teaching. However, the Bible should not be handled controversially but for the reader's spiritual growth by finding "the Word in it" or even by "feeling the very contentions between the Word and the human material through which it works."[118] Lewis summed it up this way:

> That the over-all operation of Scripture is to convey God's Word to the reader (he also needs his inspiration) who reads it in the right spirit, I fully believe. That it also gives true answers to all the questions (often religiously irrelevant) which he might ask, I don't. The very kind of truth we are often demanding was, in my opinion, not even envisaged by the ancients.[119]

Lewis's view of Scripture reveals a few serious problems: First, his principles do not account for the normative or canonical status of Scripture, claimed both by the Bible itself as well as the tradition of Christian church. Second, his insight into the nature of meaning and truth is helpful but his repeated practice of separating the two in applications, such as in his view of Scripture, seems unwarranted and artificial. Lewis himself acknowledged that they must be inter-dependent. To say a religious claim is meaningful but not necessarily true seems to betray a rationality of faith, which Lewis is deeply concerned with, and good conscience.

Third, Lewis did not sufficiently distinguish between an inferior medium and an erroneous medium in applying the principle of transposition to his view of Scripture. There is a clear qualitative difference between the two. A two-dimensional photograph is an inferior medium but not an erroneous one. In the same way, playing a key on a piano to represent a violin in an orchestral piece is fundamentally different from playing a wrong key, therefore misrepresenting the musical note. In other words, the idea of the Bible being an inferior medium to the Word of God as human literature must be distinguished from it being an erroneous medium. To say that the Word of God speaks through errors, on the other hand, only worsens the problem.

Finally, Lewis did not emphasize the inseparable relationship between the Holy Spirit and the inscripturated Word. Lewis's sacramental view of Scripture does not highlight its unique authority through a special "inspiration" of the Holy Spirit. Moreover, the Bible is not a uniquely exalted

---

117. Clasper, "C. S. Lewis's Contribution to a 'Missionary Theology,'" 6.
118. Lewis, *Reflections on the Psalms*, 114.
119. Lewis, *Letters of C. S. Lewis*, 480.

medium of the Spirit's guidance: The Holy Spirit guides a person "from within . . . through Scripture, the Church, Christian friends, books, etc."[120]

As stated earlier, the doctrine of the Holy Spirit is possibly the most unspecified or underdeveloped aspect of Lewis's theology, although his theology does not ignore the role of the Holy Spirit. In fact, Lewis discussed the role of the Holy Spirit more in the context of prayer than in the context of the Word. Now we must proceed to that topic.

PRAYER

Prayer is a major topic in the writings of Lewis. This fact is a good indication of his emphasis on practical issues of theology. In *The Pilgrim's Regress*, there is no specific mention of prayer as such. However, there are the songs that make the pilgrims courageous and determined as they face many trials and temptations. As a likely reference to prayer, the songs are the expressions of the hearts' anxiety and longing and the reinforcement of the truth as they know it. In fact, in various parts of his writings, Lewis expanded the meaning and the practice of prayer to encourage his fellow pilgrims.

Two major themes emerge out of Lewis's discussion of prayer: one causal and the other existential. First, prayer is effectual and causal, therefore meaningful, even though God is omniscient and sovereignly works out his providence. Second, prayer, though it is the most intimately subjective practice, allows the most evident experience of the objective operation of God. These results are due to the nature of prayer and the promise we find in Scripture about what God does in and through prayer.

The Causal Aspect of Prayer

Lewis emphasized prayer as the means to change both the person who prays and the circumstances that he/she prays for. For example, he attributed the cause of his wife's recovery from imminent death to numerous prayers offered in her behalf, especially the prayer with the laying on of hands of the Rev. Peter Bide, who married them in a hospital room.[121] Lewis's supernaturalism quite naturally allowed him to embrace the possibility of miracles. He wrote to a friend, "My wife's condition, contrary to the expectation of the doctors, has improved, if not miraculously (but who knows?), at any rate wonderfully."[122]

---

120. Ibid., 423.
121. Hooper, *C. S. Lewis: Companion and Guide*, 82.
122. Lewis, *Letters of C. S. Lewis*, 469.

However, Lewis thought the causal aspect of prayer to be only a small part of prayer. Its efficacy must be understood in the light of the overall dynamics of prayer. It is "a personal contact between embryonic, incomplete persons (ourselves) and the utterly concrete Person."[123] Therefore, the fact that "He answers prayers is a corollary—not necessarily the most important one. . . . What He does is learned from what He is."[124]

Nevertheless, petitionary prayer is a daily reality for Christian pilgrims. Furthermore, God has commanded us thus to pray. Lewis thought that there are two difficult problems in regard to the prayer of this kind. First, the Bible seems to teach us that we should pray, "Thy will be done"; but, at the same time, we are told to pray believing firmly that our request will be granted. Second, if prayer is causal, if God hears our prayers and, at least sometimes, accordingly changes our situations, what happens to God's omniscience and his sovereign providence? In addressing these difficult problems, Lewis began by mentioning that as servants of a Master we must obey. "Whatever the theoretical difficulties are, we must continue to make requests of God."[125]

Lewis dealt with the first problem in his brief but uncharacteristically exegetical essay, "Petitionary Prayer: A Problem without an Answer." Here Lewis tries first to describe what the problem really is, then attempts to address all proposed answers, dismissing them all as inadequate, and with no more remaining options, simply says, "I come to you, reverend Fathers, for guidance. How am I to pray this very night?"[126] His honesty is shocking.

Lewis concluded that there are two basically irreconcilable patterns of petitionary prayer presented in the Bible. The A Pattern comes from the prayer taught and modeled by Jesus Christ. We should humbly say, "Thy will be done." The B Pattern includes the recurrent demand in the biblical passages on prayer that we should have "faith that the particular thing the petitioner asks will be given him."[127] Passages such as Matt 21:22 and Mark 11:23 and 24 are key texts pointing to the B Pattern. Lewis believed that in these texts "faith" could not mean "a general faith in the power and goodness of God" but "precisely that we get 'all the things' we ask for."[128] Lewis felt that the A Pattern petition poses no intellectual complication in itself.

---

123. Lewis, "The Efficacy of Prayer," in *World's Last Night*, 8.

124. Ibid.

125. Lewis, *Letters to Malcolm*, 36.

126. Lewis, "Petitionary Prayer: A Problem Without an Answer," in *Christian Reflections*, 151.

127. Ibid., 143–44.

128. Ibid., 147.

However, if the B Pattern were consistently held we would need to consider miraculous occurrences as a normative reality. The only reason why prayers are seemingly unanswered according to our petition must be that faith was lacking. To pray for a specific thing and to add "thy will be done" would turn out to be a case of "a double-minded" prayer seemingly denounced in Jas 1:8. One may argue that since we are taught to pray in "Jesus's name," in essence we are required to bring petition only in accordance with the will of God. But still the situation remains unsatisfactory. "Dare we say that when God promises 'You shall have what you ask' He secretly means 'You shall have it if you ask for something I wish to give you'?"[129]

Lewis's trouble does not stem from his lack of belief that prayers are indeed answered, though not always according to what and how we asked for: "I believe in miracles, here and now."[130] Having conceded that he has no answer to his problem, Lewis added, "Whatever else faith may mean . . . I feel quite sure that it does not mean any state of psychological certitude such as might be—I think it sometimes is—manufactured from within by the natural action of a strong will upon an obedient imagination. The faith that moves mountains is a gift from Him who created mountains."[131] He added that what naturally remains for him to do is to pray after the A Pattern since he cannot naturally pray after the B Pattern. He thought, at least in a tentative way, this met his immediate practical need.

In *Letters to Malcolm*, a book written chiefly about the topic of prayer, Lewis developed this further. The B Pattern prayer is not an elementary or "*naif [sic]*" prayer but a more advanced and mature prayer, not made by common believers at all. Therefore, "[for] most of us the prayer in Gethsemane is the only model."[132] He emphasized again that the quality of faith is not something that can be manufactured by working up a subjective state. So he concluded that "such promises about prayer with faith refer to a degree or kind of faith which most believers never experience." Furthermore, such faith occurs "only when the one who prays does so as God's fellow-worker, demanding what is needed for the joint work."[133] Notice the practicality of Lewis's conclusion.

This conclusion comes with an added ingredient, which arouses our fascination. Lewis thought that such faith refers to a spiritual foresight or insight which participates in the divine foreknowledge. In other words, it is

---

129. Ibid., 149.
130. Ibid., 150.
131. Ibid.
132. Lewis, *Letters to Malcolm*, 60.
133. Ibid.

akin to the gift of prophecy. "But the fellow-worker, the companion or (dare we say?) the colleague of God is so united with Him at certain moments that something of the divine foreknowledge enters his mind. Hence his faith is the 'evidence'—that is, the evidentness, the obviousness—of things not seen."[134] There are three levels of relationship the praying person may reach with God. The basic level is that of a suitor whose prayer mainly centers around personal needs; the next level up is that of a servant who offers petitionary or intercessory prayers; and finally there is a fellow-worker who offers up partnership prayers. We cannot strive after the top level in our own strength. While we struggle to achieve and retain faith on a lower level, God nevertheless will listen to our prayers.[135] Lewis closed the section of the book with his characteristically modest comment that he had offered only guesses.

Lewis's solution here is less than satisfactory since Scripture frequently invites us to be God's fellow-workers. If the highest level relationship is almost never attained by most of us, what does it really mean to be God's fellow-worker or colleague? Does the biblical teaching ever allow us such an esoteric spiritual status? On the other hand, Lewis's frankness is both refreshing and noble. His painstaking efforts to meet the needs of common believers or even non-believers who mainly ask practical questions are impressive and admirable.

There remains a further difficult issue. If prayer is indeed causal, how can it be reconciled with God's omniscience and his sovereign providence? This question can be broken into a number of other questions of equal difficulty. What does it mean that prayer is causal? What is the meaning of God's omniscience and providence? How does providence differ from the natural sequence of events?

The most concise and directly relevant presentation is found in Appendix B of Lewis's *Miracles,* where he offers solutions to the above questions, which are consistent with all his time and eternity (or free will and God's sovereignty) questions. His basic presupposition is that God and humanity must not be considered to be in the same domain in terms of time, defined as "the mode of our perception," something like perspective.[136] Therefore, to God, who does not belong to the creaturely mode of existence, "all the physical events and all the human acts are present in an eternal Now."[137] Once again, we notice Lewis's reliance on Boethius's understanding of time and

---

134. Ibid., 61.
135. Ibid.
136. Lewis, *Miracles*, 176–77.
137. Ibid., 177.

eternity. He acknowledges that this is not a biblical idea but still qualifies as a Christian one in the sense that "great and wise Christians have held it and there is nothing in it contrary to Christianity."[138] Based on the idea of God's timelessness, Lewis drew an important conclusion: "The liberation of finite wills and the creation of the whole material history of the universe (related to the acts of those wills in all the necessary complexity) is to Him a single operation. In this sense God did not create the universe long ago but creates it at this minute—at every minute."[139]

Lewis viewed Providence as God's dynamic arrangement of a complex web of events, which includes both so-called miracles and natural events. In his view, the dynamics of answered prayer should not be thought of as "special providences" in distinction from miracles or natural events. Lewis thought that the idea of "special providence" should be abandoned altogether. Simply, there is the Providence which is in the hands of God at one level, and there are miracles, as well as natural events, which make up necessary ingredients, in complex arrangement, of Providence. Prayers as the free acts of free agents (in time) are, like other ingredients, adapted into Providence by God (in his eternal now) in his "timeless" creative act, and "this timeless adaptation meets our consciousness as a sequence of prayer and answer."[140]

Lewis used as an example Shakespeare's play *Hamlet* to illustrate the point. In the play, there are two levels of operation: One, the higher operation in which Shakespeare created and wove together the movement of the story; the other, the inter-connectedness of the events within the story, which makes the sequence of events seem logical and natural. Ophelia's death in the story at one level is caused by Shakespeare's plot arrangement; yet at another level, it is caused by the breaking of the branch she was holding on to before she fell into a river and drowned. Lewis explained the parallel between the illustration and the reality.

> All events in the play are Shakespearian events; similarly, all events in the real world are providential events. All events in the play, however, come about (or ought to come about) by the dramatic logic of events. Similarly, all events in the real world (except miracles) come about by natural causes. "Providence" and Natural causation are not alternatives; both determine every event because both are one.[141]

---

138. Lewis, *Mere Christianity*, 149.
139. Lewis, *Miracles*, 177.
140. Ibid., 178.
141. Ibid., 179.

What Lewis meant by "both are one" is that "natural causation" is a dynamic, which God incorporated in his providential arrangement. They are not in conflict or independent of each other. Natural causes find their meaning in God's providence.

Just as natural causes are incorporated into God's providence, the free acts of human beings are equally incorporated into it. The complication due to human free will is only a matter of degree in God's sight, and in the light of his omniscience, it is a minute complication if at all. In the same way, in prayer, human freedom cannot conflict with God's will. Lewis said,

> God and man cannot exclude one another, as man excludes man, at the point of junction, so to call it, between Creator and creature; the point where the mystery of creation—timeless for God, and incessant in time for us—is actually taking place. "God did (or said) it" and "I did (or said) it" can both be true.[142]

Prayer is causal in the sense that it is a free act, which God has promised to concern himself with. Although we pray in time, God's response is not bound by time.

In this sense, Lewis said that our prayer at noon can be answered at 10 a.m. This poses interesting possibilities. For instance, one may ask, "Why shouldn't we pray for a different result when we already come to know what result has taken place?" Lewis answered that such prayer "would sin against the duty of submission to God's known will."[143]

Lewis thought it meaningless to question whether an answered prayer is really an answer or just a simple turn of events according to natural causation.

> The Christian is not to ask whether this or that event happened because of a prayer. He is rather to believe that all events without exception are answers to prayer in the sense that whether they are grantings or refusals the prayers of all concerns and their needs have all been taken into account.... When the event you prayed for occurs your prayer has always contributed to it. When the opposite event occurs your prayer has never been ignored; it has been considered and refused, for your ultimate good and the good of the whole universe.[144]

---

142. Lewis, *Letters to Malcolm*, 68.
143. Lewis, *Miracles*, 180.
144. Ibid., 180–81.

Our prayers are causal, because God determined to use prayer as a means to his end. God's promise in regard to petitionary prayer is indeed a great privilege for the pilgrims who journey in the world.

The Existential Aspect of Prayer

On the other hand, we ought not to regard prayer as a mechanism or an element fitted into a machine. Prayer involves a real moment of meeting between the activity of God and the one who prays; hence, it actually and miraculously refers to the moment when time and eternity meet in a sense. Prayer belongs "right in the present reality." In prayer, "the momentary confrontation of subject and object is certainly occurring . . . the actual meeting of God's activity and man's."[145] This leads us to consider the existential meaning of prayer.

Lewis thought that the existential meaning of prayer is more significant than the causal, since prayer is essentially a personal encounter, the meeting place of God and his people.

> Here is the actual meeting of God's activity and man's—not some imaginary meeting that might occur if I were an angel or if God incarnate entered the room. There is here no question of a God "up there" or "out there"; rather, the present operation of God "in here," as the ground of my own being, and God "in there," as the ground of the matter that surrounds me, and God embracing and uniting both in the daily miracle of finite consciousness.[146]

Therefore, in prayer, a pilgrim is truly at home. The moment of prayer is indeed "the home away from home"; it is the entrance into the holy sanctuary of God's presence:

> Prayer in the sense of petition, asking for things, is a small part of it; confession and penitence are its threshold, adoration its sanctuary, the presence and vision and enjoyment of God its bread and wine. In it God shows Himself to us.[147]

Through confession and penitence, like the prayer of yielding and surrender, an actual change takes place in the person who prays. He or she is set free from the burdens of sin and guilt. The direction and the quality of life

---

145. Lewis, *Letters to Malcolm*, 79.
146. Ibid., 79–80.
147. Lewis, "The Efficacy of Prayer," in *World's Last Night*, 8.

are altered: the selfward move is diffused and abandoned and an earnest seeking of God's will, thus a Godward move is instituted as the center of the individual's desire. This is the essence of Jesus's Gethsemane prayer. For this reason Lewis wrote, "For most of us the prayer in Gethsemane is the only model. Removing mountains can wait."[148] However, "removing mountains" is not a higher level of prayer than the first. As we said earlier, it is corollary or even secondary. In another context, Lewis felt free to express it as more elementary. He mentioned the "hard saying," which he heard from "an experienced Christian."

> I have seen many striking answers to prayer and more than one that I thought miraculous. But they usually come at the beginning: before conversion, or soon after it. As the Christian life proceeds, they tend to be rarer. The refusals, too, are not only more frequent; they become more unmistakable, more emphatic.[149]

Higher than the petitionary prayer is, then, confession, penitence, and surrender of the will.

A higher level still is when such prayers are offered with a heart of adoration. Doubtless, confession, penitence, and surrender can be a painful process. But when one adds the spirit of adoration and is able to truly find joy in doing, a new dimension of prayer has emerged. It is as if a person passes through the threshold and finally enters into the sanctuary. Thus, the prayer of "thy will be done" should not be merely a submission. "They should, and if we make progress they will increasingly, be the voice of joyful desire, free of hunger and thirst"; to treat them "simply as a clause of submission or renunciation greatly impoverishes the prayer."[150] In fact, corporate worship should be filled with a joyful adoration, and anything detracting from that adoration must be considered undesirable. Furthermore, adoration, being a higher level of prayer, should not be considered an esoteric prayer.

Just as submission should be, an attitude of adoration should pervade our lives. Lewis said, "I have tried . . . to make every pleasure into a channel of adoration." He thought that "to receive [pleasure] and to recognize its divine source are a single experience."[151] He obviously was not speaking of "bad pleasures" he defined as "pleasures snatched by unlawful act." This

---

148. Lewis, *Letters to Malcolm*, 60.
149. Lewis, "The Efficacy of Prayer," in *World's Last Night*, 10.
150. Lewis, "Petitionary Prayer: A Problem Without an Answer," in *Christian Reflections*, 143.
151. Lewis, *Letters to Malcolm*, 89–90.

must mean that the problem is not with the pleasure itself but the incorporation of it into an unlawful act.[152] Every lawful pleasure, then, "is a message."

> We know we are being touched by a finger of that right hand at which there are pleasures for evermore. There need be no question of thanks or praise as a separate event, something done afterwards. To experience the tiny theophany is itself to adore. Gratitude exclaims, very properly, "How good of God to give me this." Adoration says, "What must be the quality of that Being whose far-off and momentary coruscations are like this!" One's mind runs back up the sunbeam to the sun.[153]

The adoration presupposes an even deeper and higher level of prayer: the very celebration and enjoyment of the presence of God. In the above quote, Lewis basically places no distinction between adoration and the enjoyment of his presence. However, more subtle distinctions are introduced.

The real heart of prayer, then, is to enjoy the very presence of God. Nevertheless, through the words of Screwtape, Lewis reminds us of our tendency: Our thoughts of enjoying God's presence are often misguided. Typically, we either try to localize God in some unworthy object or try to feel his presence by conjuring up certain emotions. Screwtape says, "The simplest [way to misdirect the attention of those who pray] is to turn their gaze away from Him towards themselves. Keep them watching their own minds and trying to produce *feelings* there by the action of their own wills."[154] Of course, this was the very trouble Lewis experienced as a child; the resulting anxiety was so great that it eventually contributed to his rejection of Christian faith. Lewis thought this misdirection of attention to be a devastating mistake one can make in prayer. Weary of the practice of introspection, Lewis strongly discouraged dependence on human emotion in prayer. He advised one correspondent to "avoid introspection in prayer" and "never to try to generate an emotion by will power." Rather he insisted on giving a directive "always to turn the attention outwards to God."[155] Lewis's distrust of emotion does not mean that it is insignificant; instead, he means to point out that emotion is only a corollary, not a proof or a cause of a deeper spirituality. "Emotional intensity is in itself no proof of spiritual depth."[156]

Another danger of introspection is that often the mind naturally tries to generate false images of God. If not within our hearts, we constantly try

---

152. Ibid., 89.
153. Ibid., 90.
154. Lewis, *Screwtape Letters*, 34.
155. Lewis, *Letters of C. S. Lewis*, 439.
156. Lewis, *Letters to Malcolm*, 82.

to locate God elsewhere, "up and to the left at the corner of the bedroom ceiling, or inside [our] own head, or in a crucifix on the wall."[157] Therefore, "He must constantly work as the iconoclast. Every idea of Him we form, He must in mercy shatter."[158] Therefore, we must not rely on vaguely spiritual feelings or try desperately to conjure up certain devotional moods. Nothing can be further from being a sign of God's presence. "Hence the prayers offered in the state of dryness are those which please Him best."[159]

How, then, can we enter into the presence of God in prayer? The act of entering into God's presence can be a very uncomfortable situation for us, for what it requires is a "real nakedness of the soul in prayer." Once again, Lewis directs us through the desperate words of Screwtape.

> For if [the patient] ever comes to make the distinction, if ever he consciously directs his prayers "not to what I think Thou art but to what Thou knowest Thyself to be," our situation is, for the moment, desperate. Once all his thoughts and images have been flung aside, or, if retained, retained with a full recognition of their merely subjective nature, and the man trusts himself to the completely real, external, invisible Presence, there with him in the room and never knowable by him as he is known by it—why, then it is that the incalculable may occur.[160]

There is an operative paradox in prayer: As spiritual beings, we are enthralled in the sweet presence of the loving and merciful God; but as earthly creatures our utter nakedness in prayer, which is duly required, is accompanied by pain. Also, this means that what I have previously identified as different levels of prayer can potentially be misleading. In fact, prayer is never simply confession or submission, never just adoration, never only enjoyment of his presence. Without a broken heart in repentance and submissive yielding of our will to him, our adoration is but an empty shell and our enjoyment of his presence a vain presumption. Prayer as a whole is an act of coming home, broken and needy; having come home, we are met by the Father who comforts and nurtures us. Lewis correctly reminds us that prayer is not only a means but also an end. "The world was made partly that there might be prayer."[161] It is a part of God's perfect design for the world; even in the fallen world, we find our home through prayerful approach to the throne of God.

157. Lewis, *Screwtape Letters*, 35.
158. Lewis, *Letters to Malcolm*, 82.
159. Lewis, *Screwtape Letters*, 51.
160. Ibid., 35.
161. Lewis, *Letters to Malcolm*, 56.

But, there is an even greater mystery. In the act of praying a believer participates in the outworking of the divine economy. In simple terms, Lewis suggested that "prayer in its most perfect state is a soliloquy." Why? "If the Holy Spirit speaks in the man, then in prayer God speaks to God."[162] At this point we are confronted with a very different concept than simply that in prayer God meets us mere humans; it is more. In prayer, God operates in and through us, and in this process we are not agents but instruments. Lewis's poem "Prayer" is illuminating.

> Master, they say that when I seem
> To be in speech with you,
> Since you make no replies, it's all a dream
> —One talker aping two.
> They are half right, but not as they
> Imagine; rather, I
> Seek in myself the things I meant to say,
> And lo! the wells are dry.
> Then, seeing me empty, you forsake
> The Listener's role, and through
> My dead lips breathe and into utterance wake
> The thoughts I never knew.
> And thus you neither need reply
> Nor can; thus, while we seem
> Two talking, thou art One forever, and I
> No dreamer, but thy dream.[163]

Lewis's reflection on prayer is beautifully expressed through his poetic art. In our state of dryness, it is God himself, through his Spirit, who speaks for us, awakening our dead lips. This is, clearly, a poetic rendering of Paul's words.

> In the same way, the Spirit helps us in our weakness. We do not know what we ought to pray for, but the Spirit himself intercedes for us with groans that words cannot express. And he who searches our hearts knows the mind of the Spirit, because the Spirit intercedes for the saints in accordance with God's will.[164]

---

162. Ibid., 68.

163. Lewis, *Poems*, 122–23. The same poem, with a minute difference, is printed in Lewis, *Letters to Malcolm*, 67–68. The eleventh line reads, "My dumb lips" rather than "dead lips."

164. Rom 8:26–27 (NIV).

Pneumatology, elsewhere, as we have seen, an under-developed or unspecified aspect in Lewis's theology, occupies an important place in his concept of prayer. It is reasonable to say that a person is empowered by the Spirit in prayer, because according to the very definition of prayer, the one who prays is given up to the Spirit as he prays. Through the time of prayer, we are filled with the Holy Spirit. Accordingly, we are strengthened, encouraged, and revitalized to fulfill the very purpose of our pilgrimage.

At a more complex level, Lewis introduces to us a Trinitarian understanding of prayer. While a person wholeheartedly involves him/herself in the act of prayer, it is God (the Father) who is the object to whom he prays; the same God (the Spirit) is the internal motive as well as the way (the Son) through which the prayer is communicated. In this manner, Lewis expounds the practical meaning of the holy Trinity in terms of prayer:

> An ordinary simple Christian kneels down to say his prayers. He is trying to get into touch with God. But if he is a Christian he knows that what is prompting him to pray is also God: God, so to speak, inside him. But he also knows that all his real knowledge of God comes through Christ, the Man who was God—that Christ is standing beside him, helping him to pray, praying for him. You see what is happening. God is the thing to which he is praying—the goal he is trying to reach. God is also the thing inside him which is pushing him on—the motive power. God is also the road or bridge along which he is being pushed to that goal. So that the whole threefold life of the three-personal Being is actually going on in that ordinary little bedroom where an ordinary man is saying his prayers. The man is being caught up into the higher kind of life—what I called *Zoe* or spiritual life: he is being pulled into God, by God, while still remaining himself.[165]

This is Lewis's practical approach to the notion of divine Trinity. In this sense, for him, theology is experimental knowledge. From what we have seen already, it is obvious that Lewis's notion of the experimental knowledge of God must be distinguished from mere emotional experiences.

We have seen, according to Lewis, the tremendous significance of prayer in Christian pilgrimage. Lewis placed a great emphasis on the topic of prayer. Some, for this reason, regarded Lewis as more of a spiritual director than an apologist or a theologian. Lewis stressed the importance of prayer as a means of grace. Also, he thought prayer is a measure of one's spiritual condition. A pilgrim can be easily distracted in the fallen world.

---

165. Lewis, *Mere Christianity*, 142–43.

Having been created "to glorify God and enjoy Him forever," we can consider it a mere duty to do so, not a delight. Our frequent reluctance to pray is a symptom; "[if] we were perfected, prayer would not be a duty, it would be delight." Meanwhile,

> [much] of our backwardness in prayer is no doubt due to our sins, as every teacher will tell us; to our avoidable immersion in the things of this world, to our neglect of mental discipline. And also to the very worst kind of "fear of God." We shrink from too naked a contact, because we are afraid of the divine demands upon us which it might make too audible.[166]

Of course, our problem is compounded by the very constitution of our minds as fallen creatures and by the problem they experience in apprehending God who is concrete and personal yet immaterial. Lewis expected in hope that some day God would fix this problem. For now, the quality of our praying is a good indication of our spiritual condition before God. A pilgrim, without prayer, is too vulnerable in enemy occupied territory. He or she will find the trials and temptations beyond their ability to resist, for the tempters are crafty and strong.

THE TEMPTERS AND TEMPTATIONS

Lewis's popular appeal soared with the publication of *The Screwtape Letters*. In writing this book, Lewis wanted to accomplish two things: usefulness and enjoyment.[167] In other words, he wanted it to be a practical help to which his readers would turn with delight. The strategy worked and the book was an immediate success. The September 8, 1947 issue of *Time* magazine featured Lewis as its cover story. The cover carried a photograph of Lewis with a picture of a devil in the background. The article reports of the book's phenomenal impact:

> It was an immediate and phenomenal success on both sides of the Atlantic. Innumerable ministers quoted *Screwtape* in

---

166. Lewis, *Letters to Malcolm*, 114.

167. About his conceiving of the idea for this book, Lewis wrote to his brother (July 20, 1940): "I have been to Church for the first time for many weeks owing to the illness. . . . Before the service was over—one cd [sic] wish these things came more seasonably—I was struck by an idea for a book wh. [sic] I think might be both useful and entertaining. It wd [sic] be called *As One Devil to Another* and would consist of letters from an elderly retired devil to a young devil who has just started work on his first 'patient.' The idea wd [sic] be to give all the psychology of temptation from the *other* point of view." Lewis, *Letters of C. S. Lewis*, 355.

sermons and urged it on their congregation. Catholics enjoy it as much as Protestants. One clergyman makes a practice of presenting copies to his parishioners with passages marked for their special attention. To date, *Screwtape* has gone through 20 British and 14 U.S. printings.[168]

The success was due to what Lewis was able to accomplish for those who were looking for practical spiritual insights about the nature of temptation. What Lewis called "the psychology of temptation from the other point of view" proved to be a very effective way to "scratch the itching spot." Every pilgrim is called to face up to tempters and their temptations. What Lewis provided was a practical demonology. But at the same time through his ingenious alteration of perspectives, it turned out to be an insightful study of the human mind and how it fares as the spiritual battleground. The key to Lewis's appeal is that instead of presenting his demonology as an irrelevant speculative piece of work, he successfully presented a deeply personal, disturbing, realistic, and thus effective work. At the core, it is a study about ourselves in the light of the biblical teaching about the spiritual world.

The Tempters

The evil spirits or demons are portrayed as exceedingly clever but at the same time miserably unable to achieve success in opposing the gracious operation of God in human lives. Although he thought that belief in the devil (his existence and his operation) is not essential for salvation,[169] Lewis nevertheless believed it important enough to speak and write about. He thought that there are two equal and opposite errors about devils: "One is to disbelieve in their existence. The other is to believe, and to feel an excessive and unhealthy interest in them." The devils "are equally pleased by both errors and hail a materialist or a magician with the same delight."[170] Lewis thus encouraged a healthy balance.

He believed that "[the] Devil was an archangel once," whose natural gifts were far above ours.[171] This archangel-turned-Devil was apparently responsible for leading many angels to fall by inciting their rebellion against God. The demons are "fallen angels" who are, like "good angels," supernatural "in relation to this spatio-temporal nature: i.e. they are outside it and

---

168. "Don v. Devil," *Time*, 71.
169. Lewis, *Letters of C. S. Lewis*, 446.
170. Lewis, "Preface," in *Screwtape Letters*, 17.
171. Lewis, *Mere Christianity*, 181.

have powers and a mode of existence which it could not provide."[172] A great tragedy arises out of the fact that they were once such excellent creatures. "The better stuff a creature is made of—the cleverer and stronger and freer it is—then the better it will be if it goes right, but also the worse it will be if it goes wrong." A mere brute cannot be very good or very bad, but "a superhuman spirit" can be either "best or worst" of all.[173]

Why did the Devil and the demons go wrong? Lewis did not think we could answer that question with certainty. Instead, a "reasonable (and traditional) guess, based on our own experiences of going wrong, can, however, be offered." The Devil's great sin was, consistent with Lewis's view of the human fall, an excessive self-will which caused him to lose his place; that is, putting himself first or "wanting to be the centre" or succinctly desiring to be God. "That was the sin of Satan: and that was the sin he taught the human race."[174] In other words, the sin of the Devil was the utmost evil or the essential vice Lewis identified as "Pride." "[It] was through Pride that the devil became the devil: Pride leads to every other vice: it is the complete anti-God state of mind."[175]

The demons, under the Devil or Satan's command, are deeply interested in humans. They are the food the demons feast on. On one occasion, Screwtape complains that some of them provide only a poor taste saying, "Not all the most skillful cookery of our tormentors could make them better than insipid."[176] But further, human minds are the battlefield upon which the demons confront their feared enemy, God himself, whose interest in human beings is exceedingly greater than anyone else's. Screwtape reflects upon this fact rather solemnly.

> To us a human is primarily food; our aim is the absorption of its will into ours, the increase of our own area of selfhood at its expense. But the obedience which the Enemy demands of men is quite a different thing. One must face the fact that all the talk about His love for men, and His service being perfect freedom, is not (as one would gladly believe) mere propaganda, but an appalling truth. . . . We want cattle who can finally become food; He wants servants who can finally become sons. We want to suck in, He wants to give out. We are empty and would be filled; He is full and flows over. Our war aim is a world in which Our Father

---

172. Lewis, *Miracles*, 170.

173. Lewis, *Mere Christianity*, 53.

174. Ibid.

175. Ibid., 109.

176. Lewis, "Screwtape Proposes a Toast," in *Screwtape Letters with Screwtape Proposes a Toast*, 154.

Below has drawn all other beings into himself: the Enemy wants a world full of beings united to Him but still distinct.[177]

The Devil's methods for accomplishing his aims are what Lewis attempts to explore in *The Screwtape Letters*. These evil schemes, which we may call temptations, fall under a few identifiable key principles.

The Nature of Temptations

The plot of *The Screwtape Letters* is very simple and even uneventful. A young professional, living with his mother, experiences a conversion to Christian faith. Wormwood, a junior demon, is assigned as his guardian with the responsibility to reverse his conversion and lead him to hell. Screwtape is the junior demon's uncle, and he, based on his shrewd knowledge of humans and the experiences he has compiled through many ages, composes the thirty-one letters. Most of the action takes place in the spiritual or mental realm; the young man is a patient who is being treated by a desperate, inexperienced intern who finds himself accountable to the dreadful elder demon. The young man's problems are rather mundane, common, and with little element of the spectacular. In the midst of his many relationships—with his mother, his church, friends, and a woman—and unsettling circumstances, the young man is exposed to demonic schemes. But, God ultimately triumphs at the moment of his untimely death during an air raid, which the world would see as a great tragedy.

About the plot of the book, Chad Walsh said,

> The plot of the *Letters* is nowhere concerned with magnificent sins or virtues. The young man's final destiny has as much to do with his facial expressions when he speaks to his mother as it does with the weighty decrees of the ten commandments. Like so many of Lewis's tales, it is a quest story. We have an Everyman whose goal is Heaven, but he leads so quiet a life that his pilgrimage is hardly visible except to demonic eyes and their acute vision.[178]

Walsh's judgment is entirely correct. This is another instance of Lewisian story-telling about a person's Christian journey. The fact that this plot deals with common matters makes it appealing to average people struggling with everyday temptations.

---

177. Lewis, *Screwtape Letters*, 50.
178. Walsh, *Literary Legacy of C. S. Lewis*, 24–25.

The nature of the demonic schemes introduced in the book is not easily narrowed down. Paul Ford, who labors through the book to compose "the theology of discernment," suggests the following "concise syntheses and distillations of Lewis's teaching on the difference between heaven's and hell's goals and strategies":

> At least two statements can be made: (1) the goal of Hell is *demonization* and *absorption*; its strategy is *seduction* and *confusion*; and (2) the goal of Heaven is *divinization* and *individuated interdependency*; its process is *invitation* and *clarification*.[179]

Ford, building upon this foundational distinction, goes on to identify two major spiritual laws, which Screwtape brings to Wormwood's attention. They are "the law of diversion" and "the law of undulation." According to the first law, Wormwood is charged to confuse the patient by mismanaging the internal glance. In regard to the good, the demon tempts the patient to look away from the object in excessive introspection; in regard to what is evil, the patient is encouraged to look away from the self and excessively focus on the object of temptation. According to "the law of undulation," the demon prompts the patient to react sensitively to the undulation of his emotions.[180] These analyses are helpful for our understanding.

From Lewis's teaching, several other principles about the nature of the demonic schemes can be drawn. The demonic attempts to disrupt the pilgrim's journey toward home are clever and crafty. First, the demons are well equipped with the knowledge of natural human tendencies. Therefore, temptations, according to Lewis, are cleverly based on manipulating these human tendencies. An example is the law of undulation. Humans, consisting of both spirit and body, are subjected to "a series of troughs and peaks." Screwtape observes, "Their nearest approach to constancy, therefore, is undulation."[181] What can a pilgrim do to overcome the devil's scheme to manipulate human tendencies? Lewis's admonition is that we constantly need to stand (or kneel) before God "in absolute nakedness of the soul." The pilgrim must cultivate the life of a continual approach to God in honesty and openness, being alert to his own weaknesses which the devil seeks to use as his foothold.

Second, the devil's schemes are subtle. Temptations, according to Lewis, come in cleverly controlled measures so that the fall into it will be a gradual one. In particular our forgetfulness in regard to very basic things is

---

179. Ford, "C. S. Lewis, Ecumenical Spiritual Director," 105.

180. The discussion of the two laws is found in ibid., 105–9.

181. Lewis, *Screwtape Letters*, 49.

often utilized as a strategic starting point. In *The Pilgrim's Regress,* the witch who approaches John entices him with a simple request: "Taste this once, and I will leave you." Her appeal is to basic, uncomplicated instincts—thirst and fatigue. "Just once.... You are only wasting time," she says.[182] Screwtape also lectures about the tactic of the gradual capture of the souls. He says, "In each individual choice of what the Enemy would call the 'wrong' turning, such creatures are at first hardly, if at all, in a state of full spiritual responsibility." What are the tempters to do with these small, wrong choices? "The joy of their Tempters was first, of course, to harden these choices of the hellward roads into a habit by steady repetition. But then (and this was all-important) to turn the habit into a principle—a principle the creature is prepared to defend."[183] And the unforgettable line, "Indeed the safest road to Hell is the gradual one—the gentle slope, soft underfoot, without sudden turnings, without milestones, without signposts,"[184] sums it up perfectly. Therefore, we are called to guard ourselves continuously by humble adherence to small duties in faithful and steadfast obedience.

Third, since the Devil, no matter how great, is unable to create anything (not even what is bad) his aim is only to spoil what God has made for good. Lewis, disputing the validity of dualism, asserted that evil is not as substantial as good is.

> A sound theory . . . demands that good should be original and evil a mere perversion; that good should be the tree and evil the ivy; that good should be able to see all round evil (as when sane men understand lunacy) while evil cannot retaliate in kind; that good should be able to exist on its own while evil requires the good on which it is parasitic in order to continue its parasitic existence.[185]

Thus, there is a real ontological imbalance between good and evil. Evil exists only because good exists; good on the other hand exists on it own as God's creation. Lewis stated that the Devil is "empty" and constantly "wants to suck in," to draw "all other beings into himself."[186] Using the same logic, Lewis wrote, "All Hell is smaller than one pebble of [the] earthly world: but it is smaller than one atom of [the heavenly] world, the Real World."[187] We find here Lewis's reliance on the Boethian concept of evil, which in turn

---

182. Ibid., 189.
183. Lewis, *Screwtape Letters with Screwtape Proposes a Toast,* 156.
184. Lewis, *Screwtape Letters,* 67.
185. Lewis, "Evil and Good," in *God in the Dock,* 23.
186. Lewis, *Screwtape Letters,* 50.
187. Lewis, *Great Divorce,* 122.

echoes the Augustinian view of evil as deprivation and, by definition, the very absence of being, which is good. "No man can doubt . . . that God is almighty (*omnium potens*). . . . [There] is nothing that He who is almighty cannot do. . . . [But] can God do evil? . . . Evil is nothing, since He cannot do it who can do anything."[188]

Practically, this means the demons tempt us to misuse and abuse what is good. Speaking about pleasure, Screwtape finds himself enraged at what God stands for.

> He's a hedonist at heart. All those fasts and vigils and stakes and crosses are only a façade. Or only like foam on the sea shore. Out at sea, out in His sea, there is pleasure, and more pleasure. He makes no secret of it; at His right hand are "pleasures for evermore." . . . He has filled His world full of pleasures. These are things for humans to do all day long without His minding in the least—sleeping, washing, eating, drinking, making love, playing, praying, working. Everything has to be *twisted* before it's any use to us. We fight under cruel disadvantages. Nothing is naturally on our side.[189]

The demons desperately try to disorient the coordinates of things created. Humans are tempted to take things out of proportion, push things to extremes, and force them to serve their own twisted selfish ends. The more noble the things that they misuse, the more ecstatic amusement they offer to the demons. "A spoiled saint, a Pharisee, an inquisitor, or a magician, makes better sport in Hell than a mere common tyrant or debauchee."[190] Therefore, our safeguard must be a continuous and honest adjustment of ourselves and all that we have and enjoy to the proper coordinates in relation to the Creator; only through our and their proper relatedness to him can truly meaningful existence take place. Thus, we should learn to celebrate the expressions of God's richness in the world as he created them; and we can increase our efficiency at it by learning to turn our glance continually outward from ourselves to God.

The young man in *The Screwtape Letters* is killed during an air raid. Screwtape, in frustration, describes what the young man must have gone through at that moment. "Just think," he says, "what he felt at that moment; as if a scab had fallen from an old sore, as if he were emerging from

---

188. Boethius, *Theological Tractates*, 291. This is not to say that Lewis did not go directly to Augustine. Rather, the connection is based on the fact that Lewis repeatedly acknowledged the profound influence *De Consolatione* had on his thought.

189. Lewis, *Screwtape Letters*, 106.

190. Ibid., 109.

a hideous, shell-like tetter, as if he shuffled off for good and all a defiled, wet, clinging garment." In agony, Screwtape acknowledges the final destiny of the pilgrim: "[He] saw Him. This animal, this thing begotten in bed, could look on Him. What a blinding, suffocating fire to you, is now cool light to him, is clarity itself, and wears the form of a Man. . . . He is caught up into that world where pain and pleasure take on transfinite values and all our arithmetic is dismayed."[191] What a marvelous description of what is to come; ironically, the words come out of the most miserable creatures in the whole universe. The discussion of the pilgrim's final destiny is the topic of the following chapter, "The Final Home," which not only elaborates on Screwtape's painstaking acknowledgment of the pilgrim's entrance into glory as temptations cease but also on the final judgment when the tempters themselves will be destroyed.

CONCLUSION

Our discussion of "the new life in the fallen world" according to Lewis highlighted his emphases on the corporate nature of the Christian journey, the sacramental view of Scripture, the efficacy of prayer, and the reality of spiritual warfare. Once again, Lewis's supernaturalist worldview and his redemptocentric view of Christianity became evident. Christianity offers a cure from non-Christian notions of both individualism and collectivism. Through Christ's supernatural presence with his people and church as the Body of Christ, a true "organic" life of individuality and communion is possible. We find this discussion particularly insightful. Scripture as a sacramental text confronts us with God's redemptive presence. Prayer is the very representation of God's supernatural operation in and through us. The Devil as a spiritual reality seeks to affect our everyday life, and our battle against the Devil's schemes continues through our journey in this world; but God's redemptive grace effectively triumphs over the evil one, leading us to the final home.

However, a few problems can be pointed out. Lewis's view of Scripture reveals serious deficiencies due to the radical separation of the medium (the "leaky vehicle") and the message ("the Word"), which we addressed earlier. His view of prayer reflects his earnest struggle with the practical issue, but his understanding of God's providence, as that which keeps into account all free activities including petitionary prayers, through the Boethian concept of time and eternity, remains unsatisfactory. Lewis resorted to this formula often; but the solution seems insufficient to address what

---

191. Ibid., 141, 144–45.

is largely a logical problem of reconciling God's sovereignty and human freedom. Lewis pointed out emphatically that the question of predestination and free-will is "indiscussable, insoluable," therefore "meaningless."[192] Nevertheless, we repeatedly find him trying to address it by making God's providence logically contingent to human free acts, as is the case in his view of prayer. However, as usual, the benefits outweigh the problems in Lewis, and his "mere Christianity" proves to be an important corrective to modern religious skepticism.

---

192. Lewis, *Letters of C. S. Lewis*, 426–27.

6

The Final Home

The Consummation of the Journey

The journey homeward is not only filled with trials and temptations but with precious moments of joyful play. The last section of *The Pilgrim's Regress* gives us a picture of childlike laughter and carefree fun.

> My dream was full of light and noise. I thought they went on their way singing and laughing like schoolboys. Vertue lost all his dignity, and John was never tired: and for ten miles or so they picked up an old fiddler who was going that way, who played them such jigs and they danced more than they walked. And Vertue invented doggerels to his tunes to mock the old Pagan virtues in which he had been bred.[1]

But soon they must face the solemn reality of the final brook they must cross. We might think that the crossing of the brook would only be an additional joy to the pilgrims. However, Lewis is more honest than idealistic when it comes to the issue of death. To all, the final moment of this life is a heavy and sad experience.

CROSSING THE FINAL BROOK: WHAT PHYSICAL DEATH MEANS

First of all, the reality of the death of others suddenly dawns on John the pilgrim as he reaches the empty and ruined cottage of his parents, the only thing they left behind. "But in the midst of all this gaiety, suddenly John stood still and his eyes filled with tears. They had come to a little cottage beside a river,

---

1. Lewis, *Pilgrim's Regress*, 196.

which was empty and ruinous. . . . 'I see that my father and mother are gone already beyond the brook. I had much I would have said to them.'"[2]

The prospect of their own crossing seems no less disturbing. Vertue says, "I confess that I go down in fear and sadness." Why should he be filled with such emotions? Vertue adds, "Whatever there is beyond the brook, it cannot be the same. Something is being ended. It is a real brook."[3] Death is real. No one, whether brave or timid, can regard it as a triviality. Something real and concrete is passing away. Life, as we know it on the earth, is not merely a dream, though it vanishes in time. Vertue sings,

> As Thou hast made substantially, thou wilt unmake
> In earnest and for everlasting. Let none take
> Comfort in frail supposal that some hour and place
> To those who mourn recovers the wished voice and face.
> Whom Thy great Exit banishes, no after age
> Of epilogue leads back upon the lighted stage.
> Where is Prince Hamlet when the curtain's down? Where fled
> Dreams at the dawn, or colours when the light is sped?
> We are thy colours, fugitive, never restored,
> Never repeated again.[4]

The reality of death came near Lewis when his wife, the one he shared his brief but happy marriage with, passed away. Following her loss, he tried to reflect on the meaning of death and the pain of losing someone in death.

> It is hard to have patience with people who say, "There is no death," or, "Death doesn't matter." There is death. And whatever is matters. And whatever happens has consequences, and it and they are irrevocable and irreversible. You might as well say that birth doesn't matter. I look up at the night sky. Is anything more certain than that in all those vast times and spaces, if I were allowed to search them, I should nowhere find her face, her voice, her touch? She died. She is dead. Is the word so difficult to learn?[5]

Lewis's view of the reality of death has not changed in twenty-eight years, the time gap between the two books, *The Pilgrim's Regress* and *A Grief Observed*. Is it possible that the paradigm of what death is to a human heart was already fixed on him when his mother passed away and that all subsequent

---

2. Ibid., 196–97.
3. Ibid., 197.
4. Ibid.
5. Lewis, *A Grief Observed*, 16.

experiences of death were only a repetition of the same? Again, Lewis said that "all that stuff about family reunions 'on the further shore'" is false. "[That] is all unscriptural, all out of bad hymns and lithographs. There's not a word of it in the Bible."[6] Life is a concrete reality, with specific particularities with their own integrity and uniqueness. "Reality never repeats. The exact same thing is never taken away and given back."[7] When Paul wrote the words of exhortation, "Do not mourn like those that have no hope," Lewis thought it can comfort "only those who love God better than the dead, and the dead better than themselves." For instance,

> If a mother is mourning not for what she has lost but for what her dead child has lost, it is a comfort to believe that the child has not lost the end for which it was created. And it is a comfort to believe that she herself, in losing her chief or only natural happiness, has not lost a greater thing, that she may still hope to "glorify God and enjoy Him forever."

But her maternal happiness cannot continue after the death of her son.

> Never, in any place or time, will she have her son on her knees, or bathe him, or tell him a story, or plan for his future, or see her grandchild.[8]

Thus, Lewis thought that our local and temporal attachments are not irrelevant to our spiritual life. God has a purpose for even our earthly belonging, for they create in us particular "pangs," so that we do not only know of "love universal" but "love particular" for a friend or a place. Thus, our experience of love becomes substantial, like the love of God. John the pilgrim observes,

> But Thou, Lord, surely knewest Thine own plan
> When the angelic indifferences with no bar
> Universally loved but Thou gav'st man
> The tether and pang of the particular; . . .
> That we, though small, may quiver with fire's same
> Substantial form as Thou—nor reflect merely,
> As lunar angel, back to thee, cold flame.
> Gods we are, Thou has [sic] said: and we pay dearly.[9]

---

6. Ibid., 28–29.
7. Ibid., 29.
8. Ibid., 29–30.
9. Lewis, *Pilgrim's Regress*, 198–99.

Death's sorrow is not a curse but a consequence of a blessing in which angels cannot partake. The meaning of death's sorrow is not to be underestimated or trivialized. To be saddened by our detachment from spatio-temporal things or persons is a properly human experience.

A more doctrinal discussion of death is found in *Miracles*. There, Lewis expounds the meaning of human death. The Christian view of death is neither like Stoicism, which says that death does not matter, nor like the naturalistic point of view, which, in the light of modern thought about the survival of the human species, says that death is "the greatest of all evils."[10] Lewis defined the Christian doctrine of death this way:

> On the one hand Death is the triumph of Satan, the punishment of the Fall, and the last enemy. Christ shed tears at the grave of Lazarus and sweated blood in Gethsemane: the Life of Lives that was in Him detested this penal obscenity not less than we do, but more. On the other hand, only he who loses his life will save it. We are baptized into the *death* of Christ, and it is the remedy for the Fall. Death is, in fact, what some modern people call "ambivalent." It is Satan's great weapon and also God's great weapon: it is holy and unholy; our supreme disgrace and our only hope; the thing Christ came to conquer and the means by which He conquered.[11]

Death, as a result of sin and the Fall and as Satan's great weapon, represents the disintegration of the unity of the human being. He/she is "a composite being—a natural organism tenanted by, or in a state of *symbiosis* with, a supernatural spirit." Because of sin, the two consisting parts became hostile to one another, resulting in a pathological relationship. "At present spirit can retain its foothold against the incessant counterattacks of Nature (both physiological and psychological) only by perpetual vigilance, and physiological Nature always defeats it in the end." The continuing battle is interrupted when the body, no longer able to resist the disintegration, experiences death. The human being, as a holistic organism, is defeated by mere "physical nature" and becomes inorganic. The division within the human organism, therefore, is a tragic result of sin and the Fall.

However, Satan's greatest weapon to destroy humanity has been turned against him by God and made into a redemptive principle. Human beings, having rebelled against God by the persuasion of the enemy, find a state of rebellion in their own organism (both psychical and physical nature war

---

10. Lewis, *Miracles*, 125.
11. Ibid.

against the spirit).[12] The result is in accordance with a principle, which God instituted in the act of creation itself. When humanity rebels against God, the whole order of the created hierarchy is overturned. The human spirit loses control of the natural organism. Dramatically, at the moment of death, the natural organism is conquered by inorganic nature, which is subjected to the process of decay and disintegration.[13] From God's point of view, death is a punishment because it is "horror and ignominy." But it is also a "safety-device because, once man has fallen, natural immortality would be the one utterly hopeless destiny of him."[14]

Only the second great rebellion by the perfect man can "convert this penal death into the means of eternal life." By "the perfect man," Lewis obviously referred to Jesus Christ, and "by the second great rebellion" he meant the willing self-renunciation to which Jesus Christ had committed himself, what we have called "the substitutionary repentance of Christ." But exactly how that process converted death itself is less than clear. Lewis simply stated that somehow the death of Christ opened the door for "that higher and mystical Death which is eternally good and a necessary ingredient of the highest life."[15] Lewis believed in the validity of vicariousness in the reality which God has created; he called it "the very idiom of the reality." Christ, in his vicarious death, "tasted death on behalf of all others." He added, "He is the representative 'Die-er' of the universe: and for that very reason the Resurrection and the Life."[16]

Lewis did not clearly distinguish between the spiritual significance of the act of repentance (represented most vividly by the sacrament of baptism) as a participation in the death of Christ and final physical death, the loss of organic life on earth. The spiritual meaning of both is essentially the same. He describes them in *The Pilgrim's Regress* as a crossing of the brooks. The physical death is, however, the last crossing. There is a definite shift of the human being from one mode of existence to another. Christ's death has transformed the meaning of this final physical death, so that the pilgrimage comes to a certain consummatory state. A new and higher reality awaits on the other side.

---

12. Lewis may seem here to be advocating a tripartite division of the human being, consisting of the spirit, the psychical aspect (the soul or mind?), and the physical aspect. However, Lewis in fact bound together the psychical and the physical as the natural organism, while the spirit was considered the supernatural entity.

13. Lewis, *Miracles*, 129.

14. Ibid., 129–30.

15. Ibid., 129.

16. Ibid., 130.

LEWIS ON ESCHATOLOGY: REAL OR FICTIONAL?

Much of what Lewis said about the consummation of the journey, he himself regarded as tentative or imaginative. This is not unique to his eschatology, however; our present discussion merely intensifies the potential danger that exists throughout Lewis's theology. But this is a particularly appropriate place to bring the issue to the fore.

The many sources from which this part of Lewis's Christian pilgrimage is to be constructed are imaginative rather than didactic in genre. However, Lewis's imaginative works are not entirely fictional, in the sense of having no theological facts or information. For him all types of language are informative, though they may be so in different senses.[17] Furthermore, while we acknowledge the tentative nature of his thoughts, especially regarding eschatology, whether personal or cosmic, those thoughts are nevertheless representative of the overall structure of his theology. That is to say, his mere Christianity, with its twin pillar perspectives of supernaturalism and salvationism, forms the foundation upon which his imaginative works are constructed. While respecting their proper sphere as artistic expressions that utilize in depth the Lewisian concept of myths and metaphors, we can still extract his own soteriological or eschatological vision from them.

This point requires elaboration in the light of the work of William Luther White. White rejects the possibility of constructing a dogmatic theology from Lewis's thought, arguing that to do so would be a complete violation of Lewis's own understanding of the nature of religious language. "Lewis was keenly aware of the nature of language. He consciously and deliberately made use of his understanding of metaphor and myth, whether writing theology or composing novels. The fundamentalist or humanist reader who neglects to notice this fact in Lewis fails to catch his full meaning."[18] However, it is one thing to come to accept Lewis's understanding of language, and therefore exercise caution when we approach Lewis's imaginative works, but it is another to categorize all of Lewis's religious assertions as belonging to this type of language. Unless the distinction is made, we are in danger of dismissing the possibility of any coherent theology expressing a rational statement of facts.

White says, "That the language of theology is inadequate to describe the reality of God, Lewis simply takes for granted."[19] If this is so, is there an alternative to dogmatic theology? According to White, we must follow

---

17. Our discussion of Lewis's views on ordinary, scientific, and poetic language can be found in chapter 5 under the subsection "Scripture and the Word of God."

18. White, *Image of Man in C. S. Lewis*, 37.

19. Ibid., 39.

Lewis's theological method (highlighting his reliance on the function of imagination), because the nature of language itself does not allow us to be dogmatic about the reality of God and his world. White continues, "For Lewis, as for MacDonald, the reality represented in myth and metaphor is more—not less—than a figure of speech. Lewis is impatient with those Christians who become so entangled in their sophisticated knowledge of religious language that they neglect the realities which the theological symbols imperfectly represent."[20] One may conclude that in White's Lewis, romanticism triumphs over rationalism.

On the other hand, White's real fear is "the widespread impression that Lewis was inclined toward theological fundamentalism." He expands,

> While he has been so classified both by conservative and liberal theologians and by many reviewers, this judgment represents a failure to take seriously the nature of literature and the nature of theological language, even as Lewis himself understood them. Far from being a theological literalist, Lewis developed a sophisticated theory of religious language and presented an extensive discussion on literary theory in his own works. For more than forty years Lewis produced imaginative literature reflecting his keen understanding of myth and metaphor as the essential language of religion. C. S. Lewis was a Christian remythologizer par excellence.[21]

White seems to be suggesting that without understanding the mythical and metaphorical intent of Lewis's use of religious language, it is impossible to talk about his theology. At the same time, such a view of language requires us to back away from our "obsessive" quest for exactitude or certainty in religious concepts. This means that supernatural reality must be grasped tentatively in terms of our reason, but powerfully and concretely in terms of our imagination, which can perceive the meaning of myths and metaphors.

By no means are we interested in classifying Lewis as a theological fundamentalist; in any case, it is doubtful if there is agreement on what "fundamentalist" means in a technical sense. White is right in thinking that it would be futile to categorize Lewis into a particular theological school. On the other hand, what White has concluded above is in danger of leading to theological irrationality. How can we truly know and assert anything? If there is concreteness to what people perceive with imagination, is there also uniformity to what they perceive? If not, what real knowledge (as a justified belief) is possible? If so, can these perceptions be organized into

20. Ibid.
21. Ibid., 213.

certain principles, conveying reliable analytical knowledge? White would have problems with both options. Lewis himself would not.

According to Lewis's epistemology, derived principles are a degree removed from the reality itself; nevertheless, Lewis would call them truths. He himself clarifies the difference between truth and reality. "[Truth] is always about something, but reality is that about which truth is."[22] Reality is the condition that makes truth possible; it does not invalidate it. That is why Lewis spent a large quantity of time to prove the reasonableness of the truth of Christianity. He was deeply concerned about objective truths and about objective reality. His view of myths and metaphors does not invalidate the use of language as an analytical tool in theology; at least in Lewis, they supplement and increase our understanding of the analytical use of language, placing the analytical use in its proper sphere. His constant appeal to the truthfulness (not only mythical and metaphorical but factual and historical) of the Christian message is what sets him apart from modern theologians of imagination as we have already briefly noted.

White is not ignorant of this fact. He notes how Lewis penetrated "to the core of [classical Christian doctrines], of separating the essential from the inessential."[23] He acknowledges Lewis's vehement concern for establishing "a cogent case for the Christian faith." White says, "[Traditional] Christianity has made some rather definite, affirmative statements about God and man. It was Lewis's intention to set forth these central beliefs as clearly and as forcefully as he could."[24] Thus, he concedes, "It may not be a misunderstanding to think of Lewis as a dogmatic writer"; but he quickly attaches the following conditions:

> When allowance is made, however, for (1) the abbreviated interpretation required by his popular audience and situation, for (2) the reservations which were set forth in several of his prefaces, for (3) the use of dramatic assertion as a teaching technique, and for (4) the fact that he was presenting traditional Christianity rather than spiritual autobiography, Lewis appears somewhat less dogmatic and self-righteous than would otherwise be the case.[25]

White's analysis is helpful, but one can hardly fail to notice a certain anxiety in his tone (he himself being somewhat less dogmatic and self-assured about his main argument), as he acknowledges that Lewis is often "too strong" in

22. Lewis, "Myth Became Fact," in *God in the Dock*, 66.
23. White, *Image of Man in C. S. Lewis*, 212.
24. Ibid., 87.
25. Ibid.

his arguments for Christianity and that this tendency fits awkwardly with the view of the nature of religious language he seems to espouse. But this shakes the central point of White's thesis.

We suggested that, having presupposed the limitations of theological methods, Lewis tried to convey a certain content, not mere impressions or possible impacts (i.e., substantial propositions that make all other theological thoughts possible for him). The aim has been to uncover the substantial content in Lewis's Christian thought or theology. In doing so, it has been important to note that certain things were central to Lewis. His didactic prose frequently shows his tentative thoughts, not because the nature of language requires him to be tentative but because he held these particular theological thoughts to be less central to the message of Christianity. Whether or not he was right about the status of these doctrines is a different matter.

Nevertheless, it is important to distinguish clearly between Lewis's didactic prose and his fictional or imaginative works. They both have served powerfully to convey his Christian message. However, the modes of appeal are quite distinct. In the former, Lewis ventured on descriptive theology, setting forth the articles of Christian faith in a reasonable fashion (using what he called "theological" or "apologetical" language similar to "scientific language"); in the latter, he attempted (utilizing fully his ability as a literary artist) to dramatize or imaginatively participate in the world which his theology describes, using myths and metaphors to convey the meaning of the reality (using "religious language" similar to "poetic language").[26] However, the boundary is not always clear cut. His didactic works are full of effective metaphors and analogies; his imaginative works are often accused of being too didactic. In overview, the unclear boundary is not a negative quality but a natural and positive outcome of Lewis's apologetic and artistic intention. Though they are not always mutually inclusive, they are not, thankfully, always mutually exclusive either.

So we may continue to explore Lewis's theological thoughts, freely but cautiously using both media, asserting some thoughts to be more central than others to his Christian "dogma." As observed earlier, we must rely more on his imaginative works as we come to discuss the consummation of the journey. Here we find tentative thoughts, which are nevertheless properly

---

26. Lewis said "theological language" is necessary "to state religious matter in a form more like that we use for scientific matter. This is often necessary, for purposes of instruction, clarification, controversy and the like." Also in apologetics, "you must use terms as definable and univocal as possible." But "the language of religion, which we . . . have to distinguish from that of theology, seems . . . to be, on the whole, either the same sort we use in ordinary conversation or the same sort we use in poetry, or somewhere between the two." Lewis, "The Language of Religion," in *Christian Reflections*, 129, 135–36.

Lewis's thoughts: informed speculations arising out of his knowledge of the Bible and inferences from his basic assumptions about God and his world. His Christian hopes about the future are certainly not detached from these "tentative" thoughts.

We can divide Lewis's eschatological thought into two main sections in keeping with the two works that focus particularly on this area of Christian faith: *"The Great Divorce*: Personal Eschatology" and *"The Last Battle*: Cosmic Eschatology." These two imaginative works provide broad paradigmatic presentations of the two great spheres of the future reality.

Lewis explicitly and implicitly makes reference to these two distinctive spheres of the coming reality. His thinking on the last things was considered by many shockingly or even "fanatically" orthodox,[27] particularly because he firmly held on to traditional images. He realized that using new images to replace biblical ones is simply confusing. He therefore chose to take traditional images and shed new light on them.

THE GREAT DIVORCE: PERSONAL ESCHATOLOGY

Lewis clearly favored the idea that one should not develop an obsessive interest in personal eschatology, because to do so can be a symptomatic manifestation of a compensatory motive, which he thought belongs in an inferior religious state. In *Reflections on the Psalms*, he discusses the topic, "Death in the Psalms." He was struck by the lack of "transmortal" hope in the Psalms. "They speak of Sheol (or 'hell' or 'the pit') very much as a man speaks of 'death' or 'the grave' who has no belief in any sort of future state whatever—a man to whom the dead are simply dead, nothing, and there's no more to be said."[28] Lewis, himself firmly convinced of the truth of transmortal hope, tries to figure out why this is so.

His answer is intriguing: He thought that God deliberately withheld explicit revelation of the future hope from Old Testament believers, as they were in the stage of developing further religious consciousness, because he wanted to shield them from forming the devastatingly selfish religious motive that characterized much of their surrounding religious practices. A so-called "hope of after-life" often motivates people merely to "hope for

---

27. Walter Hooper observes that to contemporary people who are preoccupied with the concept of "individual freedom and rights" Lewis's "orthodox belief in a real heaven and hell strikes us as little short of fanatical." Hooper, "Preface," in Lewis, *Christian Reflections*, ix.

28. Lewis, *Reflections on the Psalms*, 38.

oneself" without placing God in the center. God "is still important only for the sake of something else." Lewis asserted,

> It is surely, therefore, very possible that when God began to reveal Himself to men, to show them that He and nothing else is their true goal and the satisfaction of their needs, and that He has a claim upon them simply by being what He is, quite apart from anything He can bestow or deny, it may have been absolutely necessary that this revelation should not be with any hint of future Beatitude or Perdition.[29]

Lewis's thought seems to be based, on the one hand, on the idea of progressive revelation, and, on the other hand, on an anthropological or developmental notion of religion. Whether or not people's religious consciousness has really developed into a higher stage over time is certainly a disputable point. But the notion that "the hope of after-life" can often have a mistaken focus is a characteristically Lewisian insight worthy of our attention. He concludes,

> It is even arguable that the moment "Heaven" ceases to mean union with God and "Hell" to mean separation from Him, the belief in either is a mischievous superstition; for then we have, on the one hand, a merely "compensatory" belief (a "sequel" to life's sad story, in which everything will "come all right") and, on the other, a nightmare which drives men into asylums or makes them persecutors.[30]

The Realized Antithesis

In the light of the Lewis corpus, we can summarize the transmortal state as a higher degree of separation between those who surrender their will to God and those who are self-focused. "There are only two kinds of people in the end: those who say to God, 'Thy will be done', and those to whom God says, in the end, '*Thy* will be done.'"[31] The antithesis already runs deep in this life; the transmortal reality is only a dramatic extension or a deeper realization of it. This is the idea most foundational to Lewis's eschatological thought. To those who object to the doctrine of hell, Lewis presented the logic behind his firm belief in it.

---

29. Ibid., 40.
30. Ibid., 41.
31. Lewis, *Great Divorce*, 72.

> "What are you asking God to do?" To wipe out their past sins and, at all costs, to give them a fresh start, smoothing every difficulty and offering every miraculous help? But He has done so, on Calvary. To forgive them? They will not be forgiven. To leave them alone? Alas, I am afraid that is what He does.[32]

It would be redundant to engage in a full discussion of Lewis's description of hell and heaven. Clarence Francis Dye has done this adequately in two full chapters of his dissertation "The Evolving Eschaton in C. S. Lewis." Apart from the fact that he seems to over-stress the importance of "man's free will" (the central thesis for him) and underestimate Lewis's emphasis on the meaning of divine grace (although he is right in pointing out that Lewis tried to avoid the term "grace" because of its ambiguity to modern readers[33]), Dye has adequately detailed the images of heaven and hell presented by Lewis.

Here, in distinction, we will focus on the idea of separation as the key. For this, we turn to Lewis's imaginative work about the transmortal reality, *The Great Divorce*. Like his *Pilgrim's Regress*, it is a dream. Lewis warned his readers: "I beg readers to remember that this is a fantasy. . . . [The] transmortal conditions are solely an imaginative supposal." On the other hand, Lewis clearly states, "It has of course—or I intended it to have—a moral."[34] However, knowing Lewis, the moral is not just an abstract thought, but a certain concrete reality with particular details. We should not expect the moral to be merely like that of one of Aesop's fables.

The central moral of *The Great Divorce* is documented in the preface. Lewis points out that this work is a reflection on Blake's *The Marriage of Heaven and Hell*. It is not a direct response to Blake's work, because the meaning of his work is not crystal clear. However, Lewis desires to correct the perennial attempt to make a marriage of heaven and hell.

> The attempt is based on the belief that reality never presents us with an absolutely unavoidable "either-or"; that, granted skill and patience and (above all) time enough, some way of embracing both alternatives can always be found; that mere development or adjustment or refinement will somehow turn evil into good without our being called on for a final and total rejection of anything we should like to retain. This belief I take to be a disastrous error.

---

32. Lewis, *Problem of Pain*, 128.
33. Dye, "The Evolving Eschaton in C. S. Lewis," 202.
34. Lewis, *Great Divorce*, 7–8.

Continuing on from this, Lewis corrected the mistaken view of what life's journey is like.

> We are not living in a world where all roads are radii of a circle and where all, if followed long enough, will therefore draw gradually nearer and finally meet at the centre: rather in a world where every road, after a few miles, forks into two, and each of those into two again, and at each fork you must make a decision.[35]

Lewis's point could not be clearer. The idea of separation or the consummation of the antithesis is unmistakably in view. Lewis urges us not to commit the error that the mere passage of time can heal the wrong. The only way to correct the wrong is "by going back till you find the error and working it afresh from that point, never by simply *going on*."[36] Evil can never "develop" into good. It must be undone. And only Christ has done the process of undoing, and we are invited to be united to him in faith.

In *The Great Divorce*, the grumbling "Ghosts" from hell travel to heaven hoping to improve their condition of existence. But the bus tour to heaven is not a very successful one. Out of the multitude who bother to take the trip away from hell, only one "Ghost," who at will subjected his "embarrassing" lust to death, finds himself transformed into a "solid person." Overall, the story is a disturbing tragedy; the characters, who are bent on self-seeking, are closely identifiable with our own tendencies. It shows clearly why they are in hell in the first place and why they cannot escape. "The characteristic of lost souls is 'their rejection of everything that is not simply themselves.'"[37] Lewis suggests that damned souls have no capacity for enjoying good, which is essentially "the taste for the *other*." Lewis thought that bodily death intensifies this problem, thus subjecting them to the condition of hell.

> The taste for the *other* . . . is quenched in him except in so far as his body still draws him into some rudimentary contact with an outer world. Death removes this last contact. He has his wish— to live wholly in the self and to make the best of what he finds there. And what he finds there is Hell.[38]

---

35. Ibid., 5–6.
36. Ibid., 6.
37. Lewis, *Problem of Pain*, 123.
38. Ibid.

The Second Chance

Both Dye and White want to establish that transmortal existence is a process in which souls must continuously make free choices. In fact, the idea of second chances for those who are hell-bound is considered a real possibility. White says, "Lewis stressed the urgency of present choice, but I do not think he ever committed himself to the position that no choice is possible beyond the grave. It seems to me that he left open the question of universalism, even as he recommended against relying upon its conclusions. He stated that if additional chances after death will do any good, God will provide them."[39] Dye also, having reviewed White's statement, adds, "I would be inclined to agree with White."[40] He thinks that Lewis "saw hell as a possible evolutionary process that could lead the soul back to heaven."[41]

However, Lewis's words seem to rather consistently support the conclusion that, more than anything, he emphasizes the process of differentiation. *The Great Divorce* highlights not that souls are free to choose heaven in the transmortal life, but that regardless of the opportunities given, they really cannot choose. The point is, "It does not really matter whether they get a chance to taste heaven or not." In fact, heaven would turn out to be a very uncomfortable place for them.

The one man who finds his way into heaven is not presented as a prototype but as a rare exception. In addition, Lewis deliberately described that man's problem as carnal lust, which some religious people would consider worse than the problem of pride but in fact is not. Besides, the real focus of this episode is the transformation of "lust" rather than of the man himself. This is a fabulous tale of what we ought to pray will happen in this life, not the next. The episode is set in the context of the statement, "There is but one good; that is God. Everything else is good when it looks to Him and bad when it turns from Him."[42] Turned away from God and as an agent overruling the man, lust is represented as a "red lizard" on his shoulder. "[It] was twitching its tail like a whip and whispering things in his ear." But when the Burning One, an angel, fights off its resistance, twists it and flings it to the ground, an incredible sight takes place. Not only does the man grow in stature, turning "every moment solider," but something begins to happen to the lizard. "So far from dying, the creature was still struggling and even growing bigger as it struggled. And as it grew it changed." The lizard turns into "the

---

39. White, *Image of Man in C. S. Lewis*, 203–4.
40. Dye, "The Evolving Eschaton in C. S. Lewis," 225.
41. Ibid., 205.
42. Lewis, *Great Divorce*, 97–98.

greatest stallion" the dreamer has ever seen, shining in golden glory. The "new-made man," with face shining and overflowing with tears of joy, leaps upon the horse's back, nudging the stallion with his heels. Together they vanish into "the rose-brightness of that everlasting morning."[43] Again, the conclusion of the matter focuses on "lust" rather than on the man. "Lust is a poor, weak, whimpering whispering thing compared with that richness and energy of desire which will arise when lust has been killed."[44] The "moral" of the story is self-evident; the emphasis is not on the "second chance."[45]

Lewis confirms this in plain didactic prose in *The Problem of Pain*. Having acknowledge the objection that "death ought not to be final, that there ought to be a second chance," Lewis suggested,

> I believe that if a million chances were likely to do good, they would be given. But a master often knows, when boys and parents do not, that it is really useless to send a boy in for a certain examination again. Finality must come sometime, and it does not require a very robust faith to believe that omniscience knows when.[46]

Lewis's point cannot be misunderstood. White suggests that Lewis, by saying that "if additional chances after death will do any good, God will provide them," means to highlight the possibility of the second chance; but in context, Lewis clearly expresses his view that, regardless of our desire to see endless opportunities for the lost, more chances would accomplish nothing.

What, then of Lewis's apparent acknowledgment of purgatory and limbo? Lewis, in *Letters to Malcolm* states, "I believe in Purgatory"; but he adds that his is not "the Romish doctrine concerning Purgatory." Rather, he thought that saved souls would appreciate the place of cleansing; and if it involves suffering the purpose is for purification, and is not meritorious. Nor is the suffering itself the purpose of purgatory.[47] Also, curiously,

---

43. Ibid., 98–103.

44. Ibid., 104–5.

45. We cannot ignore the fact that the idea of a "chance" or "opportunity" to taste heaven is the underlying drama of *The Great Divorce*. However, it needs to be pointed out that Lewis intended to highlight the state of antithesis which runs deeper than external circumstances. Being brought to heaven does not solve the problem. There seems to be something deeper than being forced out of heaven or being imprisoned in hell. In fact, one may still be on earth, but the reality already points to the state of antithesis. "I think earth, if chosen instead of Heaven, will turn out to have been, all along, only a region in Hell: and earth, if put second to Heaven, to have been from the beginning a part of Heaven itself." (Ibid., 7).

46. Lewis, *Problem of Pain*, 124.

47. Lewis, *Letters to Malcolm*, 108–9.

Lewis, on a few occasions, mentions a place called limbo, which Screwtape described as, "[For] creatures suitable neither for Heaven nor for Hell . . . that, having failed to make the grade, are allowed to sink into a more or less contented sub-humanity forever."[48] Certainly the setting of this comment does not invite us to turn it into a dogmatic assertion. Fortunately, we have a very clear statement by Lewis that "the concept of a 'second chance' must not be confused either with that of Purgatory (for souls already saved) or of Limbo (for souls already lost)."[49] It seems to me that Lewis's point is to recognize a degree of differentiation in "the state of divorce," rather than a continuous intertwining of meaningful "free choices." In that sense, we must be skeptical of Dye's conviction that Lewis emphasized "man's freedom," which "continues into eternity" as effecting a "dynamic process" of "evolving eschaton."[50]

On the other hand, in *The Great Divorce*, Lewis seems to open the possibility (or at least this is the way he chose to express it) that the same locality (for lack of better term) can serve as either purgatory or limbo depending on the outcome. The narrator asks in the dream to his guide (George MacDonald), "Is there really a way out of Hell into Heaven?" The guide answers, "It depends on the way ye're using the words. If they leave that grey town behind it will not have been Hell. To any that leaves it, it is Purgatory."[51] In this sense, the young man who rid himself of lust is representative of any who receive cleansing in purgatory. By the same logic, "the Valley of the Shadow of Life," where the ghosts meet the solid spirits, will have been limbo to those who choose to return to hell. However, the outcome is not arbitrary, because the differentiation begins "before death." In a sense, those who live in hell always lived in hell; and those who live in heaven always lived in heaven.[52] The idea is difficult to grasp in the framework of time and space. Nevertheless, it clarifies further the notion of differentiation and antithesis.

Hell and Heaven

What are the characteristics of hell and heaven? Lewis presents three biblical images of hell: (1) punishment ("everlasting punishment," Matt 25:46), (2) destruction ("fear Him who is able to destroy both body and soul in hell," Matt 10:28), and (3) privation, exclusion, or banishment into "the darkness

---

48. Lewis, "Screwtape Proposes a Toast," in *World's Last Night*, 54.
49. Lewis, *Problem of Pain*, 124n.
50. Dye, "The Evolving Eschaton in C. S. Lewis," 229.
51. Lewis, *Great Divorce*, 66–67.
52. Ibid. 68.

outside" (as in the parables).[53] Lewis believed that all proper interpretations of hell must incorporate the idea of it being "unspeakably horrible." He also rejected the idea of the "annihilation" of the soul in hell. He thought that the state of having all three images combined would be "a state of *having been* a human soul."

> To enter heaven is to become more human than you ever succeeded in being in earth; to enter hell, is to be banished from humanity. What is cast (or casts itself) into hell is not a man: it is "remains." To be a complete man means to have the passions obedient to the will and the will offered to God: to *have been* a man—to be an ex-man or "damned ghost"—would presumably mean to consist of a will utterly centered in its self and passions utterly uncontrolled by the will.[54]

On the other hand, hell consists of "a state of mind" or a continuous clinging to self, which produces such a state of being. Lewis pursued to its logical end his view of evil as insubstantial (in contrast to good); hell as the ultimate consummation of evil is pictured by Lewis's imaginative mind as "smaller than one pebble of [the] earthly world" and "smaller than one atom of [the heavenly] world, the Real World."[55] Why? It is because "a damned soul is nearly nothing: it is shrunk, shut up in itself."[56] This is the meaning behind the statement, "Hell is a state of mind."[57] The statement does not mean that hell is an abstraction without a corresponding reality. Rather, hell is maintained by a state of mind. "Every state of mind, left to itself, every shutting up of the creature within the dungeon of its own mind—is, in the end, Hell."[58] The result is tragic.

> Good beats upon the damned incessantly as sound waves beat on the ears of the deaf, but they cannot receive it. Their fists are clenched, their teeth are clenched, their eyes fast shut. First they will not, in the end they cannot, open their hands for gifts, or their mouths for food, or their eye to see.[59]

Thus, it is fitting to say that "the doors of hell are locked on the *inside*."[60]

53. Lewis, *Problem of Pain*, 124–25.
54. Ibid., 125–26.
55. Lewis, *Great Divorce*, 122.
56. Ibid., 123.
57. Ibid., 69.
58. Ibid.
59. Ibid., 123.
60. Lewis, *Problem of Pain*, 127.

How about heaven? What happens in heaven? In his sermon, "The Weight of Glory," Lewis delineates for us the images of heaven according to the biblical data, which he said "has authority," because "[it] comes to us from writers who were closer to God than we, and it has stood the test of Christian experience down the centuries."[61] He presents "the promises of Scripture" under five headings:

> It is promised (1) that we shall be with Christ; (2) that we shall be like Him; (3) with an enormous wealth of imagery, that we shall have "glory"; (4) that we shall, in some sense, be fed or feasted or entertained; and (5) that we shall have some sort of official position in the universe—ruling cities, judging angels, being pillars of God's temple.[62]

In all, heaven is where we find ourselves to be accepted by God, and that is made possible by the work of Christ. "To please God . . . to be a real ingredient in the divine happiness . . . to be loved by God, not merely pitied, but delighted in as an artist delights in his work or a father in a son—it seems impossible, a weight or burden of glory which our thoughts can hardly sustain. But so it is."[63]

In a memorable scene in *The Great Divorce*, we meet a solid spirit Len who is an ex-murderer. This man, "so jocund, so established in its youthfulness," making others feel like dancing, meets his former boss, now a ghost from hell. The boss is extremely disturbed to find Len in his heavenly state. He asks, "Aren't you ashamed of yourself?" Len answers, "No. Not as you mean. I do not look at myself. I have given up myself." The boss bitterly expresses his anxiety over an unexpected outcome. He believes that he should be in heaven, by his own right, and that Len should be in hell. So the boss grumbles, "But I got to have my rights same as you, see?" Len can only say, "Oh no. It's not so bad as that. I haven't got my right, or I should not be here. You will not get yours either. You'll get something far better." The boss continues, "I only want my rights. I'm not asking for anybody's bleeding charity." Len begs earnestly, "Then do. At once. Ask for the Bleeding Charity. Everything is here for the asking and nothing can be bought."[64] Of course, the ghost can never accept the proposal, because his ego is deeply hurt. He is

---

61. Lewis, "The Weight of Glory," in *Weight of Glory*, 9. Lewis here presented an interesting ground or grounds for biblical authority. One cannot help but feel an arbitrariness in this sense of authority. See the discussion on Lewis's view of Scripture in chapter 5.

62. Ibid., 10.

63. Ibid., 13.

64. Lewis, *Great Divorce*, 32–34.

absorbed in his own sense of decency, and therefore demands what by right he should get in the light of what the murderer got. Having turned away the offer of his ex-employee, the boss goes away half triumphantly. He saves something of his "dignity." The differentiation continues. The antithesis between the ghost and the solid spirit is established not by their respective actions. They are both unacceptable before God, both horribly cruel people in their own rights. But the work of Christ enters in, and the difference is heaven and hell. The unimaginable truth is not that a "decent" fellow can be confined in hell but that a murderer can find God's approval and become an object of his pleasure.

If hell is an endless "journey homeward to habitual self,"[65] heaven is a journey that turns into an endless "dance" and an endless march toward the infinite depth of God's presence. In *The Great Divorce*, the solid spirits continue their journey into the "Deep Heaven," "further and further into the mountains."[66] In *The Last Battle*, the creatures and children travel "further up and further in" into the real Narnia. The real Narnia is "deeper, more wonderful, more like places in a story. . . . The new one was a deeper country: every rock and flower and blade of grass looked as if it meant more."[67] There the Unicorn cried out the words that "summed up what everyone was feeling."

> I have come home at last! This is my real country! I belong here. This is the land I have been looking for all my life, though I never knew it till now. The reason why we loved the old Narnia is that it sometimes looked a little like this. Bree-hee-hee! Come further up, come further in![68]

They all gallop, run, and dance toward the deeper Narnia. "Faster and faster they raced, but no one got hot or tired or out of breath."[69] And there they meet Aslan, who "no longer looked to them like a lion," who declares, "[All] of you are—as you used to call it in the Shadowlands—dead. The term is over: the holidays have begun. The dream is ended: this is the morning."[70] The consummation of the journey has come.

---

65. Lewis, "The Weight of Glory," in *Weight of Glory*, 14. Lewis quoted the phrase from Keats.
66. Lewis, *Great Divorce*, 67, 72.
67. Lewis, *Last Battle*, 213.
68. Ibid.
69. Ibid., 214.
70. Ibid., 228.

THE LAST BATTLE: COSMIC ESCHATOLOGY

Lewis believed not only in personal eschatology but also in cosmic eschatology. The latter, in short, consists of two major catastrophic or "eucatastrophic" (in Tolkien's language) events: the return of Christ and the bodily resurrection of the believers. Lewis did not leave us a great deal of material on cosmic eschatology; nevertheless, there are sufficient suggestions to construct his beliefs. The journey, then, can be seen in two perspectives: the personal and historical. The first deals with each individual's pilgrimage toward the final home; the second deals with the pilgrimage of humanity as a whole.

Lewis on Universalism

The pilgrimage of humanity as a whole does not necessarily entail the notion of universalism, that all humanity will at the end be saved. However, it certainly raises the issue, one which stubbornly recurs in Lewis scholarship. In *The Problem of Pain*, Lewis made a clear statement against universalism:

> Some will not be redeemed. There is no doctrine which I would more willingly remove from Christianity than this, if it lay in my power. But it has the full support of Scripture and, specially, of Our Lord's own words; it has always been held by Christendom; and it has the support of reason.[71]

Lewis, on the other hand, realized that his undisputed mentor, George MacDonald, had held to a form of universalism. The question is raised in *The Great Divorce* when the narrator brings it out to the attention of the guide, MacDonald himself: "In your own books, Sir . . . you were a Universalist. You talked as if all men would be saved." Lewis's MacDonald, instead of asserting his Universalism, answers, "Ye can know nothing of the end of all things, or nothing expressible in those terms."

Lewis, however, argued that human freedom must be guarded against belief in Universalism, for the freedom is the gift whereby we "most resemble [our] Maker and are [ourselves] parts of eternal reality."[72] Freedom, being a deeper truth, cannot be contradicted by Universalism, which itself ironically leaves no room for individual choices. Lewis pointed out that MacDonald's (the real MacDonald) Universalism cannot be reconciled with his own high view of human freedom which should, in theory, leave room

---

71. Lewis, *Problem of Pain*, 118.
72. Lewis, *Great Divorce*, 124–25.

for final individual choices to resist God's grace. Indeed, it was MacDonald himself who stated that God may stand at the door of one's life, but he will never "force any door to enter in.... The door must be opened by the willing hand, ere the foot of Love will cross the threshold."[73] Clearly, Lewis, while holding on to a cosmic eschatology, did not adhere to a Universalist doctrine.

The Resurrection of the Body

Lewis realized that it is not a simple matter to reconcile personal eschatology and cosmic eschatology.

> I believe in the resurrection . . . but the state of the dead *till* the resurrection is unimaginable. Are they in the same *time* that we live in at all? And if not, is there any sense in asking what they are "now"?[74]

Once again, the difficult question of time and eternity impinges here, but Lewis did not feel compelled to address it in relation to the state of the dead and the coming day of resurrection; instead, he offered a serious exposition of the meaning of the bodily resurrection as an eschatological eucatastrophe.

In his chapter, "Miracles of the New Creation" (in *Miracles*), Lewis discusses the eschatological bodily resurrection. To set the stage, and to move from a known fact to what is yet unknown, he first describes the meaning of Christ's bodily resurrection. The biblical data will not allow a one-dimensional interpretation. Jesus's resurrection was indeed a corporeal one, thus having a continuity with the incarnational body; but as a picture of a new human nature, the risen body is "extremely different from the mortal body."[75] The resurrection was an ushering in of a new reality, which turned the tide of "irreversible death and irreversible entropy." Our future resurrection will involve "the reversal process universalised—a rush of matter towards organisation at the call of spirits which require it."[76] However, Lewis thought that we can know very little about "the new nature." For him to imagine it is not to predict or forecast what would really take place, but to "make room for a more complete and circumspect agnosticism," in order

---

73. George MacDonald, *Unspoken Sermons, Second Series,* quoted in Lewis, *George MacDonald: An Anthology*, 49.

74. Lewis, *Letters of C. S. Lewis*, 491.

75. Lewis, *Miracles*, 149.

76. Ibid., 151.

that we may not in rashness limit what actually can take place."[77] Lewis's commitment to radical supernaturalism comes through with an impressive intensity.

Lewis believed that the context of our existence itself will be very different in the coming age. "[A] multi-dimensional space would be different, almost beyond recognition, from the space we are now aware of, yet not discontinuous from it: that time may not always be for us, as it now is, unilinear and irreversible: that other parts of Nature might some day obey us as our cortex now does."[78] The strangeness or the newness of this reality demands the employment of metaphorical language; but at the same time Christ's resurrected body, with its newness yet partial interlocking with the spatiotemporal world, demands of us to embrace "all their literal facthood."[79]

The tension seems difficult to get over because the post-Enlightenment mind is comfortable with the picture of reality as either one story (as Naturalists believe) or two stories (as Kant would have it) consisting of "a ground floor (nature) and then above that one other floor and one only—an eternal, spaceless, timeless, spiritual Something of which we can have no images."[80] Nevertheless, Lewis said that if we are to embrace the new nature, we must be prepared to accept a multi-layered reality, which includes "floors or levels intermediate between the Unconditioned and the world revealed by our present senses."[81] The Christian message presents a complex reality, in which our new nature is being made out of an old one. "We live amid all the anomalies, inconveniences, hopes, and excitements of a house that is being rebuilt."[82]

Therefore, the new "heaven" must include "a life in Christ, a vision of God, a ceaseless adoration," and "a bodily life."[83] We are not looking forward to "some vague dream of Platonic paradises." Instead, we must claim that our current state of feeling, that "body, and locality and locomotion and time" are irrelevant to the highest spiritual life, is a "symptom" and "disease" that needs healing. Our present-day experience of spirit and nature quarreling within us shall be corrected in the new creation. "There will be no room to get the finest razor-blade of thought in between Spirit and Nature."[84] So

77. Ibid., 153.
78. Ibid.
79. Ibid., 154.
80. Ibid.
81. Ibid.
82. Ibid., 155.
83. Ibid., 159.
84. Ibid., 161.

Lewis concludes, "By teaching the resurrection of the body, [Christianity] teaches that Heaven is not merely a state of the spirit but a state of the body as well: and therefore a state of Nature as a whole."[85] The new "heaven" is not just a state of mind but a solid reality to unfold before us.

A more poetic set of expressions is used in the last letter of his *Letters to Malcolm*, where he "guesses" about the future events, first about the "glorified body."

> At present we tend to think of the soul as somehow "inside" the body. But the glorified body of the resurrection as I conceive it—the sensuous life raised from its death—will be inside the soul.[86]

The resurrection of this body must wait until that assigned time which no one knows but the Father. "This part of us sleeps in death," while "the intellectual soul is sent to Lenten lands where she fasts in naked spirituality—a ghost-like and imperfectly human condition." The "nakedness" is in relationship to what is to come, not what we are today. Then, one day,

> the new earth and sky, the same yet not the same as these, will rise in us as we have risen in Christ. And once again, after who knows what aeons of the silence and the dark, the birds will sing and the waters flow, and lights and shadows move across the hills, and the faces of our friends laugh upon us with amazed recognition.[87]

Then, we will have really come home.

The Second Coming of Christ

What did Lewis have to say about the Second Coming of Christ? In his 1952 article, "The World's Last Night," Lewis expressed his thoughts about it very plainly. He began with the premise that the doctrine, regardless of its unpopularity with the modern theologian, cannot be abandoned. "[It] seems to me impossible to retain in any recognizable form our belief in the Divinity of Christ and the truth of the Christian revelation while abandoning, or even persistently neglecting, the promised, and threatened, Return."[88]

---

85. Ibid., 162.
86. Lewis, *Letters to Malcolm*, 122.
87. Ibid., 124.
88. Lewis, "The World's Last Night," in *World's Last Night*, 93.

Lewis identified two grounds, one theoretical and the other practical, on which the doctrine has been rejected by modern thinkers. First, he thought the modern rejection to be a reaction to the apocalyptic school associated mainly with Albert Schweitzer. Reacting against Schweitzer's radically apocalyptic view of Christ, the "gentler theology" tries to do away with Christ's apocalyptic predictions altogether, saying that such remarks must be a result of Christ's inevitable participation in the spirit of his own age. Instead of focusing on such culture-specific symptoms, this reaction wants to highlight "those doctrines which 'transcend' the thought of his own age and are 'for all time.'"[89] Lewis, without using the phrase, "chronological snobbery" in this content, dismisses this assumption as a manifestation of the symptom. For this reaction is basically saying that "the thought of *our* age is correct: for of course by thoughts which transcend the great man's age we really mean thoughts that agree with ours."[90] The doctrine of the Second Coming is suspected because it "is deeply uncongenial to the whole evolutionary or developmental character of modern thought." Lewis observed, "We have been taught to think of the world as something that grows slowly towards perfection, something that 'progresses' or 'evolves.'" On the other hand, the Christian hope of Christ's Second Coming "foretells a sudden, violent end imposed from without."[91] Lewis rejected "the modern concept of Progress or Evolution" as a modern myth without any supporting evidence. He thought that Darwinism, as a biological theorem, has no fundamental connection to the "myth." Lewis observed that historically the "myth" rose prior to the arrival of Darwin's idea of natural selection. He was convinced that "our favorite modern mythology" of progress is sadly misleading. Therefore, the doctrine of Christ's Second Coming should be accepted as "the medicine our condition especially needs."[92]

Nevertheless, the expectation of an imminent Parousia lingers over us as a troublesome problem. Jesus and his disciples really expected an imminent end to their contemporary civilization. Jesus did say, "This generation shall not pass till all these things be done" (Mark 13:30). "And he was wrong,"[93] said Lewis. But he thought that this, "the most embarrassing verse in the Bible," must be read in the light of another verse, which the Gospel writer placed "within fourteen words," as if his business was to tease. "But of that day and that hour knoweth no man, no, not the angels which

---

89. Ibid., 96.
90. Ibid.
91. Ibid., 100–101.
92. Ibid., 106.
93. Ibid., 98.

are in heaven, neither the Son, but the Father" (Mark 13:32). Lewis thus concluded, "The facts, then, are these: that Jesus professed himself (in some sense) ignorant, and within a moment showed that he really was so." Then he added, "To believe in the Incarnation, to believe that he is God, makes it hard to understand how he could be ignorant; but also makes it certain that, if he said he could be ignorant, then ignorant he could really be." [94] It is clearly Lewis's intention to establish that the apparent problem is in the prediction of the time rather than the expectation of the coming itself.

The practical objection to the doctrine of the Second Coming is precisely related to the issue of timing. The doctrine has "led Christians into very great follies." "Apparently many people find it difficult to believe in this great event without trying to guess its date, or even without accepting as a certainty the date that any quack or hysteric offers them."[95] Lewis cautioned that as one believes in the doctrine, one must thoroughly rely upon the clear propositions of Christ's teaching. These are: "(1) That he will certainly return. (2) That we cannot possibly find out when. (3) And that therefore we must always be ready for him."[96] The real point of the doctrine is that we should be in a perpetual condition of readiness. This readiness should not be based on the transitory "crisis-feeling" characterized by fear; rather, "we should always remember, always take it into account," and always realize that "at every moment of every year in our lives Donne's question 'What if this present were the world's last night?' is equally relevant."[97]

Lewis utilized the personal eschatology of "death" as a paradigm for making sense of the cosmic eschatology of the Second Coming. The first is realized for each person, and the latter for the whole human race. Any person, wise in his heart, lives not in fear of death, but remembers "how short, precarious, temporary, and provisional" this life is. In the like manner, a wise civilization, if such even exists, should remember "that the whole life of humanity in this world is also precarious, temporary, provisional."[98]

Does this mean that we should abandon our efforts to build for the future and our posterity who will occupy it? Lewis warns against "frantic administration of panaceas to the world," which employ cruelties and injustices to contemporaries. Instead, Lewis urges on his readers a "quiet life"

---

94. Ibid., 98–99.
95. Ibid., 106.
96. Ibid., 107.
97. Ibid., 109–10.
98. Ibid., 110.

of faithfulness to our vocations, accompanying "sober work for the future, within the limits of ordinary morality and prudence."[99]

Should we be surprised at Lewis's orthodox position on the doctrine of the Second Coming? Not so. This is surely a logical conclusion to Lewis's "mere Christianity." His emphasis on supernaturalism and salvationism demands a fundamental alteration of the present condition of nature. The direction of God's redemptive operation logically leads not only to a personal eschatology but also to a cosmic eschatology. The clearest element of the biblical teaching on this is the return of Christ as the one who shall judge the world. In *Mere Christianity*, Lewis called this an "invasion."

> Christians think He is going to land in force; we do not know when. But we can guess why He is delaying. He wants to give us the chance of joining His side freely. . . . God will invade. . . . When that happens, it is the end of the world. When the author walks on to the stage the play is over.[100]

What is to come is a dramatic end to the reality in which we found comfort for so long. The whole universe will melt away like a dream and something unimaginably different will crash in, "something so beautiful to some of us and so terrible to others that none of us will have any choice left." Why should there be no more choices left?

> For this time it will be God without disguise; something so overwhelming that it will strike either irresistible love or irresistible horror into every creature. It will be too late then to choose your side. There is no use saying you choose to lie down when it has become impossible to stand up. That will not be the time for choosing: it will be the time when we discover which side we really have chosen, whether we realised it before or not.[101]

This last sentence leaves us with several important points to consider.

First, for Lewis, the final judgment is a time when we "discover" what we truly are. It is not necessarily getting a "sentence or award"; rather, it is "the verdict." It will be "infallible judgment" in which "an absolutely correct verdict . . . will be passed on what each of us is." Lewis thought that the pictures of physical catastrophe—"that sign in the clouds, those heavens rolled up like a scroll"—are references to the "naked idea of Judgment."[102] It is like a person trying on different clothes, "trying to judge by artificial light how a

---

99. Ibid., 111.
100. Lewis, *Mere Christianity*, 65–66.
101. Ibid., 66.
102. Lewis, "The World's Last Night," in *World's Last Night*, 112–13.

dress will look by daylight."¹⁰³ In that day, all that we are will be revealed and discovered, and none will be able to cover his or her true identity.

On the other hand, what did Lewis mean by "it will be the time when we discover . . . whether we realised it before or not"? Did he mean that some would never have known that they were in Christ, yet will be counted as "the sheep," "the wheat," "the wise virgins," and "the good fish"?¹⁰⁴ Did Lewis think there are "anonymous Christians" outside the visible Christian community of confessing believers? It is quite clear that he did. He said,

> Is it not frightfully unfair that this new life should be confined to people who have heard of Christ and been able to believe in Him? But the truth is God has not told us what His arrangements about the other people are. We do know that no man can be saved except through Christ; we do not know that only those who know Him can be saved through Him.¹⁰⁵

This could possibly be another instance of Lewis making room "for a more complete and circumspect agnosticism," which he considered to be a healthy approach to theological reasoning.

However, on this point, Lewis offered a more daring imaginative leap. In *The Last Battle*, he introduced a character named Emeth, a young Calormene (a natural enemy to Narnians), who has earnestly searched for Tash (the false deity of the Calormenes) all his life. He says, "For always since I was a boy I have served Tash and my great desire was to know more of him, if it might be, to look upon his face."¹⁰⁶ Emeth, at the end, is saved and is invited into the blessings of the new Narnia. Lewis portrayed Emeth as a virtuous Pagan, who served the truth for its own sake (he is named after the Hebrew word for truth), and as a result served the Lord of the truth without knowing it. Aslan declares, "Son, thou art welcome. . . . Child, all the service thou hast done to Tash, I account as service done to me."¹⁰⁷ Emeth in amazement asks, "Lord, is it the truth . . . that thou and Tash are one?" Aslan answers,

---

103. Ibid., 113.

104. The expressions come from Lewis's own words: "If there is any concept which cannot by any conjuring be removed from the teaching of Our Lord, it is that of the great separation; the sheep and the goats, the broad way and the narrow, the wheat and the tares, the winnowing fan, the wise and foolish virgins, the good fish and the refuse, the door closed on the marriage feast, with some inside and some outside in the dark." Lewis, "The Psalms," in *Christian Reflections*, 123.

105. Lewis, *Mere Christianity*, 65.

106. Lewis, *Last Battle*, 202.

107. Ibid., 205.

It is false. Not because he and I are one, but because we are opposites, I take to me the services which thou hast done to him. For I and he are of such different kinds that no service which is vile can be done to me, and none which is not vile can be done to him. Therefore if any man swear by Tash and keep his oath for the oath's sake, it is by me that he has truly sworn, though he know it not, and it is I who reward him. And if any man do a cruelty in my name, then, though he says the name Aslan, it is Tash whom he serves and by Tash his deed is accepted.[108]

This surprising declaration is still difficult to believe for Emeth, so he utters, "Yet I have been seeking Tash all my days." Aslan responds, "Beloved . . . unless thy desire had been for me thou wouldst not have sought so long and so truly. For all find what they truly seek."[109]

Emeth's tale is a rare exception in the story, but it is nevertheless an expression of Lewis's "circumspect agnosticism" (i.e., leaving room for what may be possible), or rather a positive statement about his hopes for the virtuous Pagans. Lewis's point is grounded on his view that the quality of truth and goodness is objective, that God's law is not an arbitrary command without being firmly grounded in goodness as an objective quality. In *Reflections on the Psalms*, he points out, "He enjoins what is good because it is good, because He is good." From this, he sheds light on the meaning of the name Emeth: "Hence His laws have *emeth* 'truth,' intrinsic validity, rock-bottom reality, being rooted in His own nature, and are therefore as solid as that Nature which He has created."[110] Lewis is convinced that that which is truly good remains good in whatever circumstances and that good will not come to an evil end, for they belong to radically different camps. He obviously did not set himself up as the ultimate judge of the good; the impartial, infallible Judge stands at the door. He will establish truth and righteousness, because He is the Truth and Righteousness.

After the raging of the Last Battle, night falls on Narnia. Aslan stands as the great sifter, and every face must pass by him.

> And all the creatures who looked at Aslan in [fear and hatred] swerved to their right, his left, and disappeared into his huge black shadow. . . . But the others looked in the face of Aslan and loved him, though some of them were very frightened at the same time. And all these came in at the Door, in on Aslan's right.[111]

108. Ibid.
109. Ibid., 205–6.
110. Lewis, *Reflections on the Psalms*, 61.
111. Lewis, *Last Battle*, 193.

Those who come through the door enter into the dawn of a new Narnia. A voice cries out with a great sigh of relief and satisfaction, "I have come home at last! . . . I belong here."[112]

This is Lewis's vision of the final home, but then he reminds us that this is by no means the end. It is the beginning of the great story:

> And for us this is the end of all the stories, and we can most truly say that they all lived happily ever after. But for them it was only the beginning of the real story. All their life in this world and all their adventures in Narnia had only been the cover and the title page: now at last they were beginning Chapter One of the Great Story which no one on earth has read: which goes on forever: in which every chapter is better than the one before.[113]

In fact, the real journey is just beginning.

CONCLUSION

Among the stages of Christian pilgrimage Lewis portrayed, his description of "the final home" turns out to be most biblically based. Ironically, what was considered to be the most imaginative aspect of his theology turns out to include relatively frequent appeals to biblical data. Lewis's picture of the eschaton is not merely speculative. His didactic writings on the topic contain numerous attempts to abide by the relevant biblical teaching. Particularly in his *Miracles*, he seeks to consider all the relevant biblical data he could gather. Even the "embarrassing passages" are not discarded; Lewis effectively dispelled the ghost of Marcion.[114]

But what about Lewis's "circumspect agnosticism"? It is interesting to note that for Lewis the agnosticism does not make him say "I have no clue!" but "Let me suggest some possibilities!" In this sense, it is a proactive agnosticism, a flexing of the imagination in the light of previously held convictions. In terms of "the new nature" of the resurrection body, Lewis is deeply committed to his supernaturalism. In terms of the virtuous Pagan, he highlights the objectivity of goodness. Lewis's idea of the virtuous Pagan is a compromise between Universalism, which he could not tolerate because of his strong view of freedom, and the idea that salvation is limited to self-consciously Christian believers, which Lewis rejected based on his belief in

---

112. Ibid., 213.

113. Ibid., 228.

114. Marcion was an early church heretic who was known for coming up with his own version of New Testament canon based on his own liking.

universal and objective character of goodness (i.e., good is good no matter where you find it). However, it carries significant theological implications, similar to those present in Karl Rahner's idea of "anonymous Christians." The most serious one is this: if it is true that "whoever freely cooperates with the gracious presence of God in the supernatural existential can and will be saved" apart from any special revelation, "why do humans need any special, historical revelation?"[115] Is it simply to make things easier or more accessible? Does this not put a strain on Lewis's otherwise Christocentric (therefore, focused on special redemptive revelation) view of atonement?

However, his "mere Christianity" once again looms clearly before us: Whatever the future holds, our expectation of it should not be conditioned by modern naturalistic bias, which inevitably robs us of the incredible richness of what is to come. The future state of our salvation, as a complete healing of our current imperfect state as pilgrims, will be unimaginably marvelous. Lewis's "mere Christianity," with all its supernaturalism and salvationism, is at the heart of his eschatological vision.

---

115. Grenz and Olson, *20th-Century Theology*, 246.

7

"Mere Christianity"
Concluding Reflections on Lewis's Theology

In the previous chapters, I have laid out Lewis's theology in terms of the paradigm of Christian pilgrimage, trying to underline his recognizable system of thought. At first glance, Lewis's theological writings consist of loosely associated ideas, short of systematic development. This, I think, may be attributed to a few factors. First, he was influenced by diverse schools of thought. We noted from his background that he was extremely well read in various subjects, literary genres, and theological persuasions. He had immediate associations with several impressive thinkers including literary figures and philosophers, many of whom were Christian scholars. The influences they exerted upon his mind were undeniably diverse; and Lewis reflected them in his rather eclectic and perspectival approach to reality. Thus, wise students of Lewis have abandoned any attempt to categorize him strictly into a particular school or movement.

Second, his writings are largely applicational and practical; he tried to address the actual spiritual needs of the people with whom he came into contact through various means, such as his published works, personal letters, or public addresses. In this sense, he was an eminently practical, and even pastoral, Christian teacher.

However, these factors do not necessarily lead us to conclude that Lewis had no unified system which held together his specific articles of faith and even his numerous "tentative" thoughts on Christian theology. As I have contended throughout this work, it is valid to speak of "the theology of C. S. Lewis," discovering that a few unifying themes emerge from his works.

A dominant organizing principle we find in Lewis, from which this work receives its structure, is his view of the Christian life as a journey or a pilgrimage. By weaving his thoughts into this overarching paradigm, Lewis became an outstanding storyteller of spiritual significance, not only as a writer of rational and imaginative literature but as a participant, a fellow pilgrim in the story of life. We have organized Lewis's pilgrimage theology into four stages: "Away from Home," "Homeward Turning," "Home Away from Home," and "The Final Home." As a result, we have been able to present Lewis's theology as a self-contained and comprehensive panoramic vision of Christian life.

Furthermore, the idea expressed as a consistently held outlook in Lewis's vision of this pilgrimage is his "mere Christianity," which he identified as the essence of Christianity. Its "constructive motive" is evangelistic in character: to present what is essential to Christian faith without the baggage of denominational divisions and traditions. In the manner of Richard Baxter, Lewis attempted to bridge the gap between such different denominations and traditions. Its "corrective motive" is apologetic in goal: to confront the post-Christian worldview, whether in theology, philosophy, or popular culture. Lewis's theology, as a contextual theology with a prophetic edge, promotes a transcendental worldview in the decidedly immanentistic (i.e., naturalistic and humanistic) spirit of the age. Lewis's "mere Christianity" is expressed through rational arguments and imaginative discourses.

What is "mere Christianity"? Clarence Francis Dye suggests that Lewis's "mere Christianity" can be "summed up in the great creeds of the Church: the Athanasian Creed, the Nicene Creed, and the Apostles Creed."[1] Then he adds, "But when Lewis speaks about 'mere Christianity' it is obvious that he is speaking about the process of eschatology," since for Lewis "mere Christianity is more than a series of statements of what Christians believe."[2] Dye's definition seems too arbitrary and fluid to contain the prophetic edge in Lewis's message.

Chad Walsh, on the other hand, identifies Lewis's "mere Christianity" as "Classical Christianity," distinguished from "Fundamentalist Christianity" and "Modernist Christianity." Walsh's category of "Classical Christianity" is his own coinage to indicate what he thinks Lewis's "mere Christianity" means. The most important characteristic is its place "in the middle of the Christian tradition," which makes Lewis "an uncompromising defender of the doctrines telescoped into the Creeds, but chary of excessive Bibliolatry."[3] However, Walsh adds, "If occasionally he leans to one side or the other, it

---

1. Dye, "The Evolving Eschaton in C. S. Lewis," 264.
2. Ibid.
3. Walsh, *C. S. Lewis: Apostle to the Skeptics*, 75.

is perhaps more often in a slightly Fundamentalist direction."[4] Ironically, Walsh cannot contain Lewis's thought within the category he has created for him.

We have argued, on the other hand, that Lewis's "mere Christianity" is a historically sensitive or tradition-sensitive formula, expressing the major characteristics of traditionally confessed Christianity as it stands directly against modern or "post-Christian" opinion. Essentially, it is a reconstruction of the twin pillar perspective or worldview, which modern "Christianity-and-water" has rejected, namely, supernaturalism and salvationism. Thus, Lewis's theology is deeply supernaturalistic and redemptocentric as opposed to the naturalistic and ethicocentric religion of his time. His two pillar perspective, as we have seen, is not arbitrarily chosen. In addition to being a corrective to the religious *Sitz im Leben* of his and our time, it corresponds to what traditional theology has maintained as the two pillar doctrines of Scripture, namely God the Creator and God the Redeemer. Evidently, Lewis's "mere Christianity" consists of his irreducible, therefore properly basic, Christian presupposition, which we find expanded at some times more consistently than at others to its corollary points in his various works.

For Lewis, supernaturalism is a term that embraces theism (most plausibly, belief in a personal deity), creationism (that the self-existing being bestowed origin to contingent beings), and the Creator-creature distinction (that there is a fundamental distinction between the two spheres of existence).

In the light of the Lewis corpus, "mere Christianity" contains, in terms of supernaturalism, the following immediate corollaries: (1) That there is a God who is self-existent (who is the "three-personal God"); (2) this God brought all contingent beings into existence; of these, human beings are made to be free as well as contingent; (3) there is a fundamental distinction between the Creator's sphere of existence and the creaturely sphere of existence; (4) the created reality reflects and is patterned after the Creator (thus, the *telos* of creation); and (5) therefore, there exist certain objective values that are not manufactured from within the creaturely sphere of existence.

On the other hand, Lewis's "mere Christianity" contains, in terms of salvationism, at least the following immediate corollaries: (1) Humanity as we know it suffers from a radical problem, making it impossible to exist according to the *telos* (purpose and meaning) of the creation designed by the *personal* Creator; (2) humanity has no self-contained solution; therefore, the solution must come from without (the Creator himself), and it must be

---

4. Ibid.

just as radical as the problem itself; (3) the solution must involve putting things right according to the *telos* (a new humanity); (4) the solution has been offered in Christ (through the mystery of incarnation, the climactic fulfillment of the Christian vision of supernaturalism and salvationism) and "salvation" (or the *telic* existence) is granted to those who accept the solution; and (5) there exists a state of antithesis between the saved and unsaved, which will be fully realized with the consummation of *telic* existence (the full realization of the salvation). These propositions form a summary of Lewis's theology. They are essential to his understanding of Christianity. As further corollaries to these assertions, there are additional ideas many of which Lewis held to be "tentative" or "provisional."

The setting forth of specific articles of faith may seem somewhat against the literary spirit of Lewis; but, as we have contended, Lewis himself clearly desired to put forth specific "content" or "teaching." Theological abstractions have a tendency to undercut the "mythical" and "metaphorical" power that is important for Lewis, the storyteller. Nevertheless, theology as a descriptive discipline is not dismissed by Lewis, but rather is an important aspect of his theological endeavor. He reminds us, however, that descriptive work is necessarily perspectival, because the "reality" is greater than the descriptions of it. At the same time, it is the objectivity of that "reality" which constitutes the condition for a meaningful quest for descriptive "truths." For Lewis, theology is "the systematic series of statements about God and about man's relation to Him which the believers of a religion make."[5] It is like a map of the Atlantic Ocean.

> The map is admittedly only coloured paper, but there are two things you have to remember about it. In the first place, it is based on what hundreds and thousands of people have found out by sailing the real Atlantic. In that way it has behind it masses of experiences just as real as the one you could have from the beach; only, while yours would be a single isolated glimpse, the map fits all those different experiences together. In the second place, if you want to go anywhere, the map is absolutely necessary. As long as you are content with walks on the beach, your own glimpses are far more fun than looking at a map. But the map is going to be of more use than walks on the beach if you want to get to America.[6]

---

5. Lewis, "Is Theology Poetry?," in *Weight of Glory*, 74.
6. Lewis, *Mere Christianity*, 135–36.

The map would be useless if there were no Atlantic; but if we indeed have the Atlantic to cross, the map is an essential companion. Theological abstraction, for Lewis, is necessary and helpful in its proper place.

EVALUATION

To bring our study to conclusion, we must put Lewis's theology in perspective. We have already mentioned his wide popularity as a communicator of the Christian message. From a pragmatic point of view, Lewis's theology (both in "manner" and in "matter"), as a project, is a huge success. Many have been directed to Christian faith through his books. His words are effective instruments through which the gospel reached his audience. His literary instruments are generally attractive and, therefore, well-received; often readers are deeply moved by Lewis's words. His presentation of "mere Christianity" is often intellectually and emotionally attractive. His novels are powerful reiterations of the gospel: children (and adults alike), even without an understanding of the literary significance of myth or metaphor, come away from his *Narnia Chronicles* with a deep sense of good and evil, awe and terror, happiness and sorrow. As a result, they encounter the Christian view of reality.

However, we must go beyond the pragmatic results of Lewis's theology and evaluate it in terms of the soundness of its intent, its theological contribution, and of the clarity and cogency of its internal logic. First, we point out some positive aspects.

(1) As we have seen already, Lewis's motive for highlighting "mere Christianity" was two-fold: constructive and corrective. His motive points to the necessary course of theological endeavor; that is, making of proactive statements in order to teach the Christian message (the didactic, evangelistic purpose) and of reactive statements in order to defend the integrity of the Christian message from various non-Christian and pseudo-Christian elements (the corrective, apologetic purpose). In order to teach and defend, theological abstraction is a necessary enterprise. Lewis's theology of supernaturalism and salvationism should be understood in this sense. Particularly as a corrective measure, his "mere Christianity" developed in the light of a sense of contemporary urgency in which he sought to crystallize the essential meaning of Christianity.

Paul's crystallization of the Christian message in Corinth was "Christ crucified." "For I resolved to know nothing while I was with you except Jesus Christ and him crucified."[7] He preached this message when the Jews de-

---

7. 1 Cor 2:2 (NIV).

manded miraculous signs and the Greeks sought after wisdom. The Apostle John, warning against the appearance of false teachers or "antichrists," presented as his crystallized message the fact that Jesus Christ came "in the flesh."[8] Similarly, Lewis's "mere Christianity" seemed very radical in the spirit of his time. His Christianity challenged the spiritual laxity, doctrinal complacency, and scholastic irrelevance of the Western church. "Mere Christianity" was a *skandalon* to them. But to those who would believe, it was *evangelium*. Two great wars had swept through Europe and the world. Disillusionment and resentment had settled in the culture. Stability, once taken for granted, could no longer be expected. Lewis truly believed that the world needed to take a fresh look at Christianity. The heart of the Father called everyone to take a new look at the journey of life. The restless wandering must be turned into a homeward journey. He was compelled to proclaim, and as he did, he made a difference.

(2) Lewis's pilgrimage motif served his theological purpose well. It is not employed merely as a poetic device, nor as an expression of the "broadly romantic" theme of journey. In fact, the view of life as a pilgrimage has a deeply theological starting point and various implications. It grows out of Lewis's supernaturalistic and salvationistic worldview, which caused him to conclude that humanity's present inhabitancy in the world is a sojourn in an alien land. "We are not derived from [the universe]. We are strangers here. We come from somewhere else. Nature is not the only thing that exists. There is 'another world,' and that is where we come from."[9] Therefore, we do not "feel at home here," and "we have cause to be uneasy."[10] We find this incorporation of "theological psychology" to be one of Lewis's major apologetic accomplishments. In contrast to the traditional theistic arguments of natural theology, Lewis's arguments (from nature, Joy, *Tao*, the history of Israel, and Pagan redemption myths) capitalize on the state of tension inherent in each theistic pointer, as we have seen in chapter 4. Nature is not only orderly and delightful but dangerous and dreadful; one experiences Joy as both pleasure and sorrow; *Tao* reminds one of the sense of both obligation and inability; and both the history of Israel and Pagan redemption myths are incomplete in themselves. The resulting sense of alienation and incompleteness, when apprehended correctly, sets the stage for the gospel of Jesus Christ. The restless heart finds its proper object of desire in the loving Creator manifested in the incarnate Son. The consummation of salvation will bring us to the final home, when the pilgrims will cry out with a deeply

---

8. 2 John 7.
9. Lewis, "On Living in an Atomic Age," in *Present Concerns*, 78.
10. Lewis, *Mere Christianity*, 36.

felt satisfaction, "I have come home at last! . . . I belong here."[11] Lewis's insight into the tension inherent in the present life is an important theological and apologetic discovery.

However, we must go on to point out some problems. (1) An important issue we must address is the notion of epistemic justification. How did Lewis justify his truth claims? What normative control did he employ?

Lewis seems to have operated with his own multi-perspectival formula. In his article, "Religion: Reality or Substitute?" he argues that knowledge comes through three avenues: "Authority, reason, experience; on these three, mixed in varying proportions all our knowledge depends." About his assurance of the truth of Christianity, he writes,

> The authority of many wise men in many different times and places forbids me to regard the spiritual world as an illusion. My reason, showing me the apparently insoluble difficulties of materialism and proving that the hypothesis of a spiritual world covers far more of the facts with far fewer assumptions, forbids me again. My experience even of such feeble attempts as I have made to live the spiritual life does not lead to the results which the pursuit of an illusion ordinarily leads to, and therefore forbids me yet again.[12]

Here we have a tri-perspectival approach to epistemic justification.

Lewis's view of *authority* resembles the medieval notion that attributes authoritative status to the learned tradition both in the history of church and to the great philosophers of the ancient times. A certain construct of theological knowledge seems to be validated by the shared claims found in the historical and religious consensus. It is in this category Lewis placed the witness of Scripture as well. He stated that "the promises of Scripture" have authority because "[it] comes to us from writers who were closer to God than we, and it has stood the test of Christian experience down the centuries."[13] By attributing the authority of Scripture (as distinguished from the Word of God) to the consensus of "spiritually advanced" individuals who composed it, he underestimates the transcendental significance of Scripture.

Furthermore, Lewis asserts that Scripture does not have a unique status as an *inspired* revelation of God. "If every good and perfect gift comes from the Father of Lights then all true and edifying writings, whether in

---

11. Lewis, *Last Battle*, 193, 213.
12. Lewis, "Religion: Reality or Substitute?" in *Christian Reflections*, 41.
13. Lewis, "The Weight of Glory," in *Weight of Glory*, 10.

scripture or not, must be *in some sense* inspired."[14] Scripture, in its constitutive parts, is not uniformly inspired, but "the over-all operation of Scripture is to convey God's Word to the reader ... who reads it in the right spirit."[15] Lewis's view of inspiration seems to lose its focus of the theological meaning as the "God-breathed" (2 Tim 3:16) testimony which is therefore authoritative and truthful. Properly understood, the focus of the doctrine of biblical inspiration is on the process of inscripturation, which makes it trust-worthy rather than on the character of each statement. Lewis seems to have misunderstood the meaning of biblical inspiration. For example, he contrasted Paul's words in 1 Cor 7, "Not I, but the Lord" (v. 10) and "I speak, not the Lord" (v. 12), and concluded that these two statements represent different "modes" or "degrees" of inspiration. The doctrine of inspiration, however, teaches that both statements are equally inspired, therefore trustworthy and reliable in terms of what they actually say, and because of their different meanings they must be applied to the readers differently: the first as absolute divine commandment, and the latter as an apostolic recommendation. Unfortunately, Lewis's insufficient view of Scripture decisively weakens the basis for his epistemic authority.

Lewis's view of *reason*, on the other hand, leads us to the heart of his epistemology. He held quite consistently that there is a connection between reason and reality according to what he called "a kind of psycho-physical parallelism (or more) in the universe," which makes all discourse about reality possible and meaningful.[16] This coordinate of reason and reality is instituted by the ultimate reality, the Creator himself. This also means that our reason is valid because it reflects[17] God's reason, which is behind the whole universe and all universal phenomena. Lewis argued that human reason is valid because it originated from a Designer, and not from natural selection. The inherent problem of naturalism is that it cannot establish the validity of reason. If reason originated from an irrational source, then reason cannot be trusted. "No more theology, no more ontology, no more metaphys-

---

14. Lewis, *Letters of C. S. Lewis*, 480.

15. Ibid.

16. Lewis, "Bluspels and Flalansferes: A Semantic Nightmare," in *Selected Literary Essays*, 265.

17. Lewis earlier came to embrace much of Barfield's thought and actually affirmed that "mind was no late-come epiphenomenon: that the whole universe was, in the last resort, mental; that our logic was participation in a cosmic *Logos*." Lewis, *Surprised by Joy*, 209. However, with his conversion to Christianity, he developed a greater sense of the Creator-creature distinction. Nevertheless, he continued to stress a high degree of continuity between human reason and God's reason: "I think that in creating rational creatures God created things which *qua* rational are like himself." Bodleian Library, ms. facs. c. 53, Letters of C. S. Lewis, 194. Cited in Newell, "Participatory Knowledge," 185.

ics. . . . But then, equally, no more Naturalism" as a speculative science.[18] In this sense, Lewis's high view of reason is based upon his supernaturalistic worldview.

Lewis's view of *experience* highlights the reverse side (from that of reason) of Lewis's epistemology. He stressed the importance of experimental and relational knowledge in distinction from analytical, abstract knowledge. Particularly in his discussion of faith, Lewis stressed the distinction between faith as assent and as trust. The latter involves the dynamics of relational knowledge of God. God, being a person rather than a concept, establishes his relationship with us. To know God as a person, or to be known by God, is what sets Christian faith apart from other forms of knowing or believing. This quality of knowing appeals to the function of imagination more than to that of reason, although they are not mutually exclusive. Just as at one point Lewis called himself a "rationalist," he also declared, "I am an empirical Theist," because he arrived at his faith of God by reflecting upon "a particular recurrent experience."[19]

Unfortunately, these avenues of knowledge, as Lewis described, do not provide infallible ground for theological construction. Religious consensus, reason, and experience separately do not constitute objective ground for truth; collectively, they probably increase the degree of reliability but do not establish objective certainty. For instance, Lewis's claim for absolute moral standard, or *Tao*, is based on his understanding of Christian and other historical and intellectual traditions as well as the perception of the collective consciousness of humanity (consensus-based authority). It is supported by his rational argument for the rightful recognition of its objective existence contrary to subjectivistic view of aesthetic and ethical values (reason). And his claim is based on the assumption that people, including Lewis himself, have in fact experienced the internal sense of moral obligation (experience). However, this combined knowledge is insufficient for

---

18. Lewis, *Miracles*, 22. The citation originates from the chapter, "The Cardinal Difficulty of Naturalism," initially entitled, "The Self-Contradiction of the Naturalist." The famous philosophical debate between Lewis and G. E. M. Anscombe is behind the revision of the title and the last several pages of the chapter. However, contrary to what is often assumed, Anscombe's argument did not destroy Lewis's argument against naturalism, that it cannot account for rationality of human reason and thus is unable to establish the rationality of its own theory. As a philosopher of language, Anscombe pointed out that Lewis insufficiently dealt with the distinction between "irrational causes" and "non-rational causes" and confused certain key concepts such as cause, reason, and so on. An illuminating discussion of the debate can be found in Mitchell, "C. S. Lewis and the Oxford University Socratic Club," in *Lightbearer in the Shadowlands*, 341–46.

19. Green and Hooper, *C. S. Lewis: A Biography*, 113. He was obviously referring to the quality of experience called "Joy."

pointing to the transcendental character of the absolute moral law. Instead, in the final analysis it is immanentistic in that it appeals to merely historical, philosophical, and psychological considerations. Lewis's argument for objective reality is founded on collective subjectivity and thus falls short of determining its transcendental existence. The same criticism can apply to Lewis's notions of Joy and Myths.

In sum, what turns out to be Lewis's most serious problem is the lack of transcendental normativity (or an absolute standard) in his system, which is mainly due to his tentative view of Scripture. This problem fundamentally hinders his otherwise transcendental (thus, prophetic) theological vision, resulting in an immanentistic tendency, which ironically is the heart of the problem Lewis sought to challenge in the modern or post-Christian worldview.

(2) On the other hand, Lewis appeals to the revelatory significance of Christ's incarnation as a climactic justification for the transcendental meaning of the theistic pointers. In him, there is the immanence of the transcendental reality of righteousness (fulfilling *Tao*), delight (fulfilling Joy), and redemption (fulfilling Myths). According to Lewis's view of "Myth Became Fact," in Jesus Christ both myth and history converge in a perfect union, and the marriage of imagination and reason takes place. Redemption myths find their anchor in him because the stories of dying and rising gods were fulfilled in Jesus Christ.

However, in the appearance of Emeth in *The Last Battle*, who was vindicated and saved by his wholehearted pursuit of truth and goodness, Lewis's immanentistic category reappears. In his assertion, "[God's] laws have *emeth* 'truth', intrinsic validity, rock-bottom reality, being rooted in His own Nature, and are therefore as solid as that Nature which He has created,"[20] he has bypassed Christ to appeal directly to the self-evident truth inherently apprehended by "natural man." The Christian teaching of God revealing his righteousness in Christ has been reversed in Lewis's thought: Christ is subordinate to the objective reality of truth and righteousness. One may find them in Christ or elsewhere. Although Christ is God himself as Lewis argued, he becomes merely a pointer to, rather than being the author and perfector of, goodness and truth. Lewis's Christocentric view of Christianity ("Myth Became Fact") suffers a setback.

One may argue that the "virtuous Pagans" idea does not mean "bypassing Christ," because it is assumed that ultimately they are saved in and through Christ. However, this still does not resolve the tension adequately because the idea of revelation (which literally means being *revealed* so that

---

20. Lewis, *Reflections on the Psalms*, 61.

the subject can see), then, becomes arbitrary. In this sense, the salvific effect of the special *revelation* of God in Christ stands radically set apart from one's subjective apprehension of it. But, "How, then, can they call on the one they have not believed in? And how can they believe in the one of whom they have not heard?"[21]

At this point, one may be tempted to interpret Lewis's story of Emeth as an assertion that we are saved by being known by Christ and not necessarily by knowing him.[22] That being the case, salvation originates from an outside source, radically by the saving grace of God. Is this what Lewis means when he writes, "[Aslan] answered, Child, all the service thou hast done to Tash, I account as service done to me"?[23] Not at all! In fact, he points us in the opposite direction. The emphasis is on the subjective "desiring" rather than being desired by God. "Beloved, said the Glorious One, unless thy desire had been for me thou wouldst not have sought so long and so truly. For all find what they truly seek."[24] It is the quality of desiring (i.e., desiring *truly*) that occasions Emeth's salvation, although it is Aslan who grants the salvation. In the same way, "Therefore if any man swear by Tash and keep his oath for the oath's sake, it is by me that he has *truly* sworn, though he know not, and it is I who reward him."[25] In light of Lewis's immanentistic view of salvation expressed here, the danger of making *Christ-revelation* arbitrary still lingers.

As Lewis pointed out, reality is greater than our description of it. However, our theology cannot be left to speculation, imagination or fervency of the heart, because, as he said, "[only] God Himself can let the bucket down to the depths of us" and let himself be known as who he is. Otherwise, our efforts end up with creating God in our own image. "He must constantly work as the iconoclast. Every idea of Him we form, He must in mercy shatter."[26] If so, should not Lewis find revelational theology (in contrast to speculative or experimental theology) absolutely essential, particularly that which depends on the special revelation? Lewis could have strengthened his arguments by acknowledging that theology should focus on the objective embodiment of God's truth in the Word and the person of God in Christ.

---

21. Rom 10:14 (NIV).

22. In the view of some, even such a classical reformed statement as the *Westminster Confession of Faith* expresses a "larger hope." "Elect infants, dying in infancy, are regenerated, and saved by Christ, through the Spirit, who worketh when, and where, and how He pleaseth: so also are all other elect persons who are uncapable of being outwardly called by the ministry of the Word" (10:3). Shedd, *Calvinism Pure and Mixed*, 116–31.

23. Lewis, *Last Battle*, 205.

24. Ibid., 205–6.

25. Ibid., 205 (emphasis mine).

26. Lewis, *Letters to Malcolm*, 82.

(3) However, at times Lewis affirmed the priority of revelation over speculation. For instance,

> The Church claims to be the bearer of a revelation. . . . If it is true, then we should expect to find in the Church an element which unbelievers will call irrational and which believers will call supra-rational. . . . If we abandon that, if we retain only what can be justified by standards of prudence and convenience at the bar of enlightened common sense, then we exchange revelation for that old wraith Natural Religion.[27]

Lewis opposes revelational religion to natural religion. This is consistent with his supernaturalism. However, because of his *sacramental* view of reality (corresponding to his principle of "transposition") we are often faced with a confusing picture of what revelation means. By sacramental view, we refer to a perception of the created reality as a lower medium (sign), which is taken up by a higher medium (reality), thereby achieving sacramental representation. For example, according to Lewis's "transpositional view," the bread and wine of the Lord's Supper sacramentally represent the broken body and the shed blood of Christ. The lower media remaining what they are in material are taken up to represent the higher reality.[28]

The sacramental view, therefore, requires that the lower medium must contain within it a paradoxical character: While remaining a lower medium, it must represent the higher reality in a very *real* way. For example, nature as God's revelation manifests this character.

> To say that God created Nature, while it brings God and Nature into relation, also separates them. What makes and what is made must be two, not one. Thus, the doctrine of Creation in one sense empties Nature of divinity. . . . But in another sense the same doctrine which empties Nature of her divinity also makes her an index, a symbol, a manifestation, of the Divine.[29]

---

27. Lewis, "Priestesses in the Church?," in *God in the Dock*, 238.

28. This view is not identical to "Transubstantiation." However, the strong emphasis on the continuity between the sign and the reality (as we have seen in chapter 6, the relationship is less symbolic than mythic) definitely departs from the position of Lewis's own church. The Thirty-nine Articles clearly denounce "Transubstantiation," but highlight the role of faith saying, "The Body of Christ is given, taken, and eaten, in the Supper, only after an heavenly and spiritual manner. And the mean whereby the Body of Christ is received and eaten in the Supper, is Faith" (article 28). *The Book of Common Prayer*, 873.

29. Lewis, *Reflections on the Psalms*, 80–81.

Nature in the natural sense, then, is open to naturalistic scrutiny. Lewis did not object to the Darwinian theory of biological evolution. But regarding the sacramental sense of nature, naturalistic scrutiny becomes meaningless, like looking for a poem by examining the quality of the print and the paper.

The same principle applies to Lewis's view of Scripture as a "taking up of a literature to be the vehicle of God's word."[30] As a lower medium, it consists of human literature, manifesting "naivety, error, contradiction, even . . . wickedness."[31] But taken up, it carries the Word of God. This subject was discussed in some length in chapter 6. The same principle also applies to his view of incarnation: "in it human life becomes the vehicle of Divine life."[32] But "because the lower nature, in being taken up and loaded with a new burden and advanced to a new privilege, remains . . . men can read the life of Our Lord (because it is a human life) as nothing but a human life."[33]

Lewis's sacramental view gives support to his supernaturalism in so far as it describes the dynamics of the coexistence of natural and supernatural as a coherent whole. However, it contributes to his tendency to divide the reality into the lower and the higher, and to even expose the lower to the free reign of non-Christian systems of thought. Regarding his view of biological nature and religious development, Lewis opened himself to the theory of evolutionism. His developmental view of religion seems to fit poorly with his severe criticism of evolutionism as a social theory, namely what he called the "myth" of progress or developmental view of history. Nevertheless, he freely incorporated the notions of evolutionary development of humanity and that of human religious consciousness to analyze the lower medium.

In another instance, Lewis divides faith into two spheres: Faith-1 as assent and Faith-2 as trust. Faith-1, according to Lewis, is open to empirical or naturalistic analysis and can be falsified. However, Faith-2, as a personal trust of the living being, demonstrates the "power of continuing to believe," that is the "obstinacy of belief." In one sphere, Lewis acknowledges the validity of non-Christian systems of thought. In another, he highlights the internal consistency of Christian presuppositional stance. Therefore, Christianity becomes compartmentalized, the very possibility Lewis abhorred,[34] by losing its holistic claim on reality.

30. Ibid., 116.
31. Ibid., 111.
32. Ibid., 116.
33. Ibid.
34. As we have seen in chapter 4, Lewis preached a holistic Christianity in which Christ demands of us a total surrender. "Give me All. . . . No half-measures are any good." Lewis, *Mere Christianity*, 167.

(4) Finally, Lewis's view of salvation and redemption as a radical departure from the naturalistic improvement has been highlighted as a major contribution of his theology. As an advocate of a non-introspective (i.e., opposed to emotionalism), non-revivalistic (i.e., opposed to decisionism), non-developmental (i.e., opposed to intellectualism or moralism) view of salvation, Lewis's "mere Christianity" emerged as a necessary corrective to the religion conditioned by modern culture.

However, in relation to his exalted view of human freedom, his view of salvation reveals a humanistic tendency in which the outcome of salvation depends ultimately on the individual's "seeking" and "choosing," and God, in turn, *must* respond to those who freely *choose* to earnestly *seek* him. Even a natural man may earnestly seek truth and be rewarded for the effort (as we have seen in the case of Emeth). While stating repeatedly that the reconciling of human free will and God's sovereignty is "indiscussible" and "insoluble,"[35] Lewis consistently describes God's providence as that which is contingent to human free acts. In this sense, Lewis constantly placed a greater accent on human volition, despite the fact that he was compelled to acknowledge God's sovereignty as clear biblical teaching.

In the final analysis, however, Lewis does not appear to be an "amateur theologian," as he liked to call himself. He had a vast amount of knowledge that he expressed in many avenues of communication. He was a theologian who struggled in his own way to proclaim "mere Christianity" to the post-Christian world in which he found himself. As a lay-person, he successfully served God's call as a Christian author-teacher. He took seriously the work of Christ being done in his own life and was not shy to express it. Although we have traced some deficiencies in his theological formulations, he truly was a Christian intellectual of our century whose impact is likely to last, most of all because he chose to be honest rather than fashionable.[36] We all have much to learn from this don whose ambition was to lead a "quiet" yet "passionate" life for God.

---

35. Lewis, *Letters of C. S. Lewis*, 426.

36. When asked about John Robinson's controversial new book, *Honest to God*, Lewis applied, "I prefer being honest to being 'honest to God.'" Lewis, "Cross-Examination," in *God in the Dock*, 260.

Selected Bibliography

Abrams, M. H., et al., ed. *The Norton Anthology of English Literature*. 3d ed. New York: Norton, 1975.
Adey, Lionel. *C. S. Lewis: Writer, Dreamer, and Mentor*. Grand Rapids: Eerdmans, 1998.
———. *C. S. Lewis's "Great War" with Owen Barfield*. English Literary Studies Monograph Series 14. Victoria, BC: University of Victoria Press, 1978.
Aeschliman, Michael D. *The Restitution of Man: C. S. Lewis and the Case Against Scientism*. Grand Rapids: Eerdmans, 1983.
Anscombe, G. E. M. "Introduction." In *Metaphysics and the Philosophy of Mind*, vii–x The Collected Philosophical Papers of G. E. M. Anscombe 2. Minneapolis: University of Minnesota Press, 1981.
———. "A Reply to Mr. C. S. Lewis's Argument that Naturalism is Self-Refuting." In *Metaphysics and the Philosophy of Mind*, 224–32. The Collected Philosophical Papers of G. E. M. Anscombe 2. Minneapolis: University of Minnesota Press, 1981.
Arnott, Anne. *The Secret Country of C. S. Lewis*. Grand Rapids: Eerdmans, 1975.
Attwater, Donald, ed. *Modern Christian Revolutionaries: An Introduction to the Lives and Thought of Kierkegaard, Eric Gill, G. K. Chesterton, C. F. Andrews, Berdyaev*. New York: Devin-Adair, 1947.
Baggett, David J., Gary R. Habermas, and Jerry L. Walls, eds. *C. S. Lewis as Philosopher: Truth, Goodness and Beauty*. Downers Grove, IL: InterVarsity, 2008.
Barfield, Owen. *Poetic Diction: A Study in Meaning*. Middletown, CT: Wesleyan University Press, 1977.
Barfield, Owen, et al. *Light on C. S. Lewis*. Edited by Jocelyn Gibb. New York: Harcourt Brace, 1965.
Barkman, Adam. *C. S. Lewis and Philosophy as a Way of Life: A Comprehensive Historical Examination of His Philosophical Thoughts*. Cheshire, CT: Zossima, 2009.
Barrett, Helen M. *Boethius: Some Aspects of His Times and Work*. Cambridge: Cambridge University Press, 1940.
Bassham, Gregory, and Jerry L. Walls, eds. *The Chronicles of Narnia and Philosophy: The Lion, Witch, and the Worldview*. Popular Culture and Philosophy 15. Chicago: Carus, 2005.
Beach, Charles Franklyn. "Pilgrimage Patterns in George MacDonald's *Lilith* and Charles Williams' *Descent Into Hell*." Ph.D. diss., Baylor University, 1995.

Berkhof, Louis. *Manual of Reformed Doctrine*. Grand Rapids: Eerdmans, 1933.
Beversluis, John. *C. S. Lewis and the Search for Rational Religion*. Grand Rapids: Eerdmans, 1985.
Boethius. *The Theological Tractates, The Consolation of Philosophy*. London: Heinemann, 1918.
The Book of Common Prayer. New York: Seabury, 1979.
Boss, Edgar William. "The Theology of C. S. Lewis." Th.D. diss., Northern Baptist Theological Seminary, 1948.
Bramlett, Perry C. *C. S. Lewis: Life at the Center*. Macon, GA: Peake Road, 1996.
Brown, Colin, ed. *History, Criticism and Faith: Four Exploratory Studies*. Leicester: InterVarsity, 1976.
Bultmann, Rudolph. *New Testament and Mythology and Other Basic Writings*. Edited and translated by Schubert M. Ogden. Philadelphia: Fortress, 1984.
Burson, Scott R., and Jerry L. Walls. *C. S. Lewis and Francis Schaeffer: Lessons for a New Century from the Most Influential Apologists of Our Time*. Downers Grove, IL: InterVarsity, 1998.
Carnell, Corbin Scott. *Bright Shadow of Reality: C. S. Lewis and the Feeling Intellect*. Grand Rapids: Eerdmans, 1974.
———. "The Dialect: C. S. Lewis's Interpretations of *Sehnsucht*." Ph.D. diss., University of Florida, 1960.
Carpenter, Humphrey. *The Inklings: C. S. Lewis, J. R. R. Tolkien, Charles Williams, and Their Friends*. Boston: Houghton Mifflin, 1979.
Cavaliero, Glen. *Charles Williams: Poet of Theology*. Grand Rapids: Eerdmans, 1983.
Chadwick, Henry. *Boethius: The Consolations of Music, Logic, Theology, and Philosophy*. Oxford: Clarendon, 1981.
Chesterton, G. K. *The Everlasting Man*. San Francisco: Ignatius, 1993.
Chittenden-Bascom, Cathleen. "Expressions of Religious Experience in the Fiction of C. S. Lewis." MA thesis, University of Exeter, 1990.
Christensen, Michael J. *C. S. Lewis on Scripture: His Thoughts on the Nature of Biblical Inspiration, the Role of Revelation, and the Question of Inerrancy*. Waco, TX: Word Books, 1979.
Christopher, Joe R. *C. S. Lewis*. Boston: Twayne, 1987.
Christopher, Joe R., and Joan K. Ostling, eds. *C. S. Lewis: An Annotated Checklist of Writings About Him and His Works*. The Serif Series: Bibliographies and Checklists 30. Kent: Kent State University Press, 1973.
Clark, David G. *C. S. Lewis: A Guide to His Theology*. Malden, MA: Blackwell, 2007.
Clasper, Paul. "C. S. Lewis's Contribution to a 'Missionary Theology': An Asian Perspective." *CSL: The Bulletin of the New York C. S. Lewis Society* 12 (July 1981) 1–6.
Clowney, Edmund P. "Review of *The Abolition of Man*." *Westminster Theological Journal* 10 (November 1947) 79–81.
Cohen, John Arthur. "An Examination of Four Key Motifs Found in High Fantasy for Children." Ph.D. diss., Ohio State University, 1975.
Cole, Graham A. "C. S. Lewis: An Evangelical Appreciation." *Reformed Theological Review* 53 (September–December 1994) 101–14.
Como, James T., ed. *C. S. Lewis at the Breakfast Table and Other Reminiscences*. New ed. San Diego: Harvest, 1992.

Cunningham, Richard Bryan. "The Christian Apologetic of C. S. Lewis." Th.D. diss., Southern Baptist Theological Seminary, 1965.
———. *C. S. Lewis: Defender of the Faith.* Philadelphia: Westminster, 1967.
Dale, Alzina Stone. *The Outline of Sanity: A Biography of G. K. Chesterton.* Grand Rapids: Eerdmans, 1982.
"Don v. Devil." *Time,* September 8, 1947, 65–74.
Donaldson, Mara E. *Holy Places Are Dark Places: C. S. Lewis and Paul Ricoeur on Narrative Transformation.* Lanham, MD: University Press of America, 1988.
Dorsett, Lyle W. *And God Came In.* New York: Macmillan, 1983.
Downing, David C. *Into the Region of Awe: Mysticism in C. S. Lewis.* Downers Grove, IL: InterVarsity, 2005.
———. *The Most Reluctant Convert: C. S. Lewis's Journey to Faith.* Downers Grove, IL: InterVarsity, 2002.
———. *Planets in Peril: A Critical Study of C. S. Lewis's Ransom Trilogy.* Amherst: University of Massachusetts Press, 1992.
Duriez, Colin. *The C. S. Lewis Handbook.* Grand Rapids: Baker Books, 1990.
Dye, Clarence F. "The Evolving Eschaton in C. S. Lewis." Ph.D. diss., Fordham University, 1973.
Edwards, Bruce L., ed. *C. S. Lewis: Life, Works, and Legacy.* 4 vols. Westport, CT: Praeger, 2007.
———. *The Taste of the Pineapple: Essays on C. S. Lewis as Reader, Critic, and Imaginative Writer.* Bowling Green, OH: Bowling Green State University Popular Press, 1988.
Fey, Howard E., ed. *The Christian Century,* June 6, 1962.
Ffinch, Michael. *G. K. Chesterton.* San Francisco: Harper and Row, 1986.
Fitzpatrick, John F. "From Fact to Fantasy: A Story of C. S. Lewis's Use of Myth." MA thesis, City College of the City University of New York, 1972.
Flew, Anthony. *The Presumption of Atheism, and Other Philosophical Essays on God, Freedom, and Immortality.* London: Pemberton, 1976.
Flew, Anthony, and Alasdair MacIntyre, eds. *New Essays in Philosophical Theology.* London: SCM, 1955.
Ford, Paul F. *Companion to Narnia.* San Francisco: Harper and Row, 1983.
———. "C. S. Lewis, Ecumenical Spiritual Director: A Study of His Experience and Theology of Prayer and Discernment in the Process of Becoming a Self." Ph.D. diss., Fuller Theological Seminary, 1987.
———. "The Life of the World to Come in the Writings of C. S. Lewis." MA thesis, St. John's College, 1974.
Frame, John M. *Apologetics: A Justification of Christian Belief.* Phillipsburg, NJ: P & R, 2015.
———. *The Doctrine of the Knowledge of God.* Phillipsburg, NJ: P & R, 1987.
———. *A History of Western Philosophy and Theology: Spiritual Warfare in the Life of the Mind.* Phillipsburg, NJ: P & R, 2015.
Freshwater, Mark Edwards. "C. S. Lewis and the Quest for the Historical Jesus." Ph.D. diss., Florida State University, 1985.
———. *C. S. Lewis and the Truth of Myth.* Lanham, MD: University Press of America, 1988.
Friesen, Garry Lee. "Scripture in the Writings of C. S. Lewis." Th.M. thesis, Dallas Theological Seminary, 1973.

Galligan, John Sheila. "'Slow-Paced We Come': Conversion in the Writings of C. S. Lewis." Ph.D. diss., Pontificiam Universitatem S. Thomae de Urbe, 1985.

Geisler, Norman L. *Thomas Aquinas: An Evangelical Appraisal*. Grand Rapids: Baker Books, 1991.

Glover, Donald E. *C. S. Lewis: The Art of Enchantment*. Athens: Ohio University Press, 1981.

Goffar, Janine. *C. S. Lewis Index: Rumours from the Sculptor's Shop*. Riverside, CA: La Sierra University Press, 1995.

Goldberg, Michael. *Theology and Narrative: A Critical Introduction*. Nashville: Abingdon, 1982.

Green, Garrett. *Imagining God: Theology and the Religious Imagination*. San Francisco: Harper and Row, 1989.

Green, Roger Lancelyn, and Walter Hooper. *C. S. Lewis: A Biography*. San Diego: Harvest Books, 1994.

Grenz, Stanley J., and Roger E. Olson. *20th-Century Theology: God and the World in a Transitional Age*. Downers Grove, IL: InterVarsity, 1992.

Gresham, Douglas H. *Lenten Lands: My Childhood with Joy Davidman and C. S. Lewis*. New York: HaperCollins, 1988.

Griffin, William. *Clive Staples Lewis: A Dramatic Life*. San Francisco: Harper and Row, 1986.

———. *C. S. Lewis: Spirituality for Mere Christians*. New York: Crossroad, 1998.

Hadfield, Alice Mary. *Charles Williams: An Exploration of His Life and Work*. Oxford: Oxford University Press, 1983.

Hannay, Margaret P. *C. S. Lewis*. Modern Literature Series. New York: Ungar, 1981.

———. "Mythology in the Novels of C. S. Lewis." MA thesis, College of Saint Rose, 1970.

Hart, Dabney Adams. "C. S. Lewis's Defense of Poesie." Ph.D. diss., University of Wisconsin, 1959.

———. *Through the Open Door: A New Look at C. S. Lewis*. University, AL: University of Alabama Press, 1984.

Hauerwas, Stanley, and L. Gregory Jones, eds. *Why Narrative? Readings in Narrative Theology*. Grand Rapids: Eerdmans, 1989.

Hein, Rolland. *The Harmony Within: The Spiritual Vision of George MacDonald*. Eureka, CA: Sunrise, 1982.

———. "That Perilous Journey: Understanding Religious Fantasy." Class Syllabus. Wheaton College, Wheaton, IL.

Herbert, George. *The Country Parson, The Temple*. Edited by John N. Wall, Jr. New York: Paulist, 1981.

Hoff, James E. "The Idea of God and Spirituality of C. S. Lewis." PhD diss., Pontifical Gregorian University, 1969.

Holmer, Paul L. *C. S. Lewis: The Shape of His Faith and Thought*. New York: Harper and Row, 1976.

Holyer, Robert. "C. S. Lewis on the Epistemic Significance of the Imagination." *Soundings* 74 (Spring/Summer 1991) 215–41.

Hooper, Walter. *C. S. Lewis: Companion and Guide*. San Francisco: HarperSanFrancisco, 1996.

———. *Past Watchful Dragons: The Narnian Chronicles of C. S. Lewis*. New York: Collier, 1979.

Howard, Thomas. *The Achievement of C. S. Lewis*. Wheaton, IL: Harold Shaw, 1980.
———. *C. S. Lewis, Man of Letters: A Reading of His Fiction*. San Francisco: Ignatius, 1987.
Hughes, Larry Raymond. "The World View of C. S. Lewis Implicit in His Religious Writings." Ed.D. diss., Oklahoma State University, 1980.
Hunter, Lynette. *G. K. Chesterton: Explorations in Allegory*. New York: St. Martin's, 1979.
Huttar, Charles A., ed. *Imagination and the Spirit: Essays in Literature and the Christian Faith*. Grand Rapids: Eerdmans, 1971.
Jinkins, Michael. *A Comparative Study in the Theology of Atonement in Jonathan Edwards and John McLeod Campbell: Atonement and the Character of God*. San Francisco: Mellen Research University Press, 1993.
Keeble, N. H. "C. S. Lewis, Richard Baxter, and 'Mere Christianity.'" *Christianity and Literature* 30 (1981) 27–44.
Keefe, Carolyn, ed. *C. S. Lewis: Speaker and Teacher*. Grand Rapids: Zondervan, 1971.
Kettler, Christian D. "The Vicarious Repentance of Christ in the Theology of John McLeod Campbell and R. C. Moberly." *Scottish Journal of Theology* 38 (1985) 529–43.
Kilby, Clyde S. *The Christian World of C. S. Lewis*. Grand Rapids: Eerdmans, 1964.
———. *Images of Salvation in the Fiction of C. S. Lewis*. Wheaton, IL: Harold Shaw, 1978.
Kingley, George Philip. "The Doctrine of Soteriology in the Writings of C. S. Lewis." Th.M. thesis, Dallas Theological Seminary, 1979.
Kreeft, Peter. *C. S. Lewis: A Critical Essay*. Front Royal, VA: Christendom College Press, 1988.
———. *C. S. Lewis for the Third Millennium*. San Francisco: Ignatius, 1994.
———. *Fundamentals of the Faith: Essays in Christian Apologetics*. San Francisco: Ignatius, 1988.
———. *Two Arguments from the Heart for Immortality*. Grand Rapids: Calvin College and Seminary, 1989.
Lauer, Quentin. *G. K. Chesterton: Philosopher Without Portfolio*. New York: Fordham University Press, 1991.
Lee, E. George. *C. S. Lewis and Some Modern Theologians*. London: Lindsey, 1944.
Lewis, C. S. *The Abolition of Man; or, Reflections on Education with Special Reference to the Teaching of English in the Upper Forms of Schools*. New York: Macmillan, 1947.
———. *The Allegory of Love: A Study in Medieval Tradition*. London: Oxford University Press, 1938.
———. *All My Road Before Me: The Diary of C. S. Lewis, 1922–1927*. Edited by Walter Hooper. San Diego: Harvest Books, 1991.
———. *Arthurian Torso*. London: Oxford University Press, 1948.
———. *Beyond Personality: The Christian Idea of God*. New York: Macmillan, 1945.
———. *The Case for Christianity*. New York: Macmillan, 1943.
———. *Christian Behavior: A Further Series of Broadcast Talks*. New York: Macmillan, 1943.
———. *Christian Reflections*. Edited by Walter Hooper. Grand Rapids: Eerdmans, 1967.
———. *C. S. Lewis: Letters to Children*. Edited by Lyle W. Dorsett and Marjorie Lamp Mead. New York: Macmillan, 1985.

———. *The Dark Tower, and Other Stories*. Edited by Walter Hooper. San Diego: Harcourt Brace, 1977.

———. *The Discarded Image: An Introduction to Medieval and Renaissance Literature*. Canto ed. Cambridge: Cambridge University Press, 1994.

———. *Dymer*. New York: Macmillan, 1950.

———. *English Literature in the Sixteenth Century, Excluding Drama*. Oxford History of English Literature 3. Oxford: Clarendon, 1954.

———, ed. *Essays Presented to Charles Williams*. Grand Rapids: Eerdmans, 1966.

———. *An Experiment in Criticism*. Cambridge: Cambridge University Press, 1992.

———. *Fern-seed and Elephants and Other Essays on Christianity*. Edited by Walter Hooper. London: HarperCollins, 1977.

———. *The Four Loves*. New York: Harcourt Brace Jovanovich, 1960.

———, ed. *George MacDonald: An Anthology*. New York: Macmillan, 1947.

———. *God in the Dock: Essays on Theology and Ethics*. Edited by Walter Hooper. Grand Rapids: Eerdmans, 1970.

———. *The Great Divorce: A Dream*. New York: Macmillan, 1946.

———. *A Grief Observed*. New York: Bantam, 1976.

———. *The Horse and His Boy*. New York: HarperCollins, 1994.

———. *The Joyful Christian: 127 Readings from C. S. Lewis*. New York: Macmillan, 1977.

———. *The Last Battle*. New York: HarperCollins, 1994.

———. *Letters to an American Lady*. Edited by Clyde S. Kilby. Grand Rapids: Eerdmans, 1971.

———. *Letters of C. S. Lewis*. Edited and with a memoir by W. H. Lewis. New York: Harcourt Brace, 1966.

———. *Letters of C. S. Lewis*. Edited and with a memoir by W. H. Lewis. Rev. and enl. ed. Edited by Walter Hooper. San Diego: Harcourt Brace, 1993.

———. *Letters to Malcolm: Chiefly on Prayer*. San Diego: Harvest Books, 1992.

———. *The Lion, the Witch, and the Wardrobe*. New York: HarperCollins, 1994.

———. *The Literary Impact of the Authorized Version*. Philadelphia: Fortress, 1967.

———. *The Magician's Nephew*. New York: HarperCollins, 1994.

———. *Mere Christianity: A Revised and Enlarged Edition, with a New Introduction, of the Three Books, the Case for Christianity, Christian Behavior, and Beyond Personality*. New York: Macmillan, 1952.

———. *A Mind Awake: An Anthology of C. S. Lewis*. Edited by Clyde S. Kilby. New York: Harcourt Brace Jovanovich, 1968.

———. *Miracles: A Preliminary Study*. New York: Macmillan, 1960.

———. *Narrative Poems*. Edited by Walter Hooper. San Diego: Harcourt Brace Jovanovich, 1972.

———. *Of Other Worlds: Essays and Stories*. Edited by Walter Hooper. San Diego: Harcourt Brace Jovanovich, 1975.

———. *On Stories, and Other Essays on Literature*. Edited by Walter Hooper. San Diego: Harcourt Brace Jovanovich, 1982.

———. *Out of the Silent Planet*. New York: Macmillan, 1965.

———. *Perelandra*. New York: Macmillan, 1965.

———. *The Pilgrim's Regress*. Grand Rapids: Eerdmans, 1981.

———. *Poems*. Edited by Walter Hooper. San Diego: Harvest Books, 1992.

———. *A Preface to Paradise Lose*. London: Oxford University Press, 1943.

———. *Present Concerns: Essays by C. S. Lewis*. Edited by Walter Hooper. San Diego: Harcourt Brace Jovanovich, 1986.
———. *Prince Caspian*. New York: HarperCollins, 1994.
———. *The Problem of Pain*. New York: Macmillan, 1962.
———. *Reflections on the Psalms*. San Diego: Harvest Books, 1986.
———. *Rehabilitations and Other Essays*. Oxford: Oxford University Press, 1939.
———. *The Screwtape Letters*. Old Tappan, NJ: Lord and King Associates, 1976.
———. *The Screwtape Letters, with Screwtape Proposes a Toast*. Revised ed. New York: Macmillan, 1982.
———. *Selected Literary Essays*. Edited by Walter Hooper. Cambridge: Cambridge University Press, 1969.
———. *The Silver Chair*. New York: HarperCollins, 1994.
———. *Spencer's Images of Life*. Edited by Alastair Fowler. Cambridge: Cambridge University Press, 1967.
———. *Spirits in Bondage: A Cycle of Lyrics*. Edited by Walter Hooper. New York: Harcourt Brace Jovanovich, 1984.
———. *Studies in Medieval and Renaissance Literature*. Collected by Walter Hooper. Cambridge: Cambridge University Press, 1966.
———. *Studies in Words*. Canto ed. Cambridge: Cambridge University Press, 1990.
———. *Surprised by Joy: The Shape of My Early Life*. San Diego: Harvest Books, 1984.
———. *That Hideous Strength*. New York: Macmillan, 1965.
———. *They Asked for a Paper: Papers and Addresses*. London: Geoffrey Bles, 1962.
———. *They Stand Together: The Letters of C. S. Lewis to Arthur Greeves (1914–1963)*. Edited by Walter Hooper. London: Collins, 1979.
———. *Till We Have Faces: A Myth Retold*. San Diego: Harvest Books, 1984.
———. *The Voyage of the "Dawn Treader."* New York: HarperCollins, 1994.
———. *The Weight of Glory, and Other Addresses*. Edited by Walter Hooper. Rev. and expanded ed. New York: Macmillan, 1980.
———. *The World's Last Night, and Other Essays*. San Diego: Harvest Books, 1987.
Lindskoog, Kathryn Ann. *C. S. Lewis: Mere Christian*. Glendale, CA: G/L Regal, 1973.
———. *Finding the Landlord: A Guidebook to C. S. Lewis's "Pilgrim's Regress."* Chicago: Cornerstone, 1995.
———. *The Lion of Judah in Never-Never Land: The Theology of C. S. Lewis Expressed in His Fantasies for Children*. Grand Rapids: Eerdmans, 1973.
Lindsley, Art. *C. S. Lewis's Case for Christ: Insights from Reason, Imagination and Faith*. Downers Grove, IL: InterVarsity, 2005.
Lowenberg, Susan. *C. S. Lewis: A Reference Guide, 1972–1988*. New York: Macmillan, 1993.
MacDonald, George. *The Golden Key and Other Fantasy Stories*. Grand Rapids: Eerdmans, 1980.
———. *Lilith: A Romance*. London: Chatto and Windus, 1895.
———. *Phantastes: A Faerie Romance*. Grand Rapids: Eerdmans, 1981.
MacDonald, Michael H., and Andrew A. Tadie, eds. *The Riddle of Joy: G. K. Chesterton and C. S. Lewis*. Grand Rapids: Eerdmans, 1989.
MacSwain, Robert, and Michael Ward, eds. *The Cambridge Companion to C. S. Lewis*. Cambridge: Cambridge University Press, 2010.
Manlove, C. N. *C. S. Lewis: His Literary Achievement*. New York: St. Martin's, 1987.
Markos, Louis. *Lewis Agonistes*. Nashville: Broadman and Holman, 2003.

Martin, Ralph P. *The Epistle of Paul to the Philippians: An Introduction and Commentary.* Grand Rapids: Eerdmans, 1983.
Martin, Thomas L., ed. *Reading the Classics with C. S. Lewis.* Grand Rapids: Baker Academic, 2000.
McFague, Sallie. *Speaking in Parables: A Study in Metaphor and Theology.* Philadelphia: Fortress, 1975.
McGrath, Alister E. *A Cloud of Witnesses: Ten Great Christian Thinkers.* Grand Rapids: Eerdmans, 1990.
———. *C. S. Lewis—A Life: Eccentric Genius, Reluctant Prophet.* London: Hodder and Stoughton, 2013.
———. *The Intellectual World of C. S. Lewis.* West Sussex, UK: Wiley-Blackwell, 2014.
McNeill, John T., ed. *Calvin: Institutes of the Christian Religion.* 2 vols. Philadelphia: Westminster John Knox, 1960.
Meilaender, Gilbert. *The Taste for the Other: The Social and Ethical Thoughts of C. S. Lewis.* Grand Rapids: Eerdmans, 1978.
Menuge, Angus J. L., ed. *C. S. Lewis, Lightbearer in the Shadowlands: The Evangelistic Vision of C. S. Lewis.* Wheaton, IL: Crossway, 1997.
Michael, Mary. "Our Love Affair with C. S. Lewis." *Christianity Today* 37 (October 25, 1993) 34–36.
Mitchell, Christopher W. *Lightbearer in the Shadowlands.* Wheaton, IL: Crossway, 1997.
Montgomery, John Warwick, ed. *Myth, Allegory, and Gospel: An Interpretation of J. R. R. Tolkien, C. S. Lewis, G. K. Chesterton, Charles Williams.* Minneapolis: Bethany Fellowship, 1974.
Morris, Francis. "Metaphor and Myth: Shaping Forces in C. S. Lewis's Critical Assessment of Medieval and Renaissance Literature." Ph.D. diss., University of Pennsylvania, 1977.
Murphy, Brian. *C. S. Lewis.* Starmont Reader's Guide 14. Mercer Island, WA: Starmont, 1983.
Musacchio, George. *C. S. Lewis, Man and Writer: Essays and Reviews.* Belton, TX: University of Mary Hardin-Baylor, 1994.
Myers, Doris T. *C. S. Lewis in Context.* Kent: Kent State University Press, 1994.
Newell, Roger J. "Participatory Knowledge: Theology as Art and Science in C. S. Lewis and T. F. Torrance." Ph.D. diss., University of Aberdeen, 1983.
Nicholi, Armand M., Jr. *The Question of God: C. S. Lewis and Sigmund Freud Debate God, Love, Sex, and the Meaning of Life.* New York: Free Press, 2002.
Ogden, C. K., and I. A. Richards. *The Meaning of Meaning.* New York: Harcourt, 1946.
Oliver, Gary Jackson. "Language in the Theology of C. S. Lewis: Its Nature, Functions, and Forms." Th.M. thesis, Fuller School of Theology, 1977.
Otto, Rudolf. *The Idea of the Holy.* London: Oxford University Press, 1958.
Packer, J. I. "What Lewis Was and Wasn't." *Christianity Today* 32 (January 15, 1988) 11.
Patrick, James. *The Magdalen Metaphysicals: Idealism and Orthodoxy at Oxford, 1901–1945.* Macon, GA: Mercer University Press, 1985.
Payne, Leanne. *Real Presence: The Holy Spirit in the Works of C. S. Lewis.* Westchester, IL: Cornerstone, 1979.
Peterson, Michael, et al. *Reason and Religious Belief: An Introduction to the Philosophy of Religion.* Oxford: Oxford University Press, 1991.
Phillips, Timothy R., and Dennis L. Okholm, eds. *Christian Apologetics in the Postmodern World.* Downers Grove, IL: InterVarsity, 1995.

Plantinga, Alvin, and Nicholas Wolterstorff, eds. *Faith and Rationality: Reason and Belief in God*. Notre Dame: University of Notre Dame Press, 1983.
Purtill, Richard. *C. S. Lewis's Case for the Christian Faith*. San Francisco: Harper and Row, 1981.
———. *Lord of the Elves and Eldils: Fantasy and Philosophy in C. S. Lewis and J. R. R. Tolkien*. Grand Rapids: Zondervan, 1974.
Reilly, R. J. *Romantic Religion: A Study of Barfield, Lewis, Williams, and Tolkien*. Athens: University of Georgia Press, 1971.
Reppert, Victor. *C. S. Lewis's Dangerous Idea: In Defense of the Argument from Reason*. Downers Grove, IL: InterVarsity, 2003.
Robb, David S. *God's Fiction: Symbolism and Allegory in the Works of George MacDonald*. Eureka, CA: Sunrise, 1987.
Ryken, Leland, and Marjorie Lamp Mead. *A Reader's Guide Through the Wardrobe: Exploring C. S. Lewis's Classic Story*. Downers Grove, IL: InterVarsity, 2005.
Sammons, Martha C. *A Guide Through Narnia*. Wheaton, IL: Harold Shaw, 1979.
Sayer, George. *Jack: A Life of C. S. Lewis*. Wheaton, IL: Crossway, 1994.
Schakel, Peter J., ed. *The Longing for a Form: Essays on the Fiction of C. S. Lewis*. Kent: Kent State University Press, 1977.
———. *Reason and Imagination in C. S. Lewis: A Study of Till We Have Faces*. Grand Rapids: Eerdmans, 1984.
Schofield, Stephen, ed. *In Search of C. S. Lewis*. South Plainfield, NJ: Bridge, 1983.
Schwartz, Adam. "Review of *Permanent Things*, Andrew A. Tadie and Michael H. MacDonald, eds." *The Lamp-Post* 20 (Autumn 1996) 31-35.
Shedd, W. G. T. *Calvinism Pure and Mixed*. Edinburgh, UK: Banner of Truth, 1986.
Shideler, Mary McDermott. *The Theology of Romantic Love: A Study in the Writings of Charles Williams*. Grand Rapids: Eerdmans, 1962.
Smith, Roger Houston. *Patches of Godlight: The Pattern of Thought of C. S. Lewis*. Athens: University of Georgia Press, 1981.
Stevens, Ronnie Collier. "The Person and Work of Christ in the Writings of C. S. Lewis." MA thesis, Dallas Theological Seminary, 1977.
Sturgis, Amy H., ed. *Past Watchful Dragons: Fantasy and Faith in the World of C. S. Lewis*. Altadena, CA: Mythopoeic, 2007.
Tadie, Andrew A., and Michael H. MacDonald, eds. *Permanent Things: Towards the Recovery of a More Human Scale at the End of the Twentieth Century*. Grand Rapids: Eerdmans, 1995.
Taliaferro, Charles A. "A Narnian Theory of the Atonement." *Scottish Journal of Theology* 41 (1988) 75-92.
Tennyson, G. B., ed. *Owen Barfield on C. S. Lewis*. Middletown, CT: Wesleyan University Press, 1989.
Torrance, James B. "The Contribution of McLeod Campbell to Scottish Theology." *Scottish Journal of Theology* 26 (August 1973) 295-311.
Van Til, Cornelius. *The Defense of the Faith*. Phillipsburg, NJ: P & R, 1967.
Vaus, Will. *Mere Theology: A Guide to the Thought of C. S. Lewis*. Downers Grove, IL: InterVarsity, 2004.
Veith, Gene Edward, Jr. *Reformation Spirituality: The Religion of George Herbert*. London: Associated University Press, 1985.
Velarde, Robert. *Conversations with C. S. Lewis: Imaginative Discussions about Life, Christianity and God*. Downers Grove, IL: InterVarsity, 2008.

Walker, Andrew, ed. *Different Gospels: Christian Orthodoxy and Modern Theologies.* London: Hodder and Stoughton, 1988.

Walker, Andrew, and James Patrick, eds. *A Christian for all Christians: Essays in Honour of C. S. Lewis.* Washington, DC: Regnery Gateway, 1992.

Walsh, Chad. *C. S. Lewis: Apostle to the Skeptics.* New York: Macmillan, 1949.

———. *The Literary Legacy of C. S. Lewis.* New York: Harcourt Brace Jovanovich, 1979.

Ward, Maisie. *Gilbert Keith Chesterton.* New York: Sheed and Ward, 1943.

Ward, Samuel Keith. "C. S. Lewis and the Nature-Grace Aesthetics." Ph.D. diss., University of Pittsburgh, 1977.

Wheeler, Andrew. *C. S. Lewis: Clarity and Confusion.* Leominster, MA: Day One, 2006.

White, William Luther. "The Image of Man in C. S. Lewis." Ph.D. diss., Northwestern University, 1968.

———. *The Image of Man in C. S. Lewis.* Nashville: Abingdon, 1969.

Wielenberg, Erik J. *God and the Reach of Reason: C. S. Lewis, David Hume, and Bertrand Russell.* New York: Cambridge University Press, 2008.

Williams, Charles, and C. S. Lewis. *Taliessin Through Logres: The Region of the Summer Stars and Arthurian Torso.* Grand Rapids: Eerdmans, 1974.

Willis, John Randolph. *Pleasures Forevermore: The Theology of C. S. Lewis.* Chicago: Loyola University Press, 1983.

Wilson, A. N. *C. S. Lewis: A Biography.* New York: Fawcett Columbine, 1990.

Wilson, John. "An Appraisal of C. S. Lewis and His Influence on Modern Evangelicalism." *Scottish Bulletin of Evangelical Theology* 39 (Spring 1991) 22–39.

Wright, Marjorie Evelyn. "The Cosmic Kingdom of Myth: A Study of the Myth-Philosophy of Charles Williams, C. S. Lewis, and J. R. R. Tolkien." Ph.D. diss., University of Illinois, 1961.

Wright, Rosemary. "Biblical Allusions in C. S. Lewis's 'Till We Have Faces.'" MA thesis, Florida Atlantic University, 1982.

Zogby, Edward Gabriel. "C. S. Lewis: Christopoesis and the Recovery of the Panegyric Imagination." Ph.D. diss., Syracuse University, 1974.

www.ingramcontent.com/pod-product-compliance
Lightning Source LLC
Chambersburg PA
CBHW070305230426
43664CB00014B/2639